Intr

Born on a North East Cc
Christmas 1960 I had no idea t   _. would
soon lift the League and F.A. Cι   _ aοove their heads.
The Double would be achieved foι ιne first time this century.

As a child Spurs didn't mean anything. Matchbox cars
were my interest. I don't even remember the 1966 World Cup
Final win for England. But 1969 changed all that. I remember
watching the F.A. Cup Final between Leicester and Man City
and was soon hooked on football. I either bought or was
given a Spurs button badge, a strange choice you might think.
The town I lived in, Shildon, few people followed any other
teams other than Newcastle, Middlesbrough and most
prominently Sunderland.

My brother John picked up on Spurs. He was eight years
older than me, so I guess he would have chosen the best team
as a youngster, like kids still do. This is my only logic for my
choice. Spurs were to be my team.

By the 1970's my love for Spurs was getting stronger and I
was desperate to see them in the flesh, that moment would
come during the 1974-75 season. Spurs were then a team
fighting relegation, so you couldn't say I was a glory
supporter. My first match would have a huge impact on my
life, and that feeling hasn't left me, my thoughts are never far
away from Spurs.

After watching Spurs for Twenty Seasons, 1974-75 to
1993-94, I thought the time was right to get my football life
on paper, the highs and lows, the laughs, the tears, the
violence, music, fashion and everything that has skirted my
love of Spurs.

1

Twenty years seemed a nice round number, but significantly it was when football changed from the working-class game to the corporate sponsorship and the mega rich greed that football has become and would continue to be into the millennium.

The game has changed in all directions, and not all for the better. Notably the famous old terraces have gone, the Kop, the Stretford End, the Kippax, the Shed, The Northbank, to name but a few, and of course our own Shelf Side, the unique iconic terrace like no other, holding 20,000 swaying supporters.

The hooligans of the 1970's and 80's, in the most part have been eliminated from inside stadiums, but they still loiter on the outside. They will never be eradicated.

The main change to football has been the colossal amounts of money that awash the Premier League, it's the bit I despise. I don't begrudge the wages players get, if someone wants to offer you silly amounts of money you are going to take it, like anyone would in any job, but it kills loyalty. We all love our clubs, but we are fans, players are just passing through, they don't have our passion for one club.

As admission prices have escalated out of all recognition to the working class, fans from the 1970's and 80's are cast aside. A lot can't afford the ticket prices and definitely not to bring their children. Could football lose a generation of fans? Possibly not, as Sky TV show a saturated level of games for them to watch, but at what cost. Sky dictates everything, they are the cash cow, football fans are bottom of the pile. What bugs me the most is the kick-off times and rescheduling of games. People buy travel tickets as early as possible to get the best deals and then find out Sky have changed the date and time. Their money is wasted. Sky will say we have chosen, for example, Spurs away at Newcastle for a 12.30 kick-off on a Sunday to allow Spurs fans to see their team on TV. What about the loyal travelling support who would prefer a Saturday at 3pm? Stop pampering to the armchair fans I say.

So, there is good and bad with the game today, facilities are much better and safer. Hooliganism has almost gone inside stadiums. The bad I have mentioned. If I could go back to the football of the 1970's or go now, no contest, it would not be the latter.

Enjoy the read, it may well trigger memories of those times, whoever you support.

The Early Years

What are your first memories of childhood? Maybe your first bike, your first day at school? Well mine was death on two counts. Winston Churchill's funeral in 1965. I watched it on our old coin operated grainy black and white TV, sixpence or a shilling keeping it going, feeding a box on the back so that you didn't miss any of the huge occasion that brought a nation together. I was four, but I remember it well. It was as big as any Royal event. Churchill will always be synonymous with leading our country through the Second World War, deserving the outpouring of a nation.

My other memory was much nearer home, about the same time, maybe the following year, I know that because where I lived was only fifty yards from a railway tunnel, steam engines were still coming through it. The tunnel had large grassy banks either side, the spoils of the original excavation, then steep stone walls twenty feet high leading down to the track bed. The tunnel went under my hometown of Shildon. On this day I stood at the top of the embankment looking down at the tracks waiting for a train to emerge from the tunnel when I noticed the body of a man laid next to the lines. I couldn't tell if he was dead or alive, but he wasn't moving. I ran home to tell my mam. I came back to see a small crowd gathering, chatting at what could have happened to him.

A couple of hundred yards away I noticed the police and ambulance staff walking up the lines to attend the unfortunate. On their arrival they put him on a stretcher and covered his face with a blanket. No one knew what had happened to him. Was he drunk from the previous night and slipped or was he chased and pushed? This is what all the kids I knew said. It made for a better story to tell everyone at school the following Monday.

I had a happy childhood generally. I lived on a large Council Estate, it never made me feel less inferior to the kids who maybe lived in better homes. Some may look down at you if you're off a council estate, you're a bit of a scally, up to no good and in some cases there are that type, but there are many who are good hard-working people who are just keeping a family fed and clothed who are honest and cause no harm. Anyway, when I was a kid, I knew no different, it was my estate. Looking back, I was on the better side of it. When I occasionally go back for a walk on the estate for a reminder, some forty years later, it has got worse, there were a couple of shops and a pub, the pub has been bulldozed and the shops have permanent shutters to stop the attempted thefts, mainly from people trying to feed their insatiable drug problem.

I enjoyed music in the 60s and would pick up a tennis racket we had to use as a pretend guitar, why we had a tennis racket is unbeknown to me, no one played tennis out of my four brothers and sister.

I don't remember my family having a record player when I was young, that would come later, but there was always a radio playing the hits of the swinging 60's, whatever that meant in Shildon. On occasions I would go round to my next-door neighbours where the Woodward's lived, they had three girls, all in their teens, aged five to fifteen years older than myself. They always had music playing from their record player, this really was my introduction to music. The Beatles, Rolling Stones, both a big favourite to the girls, but many other groups of the time too. They regularly bought a new Single or L.P.to keep up to date with the music scene.

I now look back at The Beatles and think they were around for only eight years, 1962-1970, yet look at the catalogue of music they produced, inspiring thousands of bands and still inspiring. They have influenced so many.

My other highlight was my yearly visit to London to see my Aunt and Uncle who lived near Croydon, South London. We would visit for one week, just my Mam, Dad and myself. My older brothers and sister had all left home, all apart from John, who was then trusted to stay to look after the family home. I would go to London every year until my last year of school, I loved the place and as I got older would go into the centre to look around. I had no fear of wandering around using the trains and tube. We had an old A-Z atlas of London at home which was from the 1950's, but as London hadn't changed much by the 1970s it was still accurate, so I would plot what to visit, including marking all the London football grounds. I am sure this is another reason for my love of Spurs, I have many happy memories of London.

My only other recollection of the time was my love of Matchbox cars and toy soldiers, the 1:72 scale where you could buy so many different armies. My closest friend Gary would regularly come round to have battles with them, but I was happy in my own company at home playing alone. My possessions would always be put away afterwards, kept safe until their next use. I would give them all away as I got into my teens, shame really, as they now have a monetary value.

The late 1960's or 1969 to be exact is my first real memory of Spurs, that was the only year I know of when my parents and I went on holiday to Blackpool instead of London. I had never seen anything like Blackpool, it was so alive and glitzy, or so it seemed at the time. What I distinctly remember is that every morning I would take a Spurs tin badge off my clothing and put it on the next garment, I wore it with pride. I cannot even remember taking any notice of the results at the time, but I knew they were my team. Leeds United were probably the best team at the time and a lot of kids of my age thought they were the team to follow.

In 1970 I started to get the Shoot Magazine delivered, and to be honest in the first year I don't think I read it, I just took the posters out and taped them to my bedroom wall. My bedroom walls were painted, so any time I removed a poster it would leave ugly tape marks where it had pulled the paint off. I had to put a new one up in the same place so my mam wouldn't see the scarring. Any pictures adorned my wall, any team, any player, but the Spurs pictures would take pride of place.

It was 1971 when football started to take over my life. Gary my best mate followed Liverpool, the team to take over Leeds United's mantel. Like I say kids followed the best, but to be fair Gary has been a season ticket holder for many years now, so it wasn't a fad for him either. The two of us watched the 1971 Cup Final at my house. Liverpool V's Arsenal, I remember it well. Fortunately I don't remember that a few days earlier Arsenal beat Spurs 1-0 for the first part of their double. The same double we had won ten years earlier. I have no recollection of it at all.

The following season I was taken to a few Darlington matches with Steve my nephew. He was two years younger than myself, we were happy to run around the spartan terraces at that time, messing about, my first taste of league football. Division Four it may have been, but even at that level you get a taste and smell for football.

Apart from Darlington my other football interest was watching the local British Rail team Shildon B.R. I would watch them regularly in the early 1970's, and would travel away to watch them, travelling on the team bus to places in and around County Durham. I remember travelling to Ushaw Moor near Durham when I was twelve, and these three kids of a similar age to me noticed I wasn't a local and asked if I wanted a fight. They must have been Newcastle fans! I would probably meet them later in life. I declined the Ushaw Moor hooligans, and they went on their way.

Junior school was good, I had good friends and I never got into trouble, but that changed in my last year at school as I approached leaving for senior's. I had been playing on the school field near the sand pit, which was used for the long jump, but during lunch breaks the kids would build sandcastles in it. Well, I accidently stood on Charlie Heslop's sandcastle. He was the same age, but not in my class and a lot bigger than me. Charlie didn't take kindly to his castle being crushed and soon got hold of me. Our slight friendship went out of the window. He pushed me to the sand and sat on top of me, with his heavy legs pinning my arms down so I couldn't move. I tried to explain that I had slipped, but it meant nothing as the first punch stung into my face. This was the first punch I had ever taken in my young life and it wasn't pleasant. I lifted my head, the only movement I could make off the sand, but the next punch put it back into the sand. I could hear the sound of screaming kids around me shouting 'fight, fight, fight'. Fight it wasn't. Again, I lifted my head, and it had the same result. I wasn't strong enough to move him. I appeared to be box office, as the mass of faces looked down. They wanted more, so who was I not to give them more. I lifted my head again, another punch and another. Charlie was enjoying the adulation as he pummelled his victim. I was just thinking let this be over, then I heard the joyous voice of a teacher.

'Come on move you lot, you two in my office'. I dragged myself up, shaken. When you are eleven and you get into a fight you might have a scratch, not me, I had two black eyes after the swelling had gone down, a swollen lip and a bust nose. A good pasting you could say. We shook hands and were fine with each other. About fifteen years later I saw Charlie get into a fight with another lad whilst I was looking out my bedroom window one night. He got him on the ground and again pinned him down and continually head butted him with such ferocity. I was pleased to of been his early victim. I got home that day after school with my puffed face beginning to turn black and blue. My mother didn't even notice. Well, she did say,

'Have you caught your face?'

By 1972 Spurs results were really starting to play a part in my life, I would regularly listen to the UEFA cup matches on the radio. Living in the Northeast Spurs news was in short supply, the only time you would get a good match report in the paper was when we played a Northeast team and at that time only Newcastle were in the top division, games against Man Utd, Man City, Liverpool, Everton and Leeds would only get a small report, but the rest you would be lucky if you got a line. As for TV we had 'Shoot' which covered the Northeast, so Spurs featured hardly ever. Match of the Day was really my limit to seeing my heroes. Only two games were shown, not like today's saturation coverage.

The other big change in my life in 1972 was leaving junior school and going to the big school. One of the three schools I could go to were Bishop Auckland Grammar School. I had no chance as this was for the best scholars. I was okay at school, average all the way through, typically the school report said, 'Could do better if he put his mind to it'. The second school was the large comprehensive Shildon Sunnydale, home to around a thousand pupils, and finally the Council School, which was frowned upon as the school where you were known to be an under achiever and reputation where the toughest kids in Shildon went.

In the summer of 1972, we all received a letter to which school we were going to attend in the September. I opened the letter and it said, 'Council School'. I had to look at it again, 'Council School'! My eyes weren't deceiving me. 'They must have made a mistake' I told my friends. Only three lads were going, no girls, Council School was only for boys.

'What School Ian?' they asked.

'Council', I replied.

An intake of breath from my friends.

'Ooh, have you heard what they do to new kids on the first day?', one said.

'No', I replied.

'Head straight down the toilet, yeh, the older lads get the new ones, drag them to the outside toilets and put their heads down, then give them a good kicking'.

I hoped my six weeks summer holiday would go slow as it felt I was on death row. I found out later that the choice of school was down to where your other siblings had attended and mine had gone there, except Dave who went to the Grammar School. The fact was that Sunnydale hadn't been built when my other brothers had gone to the Council School, this news didn't comfort me in anyway.

To take my mind off the fate that lay ahead of me I decided to take a morning paper round which I would be paid one pound for six mornings. It was summer, the mornings were bright, I found getting up at 6a.m. not too difficult. I walked to the shop about half a mile away and followed an older boy who was teaching me the round but was about to leave that week. I noticed the bag to be quite large and mainly filled with Northern Echoes which was the local paper, and a broad sheet, plus the usual tabloids, Mirror, Sun, etc. I noticed the boy knew what papers went in where, nothing was written on the paper, he had it all in his head. I should have written down what went in each letter box, but I thought I would remember it. Seventy papers, and approximately fifty of them were the Northern Echo, so If I could remember the other twenty, I would crack it. The following day I followed again. The round was about a mile long. The first house was about five hundred yards from the shop which was uphill. The boy had carried the bag so I didn't even know what it weighed but it looked bulky and I was a lot smaller than him. Well tomorrow (Wednesday) would be my test.

My first day, the alarm went off, I got up almost excited, I'm at the shop by 6.30a.m. It was sunny but that would be the only bright part of this Wednesday morning. The bag was already filled, it looked massive, bigger than the previous two days.

'I've put the magazines in at the front of the bag', Sid the owner said.

At least these had the addresses on. I hadn't banked on magazines, mainly Woman's Own, almost forty adding to the weight, Wednesday was magazine day. I put the strap around my small neck an eased the bag off the bench. A few older kids had already taken their bulk and set off on their round. The bag dropped from the bench and almost pulled me over. I set myself, left the shop and began my climb, it was only a small bank, but it might as well have been Everest. The first door was a Northern Echo, I could remember that, but my memory was all over the place and the weight was intense. I needed to get rid of the weight as quick as possible.

Papers going in wrong letterboxes willy-nilly. The odd person who was up would come to the door.

'Oh, I don't get this paper'.

11

One house had a letterbox that was so tight it was a job to open, and when I did get the paper through, the dog would rip it out of my hand. You could hear it rip it to shreds with the owner shouting,

'Leave that bloody paper'. It happened regularly, it would make me smile. As I got to the latter part of the round, I would take a break and look at the tabloids, straight to the sport to see if there was any Spurs news, invariably there wasn't.

My second day arrived, I walked into the shop quite sheepishly knowing how badly day one had gone.

'We've had a lot of complaints of wrong papers', Sid said.

Sid gave me his book so that I could learn the round. Things improved. Every day I would buy a Mars bar and a packet of crisps and say to Sid to take it out of my wages. On the Saturday Sid would give me my wage of forty pence, which was what was left, not a lot for six days.

I awoke, my alarm was going off with that noise that you could do without, it was dark, the rain was bouncing off my bedroom window the bed was warm. I turned off the alarm and decided I was retired. We didn't have a phone at the time so I couldn't ring Sid to tell him I'd had enough. Later that day I got my mam to call in the shop to do my dirty work for me saying 'Ian doesn't want the round anymore'. I never went in the shop again as I was too embarrassed.

Music was also becoming part of my life. John my brother had purchased a record player, one of them typical square box types with a lid. Playing your 33, 45, 75 rpm. John's taste in music was Rock, Prog Rock, resulting in John's hair getting longer and longer much to the annoyance of my dad's stance that a man should have short back and sides.

12

Although I had a love of pop music, we had one record I often played, that record was 'Sparky's magic piano', A musical story on an old 78 record, it was about a boy who couldn't play the piano, but his piano began to talk to him, when sparky played it, he was a grand master. Of course, it was only a dream. My dreams were becoming a nightmare as September was looming large and the big school awaited.

The day had arrived, Shildon Secondary Modern for Boys. The only good news was you could wear anything, no school uniform for my parents to fork out for, just wear what you want as long as you don't wear jeans is what I was told. I trudged up to the school, it might as well have been a death march. I felt my sentence becoming ever nearer imagining some older boys beating me up and then flushing my head down the toilet to remove the dripping blood. I walked into the playground, most of the kids were dressed in flares, Doc Martins and jumpers that weren't quite long enough, I made sure I didn't catch anyone's eye. I met up with a few friends from junior school who were like me, new starters. The bell rang and we were all put into lines in the playground, our names read out and that was our class for the year. We went into school, which was like my junior school, built in the same era, about 1920.

We settled down for lessons, but I had this thought, the first playtime and then I would go down the toilet. The bell rang at approximately 10.30a.m. we left our desks and headed for the yard where nothing, absolutely nothing happened. Most of the older lads were looking for any decent place to have a smoke, they couldn't care less about the little kids.

The next three years were the happiest days of my school life. Of course, there were fights, I even had two minor scuffles, but the class was close knit and didn't get split up in all the three years, classmates became good friends, many I still see to this day. With school being good and never getting homework, a bonus, having no paper round to get up for, I could now listen to radio Luxembourg on a night in bed. I really liked the show. You would get to hear new bands and tracks you had never heard before, the only problem was the reception would fade out all the time. You would hear a song you liked then the song would get quieter and quieter until it disappeared then it would slowly come back, by which time the song had finished and you were none the wiser who had sung it. But still a great station to listen to.

'Son of my Father' by Chicory Tip, a hit in 1972, I remember it well for one reason. They say music is a way of remembering events, well, this was my first taste of the opposite sex. My best mate Gary would come around my home to see me, I have known him all my life, we were pushed around in our prams by our parents. Gary and I went around the corner from where I lived to see Michael Stark, a new kid who had moved in that summer of 72. Mike was a year older than me but seemed a nice lad. I remember his dad always smoking and once painting his car with a paint brush, the whole car!, in light blue paint, he did work at a paint factory so it must have been surplus to requirements. Mike, Gary and I would often trawl through the streets of Shildon and beyond, there wasn't the worries of today, our parents didn't think anything of it, life seemed safer.

We bumped into a group of girls that Mike knew from school. Mike was at the Grammar School. They were his age or a year older, either thirteen or fourteen. For the next two or three weeks we would meet regularly, there were usually four of them. We would go to one of the girl's houses, her parents never seemed to be in. At first we would just talk, then things moved onto games which seemed to have some form of chasing, then we would end up kissing, which I had never

14

done but was happy to learn. I am sure the girls were just using us to gain experience for when they moved on to older boys. It became a strange meet up where we would swap from girl to girl and move from room to room for the next two hours. Chicory Tip on TV while I was in the living room. It never went much further than kissing. Occasionally you would get to touch a breast. Mike would try more, and you would hear the occasional.

'Try that again and you can go home' from one of the girls.

This is how 'Son of my Father' is so ingrained into my memory, sitting on a sofa snogging a girl two years older than me. It all ended as quick as it began with a polite 'don't call anymore'. Shame, but fantastic while it lasted.

Glam Rock was now all the rage at school. By 1973 bands like T-Rex, Slade and Gary Glitter all vying for the number one slot. Gary Glitter would later be outed as a pervert who prayed on young kids, much like D.J. Jimmy Saville. My prcference was Wizzard who were led by Roy Wood, former singer of The Move and a large influence on the Electric Light Orchestra.

'See my Baby Jive', was the first single I ever bought, but with my brother John's influence I liked an album by Pink Floyd, 'Piper at the Gates of Dawn' which was their 1967 debut album, a mix of psychedelic, with almost childlike nursery rhymes. No one in my class had heard of them and I got the usual 'Pink who!'

The fashion at the time was hideous, but you were part of it, you knew no different, but I drew the line at platform shoes. Looking back I am so pleased I haven't any photos from those times. My hair was fairly long, down to my shoulders with no style whatsoever, I knew it needed cutting. I was playing a lot of Subbuteo at the time and would lay the pitch out on the carpet. As I was leaning over to play my hair would constantly fall over my eyes, something had to be done, anyway I didn't want to end up like John, getting constant digs about my long hair off my dad. My other problem, like I said I didn't like platforms shoes and trying to find anything normal was becoming very difficult. The shoes I was wearing for school were starting to get a hole in them, not at the usual front, but on the top, approximately where your big toenail would be, caused from playing football in the school yard at break times. The hole was growing by the day as the ball erased the leather from my shoe. The shoes were black so I could wear black socks to hide the hole, sort of camouflage it, but if I could not find black socks, I would use black polish on that part of the sock to colour it. I had to find a new pair!

During the school holidays of that summer having completed my first year of senior school I finally found a black pair of shoes I liked. I also bought a pair of bright purple flared trousers, which looked the business with my new large collared shirt. I also went for a haircut which unfortunately didn't come out as I was hoping. Yes, it was shorter on the fringe, but then sharply cut vertically, then cut horizontally and finally a small vertical cut. When I returned home, John summed it up when he said.

'Why did you ask for a German Second World War helmet hair style!'. He wasn't far wrong.

My football interest was still growing, with Spurs at the forefront. I was a regular listener to Sport on Two, as it was known then, nowadays it's Five Live. Peter Jones, one of the best commentators around, would paint a picture of the match so vividly with his description of his surroundings.

Spurs had an average season finishing mid-table and it was evident that Bill Nicholson's team were growing old, and the replacements were not good enough, but in contrast the European campaign was going well. As a result of beating Norwich in the League Cup Final the previous season Spurs entered their third consecutive season in the UEFA Cup. The two previous seasons Spurs had won the trophy 1972 and reached the Semi-Final in 1973. The cup run from 1974 would see Spurs play Feyenoord in the Final but would reach a new low for Spurs and football.

The first leg of a two-legged Final at White Hart Lane went off relatively trouble-free, ending in a draw. The second leg played in Rotterdam was carnage. Around 5,000 Spurs fans housed in two tiers behind one goal were taunted throughout by the Dutch. They burnt Union Jacks in front of the Spurs contingent who stood behind a chicken wire mesh fence which divided the two factions. Spurs fans charged the fence pulling it down, which had most of the Dutch fleeing, but some fought, several Spurs fans were stabbed. The Dutch police waded in indiscriminately hitting any English person, man, woman, child, no one was freed from the flaying batons that the Dutch police lashed out with. Bill Nicholson came on the tannoy at halftime to try and quell the trouble, but it was too late. The game ended 2-0 to Feyenoord but the result was almost an afterthought. I watched the news that night, Spurs being the headline for all the wrong reasons, I was shocked to see so many Spurs fans being interviewed, with bandages and slings adorning their bodies, many saying the Dutch police had been overzealous, either hitting them or pushing them down the steep tiers, many breaking bones as they fell. The following morning the Daily Mirror's headline read 'Spurs hooligan fans causing mayhem'. I didn't want to see that sort of news, I was constantly looking for snippets of Spurs news, well now I had many pages of it. The kids at school who liked football, mainly Sunderland, Newcastle, Leeds and Man

Utd, chatted to me about it, I was the only Spurs fan after all, this the first hooliganism I had seen, but reading later about trouble on the terraces it wasn't uncommon, and Spurs were right up there, having skirmishes with Chelsea, West Ham, Arsenal and Man Utd at White Hart Lane. Starting in the early to mid-60s, trouble was only sporadic and before the segregation of supporters, but it would escalate year on year to its height in the 1970's and early 1980's.

It was about this time John and I started playing football in the house, not with a ball, but with a glove or a sock, rolled up and then put into a nylon stocking, using the stocking to tie it up into a tight ball. We called it 'Sock Ball'. In our kitchen we used a chair for one goal, trying to get it between the legs, and at the other end, approximately ten feet away, the other goal, underneath one of those iconic kitchen cabinets from the 1960s. It had a glass sliding door at the top, and a pull-down hatch which you could store items inside, at the bottom it had two further sliding doors made of plywood. The small legs that it sat on made an ideal goal about eight inches high and approximately three feet wide. We would play each other, dribbling and shooting, John running around with his hands permanently holding his ever-growing hair to stop it covering his eyes, but often I would play on my own pretending to be Chivers or Gilzean, just shooting at the cabinet or picking up the ball and throwing it up for headers, imagining I was them. It was always difficult to play when my dad was in, as any high shot would clatter the plywood doors and make a terrible din, with my dad shouting from the living room.

'Stop kicking that bloody sock about.'

It wouldn't be long before after hitting the plywood doors again my dad would rush in, pick the sock ball up and put it on the coal fire with me watching it burn brightly, I'm thinking, 'nylon stockings burn really well'!

My mam would often say.

'I don't know where all my nylon stockings are going to'.

'Don't ask me', I would reply, not having the heart to say they were a constant heat source.

The start of another term at school was here, and my third year at Secondary, or, as now they say year nine, but to me it was 1974-75 season. The season I became a paying customer to watch the famous Lilywhites. I headed off to school that morning knowing this would be my last year at the Council School. Due to lack of funds, it wasn't viable to keep two Secondary Schools running in Shildon. As Sunnydale was bigger and modern, the Council School would be no more and by 1975 it would merge with its big brother.

With my new attire and haircut, I thought I looked the height of fashion, to be fair my mates did to, but once in the school yard my wide bottomed trousers did cause some concern while dribbling with the ball.

The teachers at the Council School were quite hard with the pupils, but fair. Remember this was the time of getting caned for any inappropriate behaviour, but of course there was one teacher who was weak, and this weakness was soon picked up on, and like any pack of wild animals looking for food they will soon find their prey. Mr Dickinson was their quarry, a Donald Pleasance (the actor) lookalike with round glasses, he soon lost control of all his classes and ours was no different. Putting it bluntly we ran amok. His only saving grace was the class next door, the Art class ran by Mr Minto, who could cane with such ferocity that you were almost crying before your fate. Luckily, I never befell to it, but I saw many who did, and you could only wince at their punishment.

At times I had empathy towards Mr Dickinson, it must be hard at the best of times to teach pupils mathematics, but Mr Dickinson was weak, even his caning was weak, in fact he probably spent more time using his cane than his chalk. It was quite normal for the whole class to be lined up, around twenty-five of us, usually for throwing paper planes and the like, his cane would clatter his desk and he would shout.

'Right, all of you get out in a line'.

Cheering would go up from the class.

'Me Sir?' Phil Horner would say, him being the swat of the class.

'Yes Horner, you as well'.

More cheering. Tony 'Toppo' Caygill would head the line, putting his hand out in anticipation but would always withdraw his hand as the cane made its downward stroke, this being repeated five or six times. Mr Dickinson would become irate. Toppo would be passed until the end, letting the rest of us be caned first. He would eventually get his turn. Toppo had the record of being caned the most times in a one-hour lesson, nine times, all separate canings. The class was chaotic. I remember one lesson where a lad was sat at the back of the class, his chair on two legs as he leaned against the back wall, and he was masturbating! Yes, it was chaos, but the happiest days of my school life. At the end of that year, we moved to Sunnydale for the last two years. Basically, I hated it and don't need to talk about it.

It's a Conn Trick

Spurs had played at Newcastle on the last league game of the 1973-74 season which I had hoped to go to but there was no room in the car, so I missed out. Lenny my oldest brother had arranged to take me to a couple of games at Newcastle the following season, both cup games, one in the short-lived Texaco Cup against Birmingham, and a League Cup game against Fulham, both games played in front of around 20,000, the biggest crowd I had ever been in, but relatively small for Newcastle, but to me it was wonderful, both under lights which creates an atmosphere all by itself. I didn't care who won, I was just excited to be sitting at a Division One ground (or Premier as is now). But now I had pencilled in January 11th when Spurs would visit St. James' Park.

The day had finally arrived, my first ever Spurs match. I was filled with excitement and trepidation. I was always nervous before any Spurs game, the result was so important and with the club fighting relegation, gaining much needed points was already a concern.

I made my way from Shildon to Darlington, the nine-mile journey to my brother Alan's home. He had managed to get me a lift with his friend Tommy who was taking his son Colin to the match, also Alan's son Stephen (my nephew), two years my junior but more like a kid brother. Alan followed Newcastle and regularly supported their home games in the early to mid-70's. Stephen had followed suit like his dad and had started going to games quite regularly. Colin was a fellow Spurs supporter so even though I had just met him we got on really well, talking Spurs on the thirty-five-mile drive to Newcastle.

The journey was quick, hardly noticed crossing the Tyne and seeing the iconic Tyne Bridge. It was the first time I had seen it properly, as the other two occasions I had been to Newcastle it had been dark. We pulled into the car park near the Central Station at around 2p.m., an hour before kick-off. Parking in those days was relatively easy compared to now.

The day was mild for January, but I was warm wearing my khaki parka, the type with a bit of fur around the hood, which nearly every kid had in those days. Walking up the back alleys past heaving pubs, hearing that strong Geordie accent ringing out of doorways. I bought my first ever football programme involving Spurs, folded it and stuffed it into my parka and continued my the fifteen-minute walk to the ground.

Approaching St. James' Park, I could now see the back of the open Gallowgate End, but we made our way to the West Stand, which was an old construction with a barrelled roof built at the turn of the 20th Century. We all entered the paddock, a terrace in front of a traditional stand of the time, with around 3,000 seats above. We were towards the Gallowgate End. Colin, Steve and I made our way to the front of the terrace about in line with the eighteen-yard box. The ground filled until just over 38,000 were present. The ground was totally different to how St James' Park now looks. The only part visible from then to the present day is the East Stand opposite the TV cameras, which is where I sat earlier in that season, that being built in the early 70's and is now difficult to replace owing to the listed buildings behind it.

The teams were read out over the tannoy, the names all familiar apart from one, Alfie Conn making his full debut, having had one sub appearance earlier in the season also against Newcastle. Conn was Bill Nicholson's last purchase for Tottenham before stepping down after a terrible start to the season after Spurs lost the first four matches. It was always said the disgraceful scenes at Feyenoord the season before had played a massive part in his decision. He will always be Mr Tottenham to the Spurs faithful though.

What was strange about the Conn signing was that Conn had very long hair, a thing Bill Nicholson was said to hate, but Conn's reputation of being a skilled, charismatic player must have sold him to Nicholson and he was the type of player Spurs were brought up on.

'The players came out, the floodlights already on, like most grounds of the time, four metal girders shining a light on the arena. The Geordie faithful making plenty of noise, mainly from the Leazes End which at that time had a large terrace, but unlike the Gallowgate End, a large shed over its entirety so the noise reverberated. It seemed that Colin and I were the only two Spurs fans in the ground, but I suppose there would have been a couple of hundred there, dotted around but none in evidence. Just before kick-off Mcfaul, the Newcastle keeper received an award for his recent good displays, a trophy he would want to return after this match.

Kick-off, Spurs kicking into the Leazes End, Alfie Conn a real menace, his long flowing locks looking more like he should be playing guitar in a Glam Rock band. Spurs take the lead, Colin and I jump up, the rest of the ground in silence. Soon after 2-0, a second for Conn. Colin and myself are in heaven, Steve not so. By half-time we are four up including a very soft goal by Cyril Knowles. Colin and I waving our scarves around in total joy. The second half, and to give credit, the Geordie crowd really got behind their team, soon pulling a goal back. I still felt nervous as our defence could be quite porous, but no, straight up the other end, 5-1, Newcastle hit back to conclude the score at 5-2. A brilliant display from keeper Pat Jennings, but the man of the match had to go to Alfie Conn with a 'Hat-Trick'.

Once the Spurs faithful were to see Alfie, they loved him, and he became a cult hero. His skill was like the Q.P.R. player Stan Bowles, he would drive at defences at speed, there was always excitement when he received the ball. Alfie played to the crowd, the love affair was mutual. Alfie was signed from

Glasgow Rangers and after his short spell at Spurs 1974-77 he left for Celtic, which was a rarity, crossing the Glasgow divide. When a Scottish reporter once asked, who did you enjoy playing for the most, Rangers or Celtic, Conn's answer was an emphatic 'Tottenham' Whether he was just being diplomatic now he was living in Glasgow. It was said by Conn that he was hounded out of Tottenham by 'The Cockney Mafia', of Perryman, Pratt, and Naylor. Steve Perryman admitted in his autobiography that he didn't get on with Conn because he didn't give his all for the shirt. But he had a special bond with the Spurs crowd, only playing thirty-five league games, but adored by the Spurs faithful.

I left St James' Park on cloud nine, probably the happiest day of my young life, it would be a happy drive back to Darlington and then the bus home to Shildon.

My first job on returning was to get my haversack, and emulsion the opening flap, and paint on Tottenham Hotspur F.C., with a cockerel at the side. I wore it with pride to school the following Monday.

The season didn't carry on in a similar vein, as results were disappointing. Going into April we had some big games to try and pull away from the relegation zone. Chelsea were the visitors, in what was said to be winner stays up, loser goes down. Spurs won 2-0 but the game was marred by vicious fighting on the terraces as Spurs fans clashed with Chelsea fans who were driven to the front of the paddock until they piled on the pitch with Spurs fans following. Hundreds were on the pitch, mainly Spurs beating and kicking their foe. Less than a year after the Feyenoord episode Spurs were in the news for the wrong reasons again.

Losing to Arsenal in the next match at Highbury meant Spurs went into the last game against Leeds at White Hart Lane needing a draw to stay up, to send Chelsea, Luton and

Carlisle down. Just under 50,000 turned up in what was said to be one of the best atmospheres since the glory days of the early 1960's. Leeds a force in those days but having a European Cup Final looming took their foot off the gas and Spurs ran out 4-2 winners. Alfie Conn endeared himself to the Spurs crowd by sitting on the ball during the game to taunt the Leeds midfield to try and get it off him. For me, sat at home listening to the match on the radio I was ecstatic as I ran to celebrate with John my brother, it was going to be a good summer after all.

Roy Wood and his band Wizzard were about finished by 1975 and I was listening to more of what John had in his collection, a particular favourite was an album by America titled quite simply 'America'. They had one hit 'Horse with no name', but the whole album is a beautiful acoustic joy, the only album I have bought on vinyl, C.D and tape, and one I still play regularly to this day. On a more commercial side Queen, who I had liked from their first big hit 'Seven Seas of Rhye' were now making it big. Two albums, 'A Nights at the Opera' and a 'Day at the Races', showed off their musical talent which would inspire them to write 'Bohemian Rhapsody'. Has there been a better frontman than Freddy Mercury? Their New Year's Eve concert from the Hammersmith Odeon which the BBC showed live in 1975 would be a first and was fantastic, especially after watching the blatant miming on Top of the Pops, a treat and a talking point when back at school, for the few of us who enjoyed music.

The 1975-76 season was much better in term of results for Spurs, finishing mid-table and reaching a League Cup Semi-Final, but Terry Neill the Spurs manager who had taken over from Nicholson the previous season wasn't liked, he was

Arsenal through and through, having played there for many years in the 1960s, it was like when Spurs appointed George Graham twenty odd years later, he was seen as the enemy.

The Spurs/Arsenal rivalry started in the 1920's when Arsenal moved from Woolwich in South-East London onto Tottenham's North London patch, but the real blow to the Tottenham faithful was earlier. Spurs finished twentieth in the 1914-15 season in a twenty team Division One. Arsenal had finished sixth in Division Two. After the conflicts of World War One ended, the league went to twenty-two teams, the Directors of Tottenham thought their relegation would be cancelled, but the football league decided to relegate Spurs and Arsenal were asked to join the first division in place of Tottenham. There was an outcry, but the league officials stood by their decision, so when they moved to Highbury that rivalry was sealed and has been fierce ever since.

Gary and I started to watch a lot of Darlington games in 1975. Steve my nephew would also attend when his dad wasn't taking him to Newcastle. We would all stand in the Tin Shed, the home of the more vociferous supporters. Darlington seemed to be embedded in the old Fourth Division so away supporters who travelled to Darlington weren't in big numbers, but the likes of Doncaster, Huddersfield and Stockport would generally bring around 2/300. They were also housed in the Tin Shed which would create a lively atmosphere. On rare occasions the two factions would charge each other, filling in the void the local constabulary had declared a no-go area. You would get a couple of away fans dragged out by the police kicking and screaming. It made the day more exciting, though Gary and I were always cautious after the game when heading back to the railway station not to be caught in any agro.

Managing to get to two Spurs games that season, away at Middlesbrough and at Newcastle, the Boro game we lost 1-0.

I went with Colin, who'd gone with me to Newcastle the season before. We stood in the boys' enclosure which was a small strip of terrace above the main terrace behind the goal. I had gone in there the previous season when my dad took me to the one and only game he ever took me to, against Sheff Utd. We had travelled on a coach from Shildon ran by Boro fans. When we got to the turnstiles my dad told me to go in the Boys' bit and he would go in the adult turnstile. We weren't even stood together, I was ten feet above him against a wall. Luckily, he spotted me and stood below me. Probably saved him 20p which would have bought him half a pint at the Workingmen's Club later that evening along with the other seven or eight pints he would have had.

The other game I attended at Newcastle was in the October. Steve came with me, he liked to stand in the open Gallowgate End which was fine by me. As we entered the open terrace I glanced across to the paddock to where I had stood in the January to see Alfie's hat-trick, a happy feeling filled my body. Unfortunately we were soon 2-0 down, half-time couldn't come quick enough, it looked like revenge for the Magpies. The second half was different, and we got a goal back, Spurs pushed for the equaliser, and it came, a beauty from John Pratt into the Gallowgate goal. I jumped in ecstasy and noticed another lad jump up just in front of me, not more than five yards away. I moved towards him wanting some solidarity. As I moved, I heard a voice behind me.

'I fuck off ya cockney bastard'.

I ignored it and walked to the small lad.

'You a Spurs fan?' I asked.

'I, from Murton, near Sunderland'.

I told him I was from Shildon near Bishop Auckland. We chatted until the game ended, 2-2.

'I might see you about', I shouted.

27

This was my first introduction to Harry Dixon or Little Harry as he is often known. It wouldn't be too long before I would be travelling the country with him. You would often hear Harry before you saw him, shouting,

'Geordie Spurs we are here'.

As the years past Harry became well known to the travelling Spurs support. You would hear regular shouts of 'Alright Geordie' from Londoners. Harry moved to Luton in the early 1980s and would travel to games at the Lane on his trusty Honda 50. He would wear as many coats as he had, to keep warm. The weather didn't seem to matter, whether it was hot or cold three jackets were the norm. Harry also liked to wind the Spurs fans up when things were quiet during away games, Harry would often start chanting.

'Can you hear the cockneys sing, I can't hear a fucking thing'.

Anyone that knew him would shout,

'Sit down you Geordie cunt'.

All in good nature though, yeah Harry's a good mate.

Relegation

In the Summer of 1976, that long hot summer, John my brother decided it was time to leave home and move to Leeds. He had got a place at Leeds University, he was always a bright lad. After leaving school he worked at an engineering company which he hated. It wasn't him, he was articulate, artistic and working with metal wasn't his goal in life. He moved to another factory producing plastic pellets which were then sent to be moulded into anything made of plastic, but his calling was to get a better education, so managed to take his A levels at Darlington College. John was delighted to go to the next level when offered a place at Leeds University, he took the opportunity and moved to Leeds.

As much as I loved my brother it was a blessing that he was leaving the family home. My dad and John were never going to see eye to eye, once John had reached the age of eighteen he became a member of the Workingmen's club, the same club my dad would go to. John would play snooker and was a decent player, but to get to the snooker room he would have to go through the bar area where my dad would sit with his clique. My dad would be embarrassed at the length of John's hair, especially with my dad's friends probably saying, 'he looks like a girl'. I would go to bed about 10p.m. but soon after they would come in, never together and the arguments would start, invariably about John's hair. The argument would be fraught with my mother screaming trying to get in between them to stop them from hitting each other. I would put the blankets over my head to eliminate the tension directly below me, occasionally with tears in my eyes hoping no one would get hurt.

As the years passed nothing changed, except I would be the peacemaker, along with my screaming mother trying to intervene. Our living room had a bay window which had long velvet curtains from ceiling to floor, not around the bay but in front of the bay. They were closed on this particular evening, when as usual the topic of John's hair rose its ugly head. Watching TV totally out of the blue, my dad said,

'When you getting your hair cut?'

John's hair had been the same length for five years, he wasn't going to change it.

'I'm not', John replied.

'It's like a girl's hair,' my dad said.

'Don't care what you say', John replied.

The argument continued until they were facing each other. I watched, thinking here we go again. First a push, John telling my dad to back off, but it didn't happen. Pushing each other like two stags ready for the rut. John's final push had my dad reeling into the long heavy velvet curtains. Before my dad could do anything, John spun my dad and continued until my dad was entwined in velvet, the hooks popping from their moorings. If it wasn't such a serious situation it would have been comical.

'I'll kill you; I'll kill you', my dad shouting in a muffled tone.

John made an exit from the house as we unravelled my dad.

In the summer of 1976 Arsenal came a calling and took Terry Neill as their manager, a glass was raised in London N17 as Spurs fans rejoiced. The successor to the White Hart Lane hot seat was Keith Burkinshaw who was Terry Neill's coach. He had never managed before, had played for Workington, and had been Newcastle's coach the season they lost to Liverpool in the 1974 F.A. Cup final. He was highly respected as a coach but was he the right man for the huge job at Tottenham, only time would tell.

My first game that season I got too was in the League Cup at Middlesbrough in the 2nd Round, yet again going with Steve and Colin. This the last time I would see Colin other than at Darlington matches. Once again standing in the boy's enclosure, we would be the only two jumping up when we scored, the Boro kids around us looking surprised. In the Paddock on the side, a group of Spurs fans, not more than fifty also celebrated, the first time I had seen Spurs fans at a match I had attended. It felt good to hear the chant of 'Come on you Spurs' even though it wasn't deafening. Ian Moores scored on his debut in a 2-1 win, but it must be said one of the worst Spurs strikers to have worn the Lilywhite shirt, his short Spurs career was hounded by the hard to please Tottenham public. His one and only glory was scoring a hat-trick when beating Bristol Rovers, but even then he was out done by Colin Lee who hit four in the same game in an emphatic 9-0 win.

After the game I met up with Harry at Middlesbrough station who was with another fellow Spurs fan, his name was John Trewitt, who would become another regular on my Spurs adventures.

John, a couple of years older than myself was also from Murton, the same pit village as Harry. John was always a confident lad and would always make his stories that bit better than they really were to make them more interesting and funnier. I think John thought he was a bit of a lad, and as the years passed he sort of distanced himself from his Northern Spurs mates to meet up with lads from London. We would often go for a few beers around Kings Cross when in London. You would look around and John had gone, he might say he was off to meet a well-known lad who would run a coach to Spurs away games. Let's just say not all his passengers were just there for the game. But all in all I like John, he now lives in Wakefield, following Spurs home, away and abroad.

Darlington matches were still part of my life, I was getting to most home games in 1976-77. They were having a good cup run, which included an eventful game with Sheffield Wednesday who were in Division Three at the time, but still well supported. It was an evening kick-off under the lights, and for once I didn't stand in the Tin Shed, but on the side, watching Wednesday supporters take over the ground. Darlo fans in the centre of the Shed surrounded on both sides by

31

Wednesday fans who were everywhere around the ground. It wasn't long before Darlo fans at the front of the Tin Shed broke the hoarding and were on the pitch. The atmosphere crackled with the vociferous Yorkshiremen. But it was a long-range screamer that gave Darlington a 1-0 win. Before every game I would visit the programme hut, which stocked quite a few programmes from Division One clubs, Tottenham being one of them. I would buy any that they had in. They may have been three or four months after the games had taken place, but I didn't care, I digested every word in the sixteen pages. What stood out in the Spurs programmes were the quality of the photographs. They showed action from a previous match with the backdrop of the stadium showing the Shelf Side, the iconic terrace which I knew nothing about, but I knew if I got to White Hart Lane it would be where I would stand, but for now watching Spurs in the north was all I could afford.

Shildon Sunderland Supporters Club have always run a coach to matches as long as I can remember, so in the November of 1976 I boarded to see Spurs at Roker Park, another new ground to visit. Spurs were having a season like two years earlier, hovering above the bottom three. Sunderland who had only just won promotion the season before were doing even worse than ourselves and looked set for a quick return. Spurs being Spurs gave Sunderland the three points in a 2-1 defeat, Alfie Conn having a late shot cannoning off both posts summed the day up, it was going to be a tough season.

In the February, the fixtures threw up a series of games in the North, the first at Middlesbrough. I made my way to Darlington and waited for the train to Middlesbrough. While I waited, an Edinburgh bound train rolled in on the adjacent platform, the train stopped and the doors were flung open, a roar reverberated around the station.

'Tottenham, Tottenham'

It was like music to my ears, people moved to one side, kids pointing as the Tottenham boys walked down the platform to the awaiting Middlesbrough train, which I hadn't even notice come in. I had my Spurs silk scarf already around my neck as I boarded with them. Many of them were wearing Doc Martins and Donkey Jackets, with the cockerel badge adorning their lapels, most with straggled hair, the sort where you have had an early start and a comb wasn't part of the morning routine. A few skinheads also, the majority still carrying cans of beer. I listened to the conversation, talking in their London accent, an accent I had heard plenty of times from my numerous London visits. Most of the chat was how we had to start getting results as we were now in the bottom three. The thirty-minute ride passed quickly, quicker than I wanted, and it was good to listen to exactly what Tottenham fans were going through. As we pulled into Middlesbrough there was a repeat of what happened at Darlington. The doors flung open and the two carriages of Spurs fans, about 150 leapt off with the same chant.

'Tottenham, Tottenham'

We walked from the station in a large mob, hardly a copper about, only onlookers, looking surprised at the blue and white scarfed Londoners walking towards the ground. I knew the way from previous visits, I was at the front and after a minute or two I looked back and saw I was on my own. It was 1.30p.m. they weren't going to the ground, they craved beer and the first pub they saw they were in. I strode on regardless and was at the ground just as it was opening its turnstiles. I had decided to stand in the Paddock where I had seen the group of Spurs fans in the League Cup. I thought that's where they would congregate. I went into the empty Paddock. I must have been practically the first in and leaned on a crush barrier and read the programme. At around 2.15p.m. I looked to my right at what was to become the away corner at Ayresome Park and noticed about ten Spurs fans who were on the train earlier. That's where I needed to be if it was where the Spurs contingent were going to stand. I walked over to a steward and explained I had entered the wrong section, he obliged and let me in the corner terrace. The ground filled, the corner did likewise, but it became apparent the 150 Spurs fans were not coming in here, in fact the ten I had seen earlier had vanished, the corner was all Boro fans.

Harry showed up just before kick-off, I gave him a shout as I saw his small figure wandering through bodies, a flask in his hand, his three coats filling him out. I noticed the top of his Spurs scarf inside his coat, less evident than mine, which was blatantly on show. I, still ignorant of the hooliganism which was gripping football. The week after this game there were violent scenes inside and outside of White Hart Lane when Man United's mass red army took on Tottenham, on and off the field.

The game kicked off at Middlesbrough. There appeared to be a hostile atmosphere, you could sense it by the abusive language directed at the Spurs team. I tried to concentrate on what was happening on the pitch but soon felt a tap on my shoulder as three Boro lads, about eighteen years old started talking to me. I was sixteen, still small, looking a couple of years younger, they looked big.

'Come up on the train mate?' one said.

'Just come from Darlington' I said.

I couldn't really say Shildon, who the hell had heard of Shildon unless you were a railway enthusiast.

They were surprised not hearing a Southern accent.

'Why do you follow Spurs?' they asked.

I gave them the reason, a reason I have recounted so many times. Harry had slipped off down the terrace, his many coats had hidden his scarf, I didn't blame him.

'Hereford were up here last week in the cup' another said. As if I would be interested.

'Gave them a good kicking'.

He wasn't meaning on the pitch. My early inclination of what was happening was becoming reality.

'All we want is the scarf you're wearing'.

The game was becoming so secondary I wouldn't have noticed if a goal had gone in.

'And if I don't?'

My first and only scarf meant something to me.

'Nothing yet, but we will keep an eye on you and give you a good kicking after the match, once you're outside'.

The scarfs appeal was waning and three onto one was a mismatch. I had no alternative, I released the scarf, sad to see it depart but not worth a beating. The three lads moved on, as they said they would wearing their trophy. Stunned and shocked my appetite for the match had gone. I looked down the terrace and saw Harry being chased. He managed to get out at half-time, scarf and flask intact. I stayed and watched the second half, but my thoughts were more for home, another defeat 2-0.

Two weeks later Spurs were playing Leeds at Elland Road. John my brother was now settled in Leeds and shared a house with a couple of other students in the Headingly area. John had arranged to meet me and show me his new home. We had made all of the arrangements when he had come home for Christmas, so he knew what train I would be coming on. As usual the atmosphere at home had been fraught, with my Dad and John, like a tinder box ready to explode, so I was pleased in a way when he went back to Leeds.

This was to be my first game outside the North-East, not that Leeds was far, about an hour on the train. John wasn't that bothered about going to the game, but I insisted, after all he had got me into Spurs and it was time he got to see the team he had adopted as his, although this incarnation was much inferior to the Danny Blanchflower led Spurs of 1961 who did the double when lifting the coveted League and F.A. Cup.

Boarding the train at around 10a.m. on a cold February morning I sat in the first-class compartment, not that I had bought a first-class ticket. In those days first class was a carriage with a long passage down one side and then made up with around ten separate compartments holding eight, with a sliding door to enclose you from the long passage. The journey was quiet, me being the only one in the compartment as I looked out the window watching the countryside fly by with the drone of the diesel engine pulling us along, my mind skipping from what had happened two weeks earlier and the forthcoming match against a very average Leeds side. They were mid-table, and an awfully long way from the Leeds of a few years earlier. They still had good players, Harvey, Lorimer, Jordan, Clarke etc. but they were ageing, the same happened at Spurs, but quality recruits were not bought.

The train entered York, I could see about thirty Leeds fans on the platform, you couldn't miss them, everyone appeared to wear half a dozen scarves, a couple around the neck, one around each wrist, one around the waist. I know it was winter, but they looked ridiculous. I'm sure Leeds souvenir shop must of had a roaring trade. It wasn't long before the sliding door of the carriage was slid open, fortunately I was scarfless, not yet replacing the one lost two weeks earlier.

Five noisy woollen bodies sat down talking amongst themselves. I gazed out of the window as the train pulled out of York, listening to their chat. A pause and one spoke.

'Where you off, Tut match?' in their Yorkshire drawl.

'No' I replied, 'I'm off to see my brother in Leeds',

Which was strictly true. Still a little wary after Middlesbrough.

'We are going tut match', as if there was any chance of going anywhere else looking like they did.

'Playing Spurs today, Cockney bastards, we'll slaughter them'.

I just shook my head in agreement. A rendition of 'Marching on Together' was sung as we entered Leeds station.'

Meeting John as arranged, he took me to where he lived, a good half hour walk, and showed me around his flat which he shared with two others. Basically what I expected, a bit messy but ok. A quick drink and we were off again on the three-mile walk to Elland Road. Luckily it was a bright crisp day, so it was a nice walk. Approaching the ground, you could see the tall floodlight pylons, said to be the tallest in the country. Unlike today, Elland Road hadn't yet laid down the road network that you see sprawling around the ground, then it had a large grassy area serving the terraced streets nearby. We walked up to the ground and bought the obligatory programme to add to my growing collection and looked for the nearest turnstiles, which happened to be on the Lowfields Road Terrace. The stadium was good and quite modern. Elland Road had rebuilt a large part of the stadium in the 1960's and 70's. John and I stood almost on the half-way line. I looked to my left and to my surprise a decent Spurs following were present, housed in one half of the terraced end, around 1000 singing their songs. It was good to know the team had a bit of backing. Leeds fans were in other half of the terrace, the two factions traded verbal's. I distinctly remember an annoying jingle over the tannoy for 'Brut aftershave', which seemed to be played as much as possible in between team news and birthday wishes.

The teams came out with the Leeds Kop to my right shouting,

'We hate the Cockneys'.

It was apparent that Spurs and probably every London club were disliked by Northern fans.

Spurs played well in the early stages but were soon a goal behind, but we kept pushing and a goal from Gerry Armstrong, (The Northern Ireland player who would become an icon five years later, when he scored the winner against Spain in the 1982 World Cup.) drew us level. I jumped up in delight, John just smiled, no one around me said anything, after all I am just a small kid. I looked to my left, it was bedlam in the Spurs section as they leapt about. Oh, to have been in with them, but it wasn't to last as Leeds made it 2-1. That's how it ended, with Leeds fans chanting, 'Going down, going down, going down' to the Spurs faithful.

I still believed we could get out of this mess, but as Man United had done three years earlier, big clubs go down. John and I walked out into the almost dark surroundings of Elland Road, Spurs supporters let out at the same time. In the partially lit park everyone mingled together, two Spurs fans in front of us were kicked, one turned to face the instigator.

'Come on then', he shouted in his strong London accent.
I looked around, fights were breaking out everywhere, fans charging at each other. I had seen the images on TV of the trouble in Feyenoord in 1974 on our black and white TV, but this was colour, in high definition, and it was brutal. Punches and kicks raining in, the Donkey Jacketed Spurs fans giving

as good as they got against the multi scarfed Yorkshiremen. John was shocked, me a little less so, after all I had seen this behaviour before.

We moved away from the aggro and headed for the railway station, arriving safely. I said my farewell to John and made my way to the platforms, looking up at the large sign above my head 'Welcome to Leeds'. I smiled and boarded the train with the sound of barking Alsatians fading in the distance as the train left for York. I sat thinking, another loss, but had the satisfaction of a good story for my fellow classmates.

The following week it was Newcastle at St. James's Park and another defeat 2-0, which sent us to the bottom of the league. The only good thing with getting nil is you're not sussed out as an away fan.

Spurs were relegated at Man City, although we were sent down the game before. We had to win at City by a large score, we lost 5-0.

The last game of the season we won at home to Leicester. The win meant nothing, but it's the fans reaction that surprises the Players and Club Officials with an outpouring of support and loyalty. As the final whistle blows the fans go on the pitch with two of them holding a flag reading 'We Will Return'. It's caught on camera and makes many of the back pages the following day. Thousands of supporters climbed into the West Stand seats and chant for the team to come back out.

Steve Perryman, in his testimonial programme in 1979 said that reception was a special moment in his career. He knew the support would be there for Division Two, and what a season that was!

White Hart Lane

In the August of 1977, I spent my usual week-long holiday in London. On one of the days, I travelled to Plough Lane the then home of Wimbledon to watch Spurs play in a pre-season friendly. When I arrived it had been cancelled, which was disappointing, and although relegated my desire to watch Spurs never waned, in fact the opposite. I needed to get to White Hart Lane, the sooner the better.

Having left school at the beginning of June I hadn't a clue what I wanted to do. My exam results were all average, apart from one grade one in English Oral. You had to read aloud and discuss a subject of your choice. I chose Spurs as my subject. The examiner had to stop me talking as I reeled off the history and my own experiences of Tottenham.

She said, 'You seem to know what you are talking about'.

To be honest I was disappointed to be stopped, my subject was so easy to talk about.

I signed on the dole for my weekly nine quid allowance, queuing up with a load of what appeared to be old men. My mam would swiftly lighten it by six, as she said, 'you have to pay board now'. Still three quid wasn't bad, a six hundred percent pay rise from my fifty pence pocket money. I didn't grumble.

On July 4th I started work at a small printing works, so small I was the only employee. It was run by Alan who had recently started his own business after working for a larger print company. He wanted to train a youngster on the one machine he had. Starting on a Youth Training Scheme (Y.T.S.) my first wage was sixteen quid for a forty-hour week, which was reduced by my mam taking nine quid board.

At work the radio was constantly on, even though I couldn't hear it most of the time due to the one machine we had trundling away, but I did hear in the August of 1977, when it was announced Elvis Presley aged only forty-two had died. I wasn't an Elvis fan, but you know the influence he had on a generation of musicians. They said in the all the papers 'The King was Dead'. The Sex Pistols said, 'God Save the Queen, the Fascist Regime', how the music scene had changed from Elvis in 1957 to the Pistols in 1977. Punk was trail blazing across the U.K. I had seen it on my visit to London that summer, the leather clad, studded and pinned clothing, and the Mohican hair made them stand out from the flared trousered, wide collared society. The tourists couldn't get enough of them clicking their cameras to capture the new culture, but my interest was more on the forthcoming season.

The fixtures were out, it seemed strange to skip past Division One and concentrate on Division Two. Sheffield United were Spurs opening game at the Lane, and I wanted to be part of it.

Two weeks before the game I went to Dowsons Newsagents in Shildon where you could obtain coach travel to London. It seemed strange you could get a coach from my little town of thirteen thousand people to the capital of Eight Million. The shopkeeper looked surprised when I asked for a ticket to London. He asked how old I was?

'Sixteen', I said.

'I'll put you down for a half as you look younger, a half goes up to fifteen years old', he said.

I didn't argue, anything to save a few quid was good to me,
I was more than pleased.

The ticket was purchased for four quid. I read the information on the ticket.

'Leave from the shop at 11p.m. on the Friday, return from London Victoria Coach Station on the Saturday evening at 10.30p.m'.

It was finally happening, White Hart Lane was calling.

For the next two weeks I studied the London A-Z book I had, digesting streets and train stations. How I wished school had been so interesting, my route was set. On arriving at Victoria, I would walk along Victoria Street, pass the Houses of Parliament to Westminster Bridge, follow the River Thames along the Embankment to Blackfriars, onto Queen Victoria Street, Threadneedle Street, Bishopsgate and finishing off at Liverpool Street Railway Station. The walk was approximately four miles. I could of course have got the tube from Victoria to Seven Sisters, but I had loads of time to kill. It would be nice in the late summer/early morning sunshine to stretch my legs after a seven-hour coach journey.

In the Autumn of 1975, I watched a documentary on TV, not intentionally, it was just on, but I was soon engrossed, the programme was called 'Johnny go home', about a young Glasgow kid who had such a tough upbringing he leaves home, he doesn't tell anyone, just gets on a train and bunks a ride to London with his small bag. Cigarette hanging from his lips he wanders around the bright lights of London's West End with hardly any money, he sleeps rough. He's aged twelve! It wasn't long before a man comes along and starts chatting to Johnny and offers him a bed for the night. This leads to what you think.

Johnny has to give favours for his keep.

I hadn't given a thought to the seedy side of London, or for that matter any major town or city. The documentary stayed with me and two years later came to the fore.

August 19th had arrived, the eve of my first home game. I clock watched as I got ready, it was a cool night, the stars out, it almost felt Autumnal.

I decided I would wear my snorkel parka coat, the type that had superseded the khaki variety. Snorkel parkas were again worn by most kids, usually the navy blue and orange lined type. What was different to the series one version was that when fully zipped up the hood would turn in to a sort of snout leaving only a six-inch diameter view, there was no peripheral view. They were deadly when crossing a road as your head had to turn a full ninety degrees. The snorkel parka was to be a bad decision especially on what would be a hot August day in London.

I set off, with my mam saying be careful what you're doing. I strode the half-mile seeing numerous pub revellers, pubs closed at 10.30p.m. then. What I did notice is how loud people talked to each other when they were pissed, even though they are only two yards apart. I reached my destination outside the newsagents, surprised to see another person waiting, it made me feel more at ease. The coach arrived quite full, it had started its journey from Ashington north of Newcastle. I boarded and soon dozed off managing a couple of hours of sleep, waking as we stopped and started in London's numerous traffic lights. It was 6a.m.

Leaving the coach, I checked the exits from the coach station, I needed to get the correct exit to start my journey to Liverpool Street Station some four miles away. But first a drink in the coach station café, which was just opening. I entered, the first person in, it was still quiet but coaches were arriving. I asked for a tea.

'You'll have to wait', came the reply. 'We need to get everything heated up'.

I sat down, perused the station, noticing the sign saying, 'Exit for Victoria Street'. At least I knew my exit route was correct.

'Your tea's ready', the lady said.

I sat, having paid for my cuppa, expensive I thought, but this was London after all. The canteen was still empty, until a man came in, probably in his early forties, It's hard to tell when you're young. He walked over and sat at the table I was sat at, there were about twenty other tables he could have chosen.

'Hello', he said in a polite manner.

'Would you like a drink of tea or coffee'.

'No' I replied, I still had half a cup left.

'How about a bacon sandwich', he says.

'No thanks', I said, staying calm, but all the time I'm thinking of Johnny the kid from Glasgow.

I got out my seat and left the café, heading in the direction of the sign for Victoria Street. Leaving the coach station I walked up Victoria Street, I looked back and there was the bloke from the café about a hundred yards behind. This could not be a coincidence, my pace quickened. I turned my first corner, reading the street sign, making sure my thirty-year old A-Z book was still accurate. Looking back again he was still there. I decided, the next corner I would run. As I turned the corner, I legged it, I ran for about four hundred yards. I'd shook him off. I felt much better once I got to the Houses of Parliament and Big Ben, a landmark I had seen many times before, and busier streets than I had left. I crossed the road and onto the banks of the River Thames. I had calmed now and looked forward to this part of the walk. I had never done the walk before but had done the river cruise, Westminster to the Tower of London on a couple of occasions, so it was similar, just on foot this time. I occasionally looked over my shoulder just in case.

The walk went to plan perfectly. The A-Z was spot on. I entered the large expanse of Liverpool Street Station which serves the community belts of North London, Essex, Suffolk and Norfolk.

Buying a paper, I settled into the small but busy café. I needed busy after that morning's experience. It was still early, 9a.m. I read the paper and the large article on Tottenham and how we would fare in Division Two. It was good to read something about your team knowing that there wouldn't be even one line in the Northeast paper about Spurs. I checked out the train times to White Hart Lane Station, wearing my new scarf, which to be honest wasn't a Spurs scarf, as it was more a royal blue, yellow and white rather than navy blue which Spurs played in, but it was the nearest I could get to the colours of Spurs in the northeast. Whatever colour my wool scarf was it was being hidden as hundreds of Arsenal fans converged onto the station on their way to Ipswich for their opening Division One game.

I boarded the 10a.m. train and I was off, the final eight miles. I had seen many photos of White Hart Lane so I had a good idea of what it would be like, but you imagine what the surrounding area would be like. As the train went through Bethnal Green, Hackney, and Stoke Newington, past thousands of Victorian terraced houses my anticipation grew. Seven Sisters, Bruce Grove, White Hart Lane was next. I had purposely sat on the right-hand side of the carriage so I would see the ground from a distance. I looked, seeking out the flood light pylons, then caught sight of them. As the train got closer you could make out the lettering on the old West Stand 'Tottenham Hotspur Football Club'.

The train soon stopped, and I opened the train door. I looked at the station wall and emblazed in spray paint it read 'Alfie Conn is God'. This made me feel more than anything, that I had arrived. Unfortunately Alfie had left for Celtic. White Hart Lane station was small, just a stop off station for the community who would use it to commute into the heart of London for work or pleasure, but on match days it would throng with thousands at peak times.

I walked down the steps and out of the station and headed towards the floodlight pylons, joining Tottenham High Road, a long high street with shops towards Bruce Grove, but this part of the High Road was comprised of numerous cafes, chip shops and a few pubs, notably 'The Bricklayers Arms', 'The White Hart', 'The Corner Pin' and 'The Bell and Hare', the latter two both on the corner of the Park Lane End. Calling in a café I ordered breakfast and got talking to a street vendor who sold scarves and badges. He was having a cuppa before hopefully having a busy afternoon selling merchandise. He talked about the glory days of the past and the huge attendances, talking about the many players which adorned the walls of the café, photos of Greaves, Blanchflower and the like. I wished him well and left, calling into the souvenir shop to get a programme, a bit disappointed that they hadn't kept the small size that they had had for many years, replaced now by the standard size of most other clubs. I walked around the ground, down the Park Lane End, and then around the corner onto Worcester Avenue and saw the vastness of the East Stand standing proud built with thousands of bricks. This was 'The Shelf', where I would queue up for.

Making my way to the turnstile at the centre of the stand I sat down on the warm pavement, which already made me regret my decision to wear my snorkel parka.

It was 1p.m. the ground wouldn't open until 1.30p.m. I got talking to a couple of young lads also waiting to go in, Paul and Panno, they were from the Chingford area. They were really impressed I had come all the way from the North-East. I would stand with them for the next couple of years, two lads who really made me feel welcome.

The bolts were released on the inside of the turnstile doors, anticipation growing, Paul explained to me to follow him into the ground but be quick. I paid my fifty pence entry. It always amused me over the years how many bearded men would go through the juvenile turnstiles to save a little money, then queue for a beer once under the stand, the operators turning a blind eye as they can't be arsed with arguing who is sixteen or over. Pushing myself through the turnstile barrier, which had seen thousands doing the same over the countless years, I ran, following Paul and Panno, briefly looking at the long expanse of the underbelly of the stand, noticing a few kiosks that sold Bovril and pies. I climbed about ten steps bringing me onto the lower terrace, then up another ten steps and onto the upper terrace (The Shelf). The three of us got to the front wall which separated the Shelf from the lower terrace.

Standing over the halfway line I could now peruse my surroundings and I wasn't disappointed. Designed by the Scottish architect Archibald Leitch who had designed many of the Grandstands at British football stadiums, Tottenham would employ his services to build a ground like no other.

Starting the project in the early 1900's the stadium began to resemble the ground that we would recognise, but Leitch was to deliver his masterpiece in the mid-1930s with the construction of the East Stand. A two-level terrace with seats above, and a press box perched on the roof, no stand looked like it. The stand was completed in 1937 holding an estimated 30,000, this capacity being reduced to 25,000 in the 1960's. 20,000 were on the two-levels of terrace, the upper level was soon affectionately known as 'The Shelf' by the supporters. The ground changed little from then until 1980, except for the two standing ends having seats put in at the rear in the early 60's and the West Stand link ups to the two ends in the early 70's.

I took in the view before me. The beautiful, manicured pitch, the stands which showed their age but were neat and newly painted. The three sides I viewed looked smaller than on TV, all grounds did. Then I turned my head and took in the vastness of The East Stand. It reminded me of a huge battleship, many said it was a glorious wedding cake, three levels and the press box on top like a bride and groom. Interestingly the press box was rarely used, the pressmen preferring to be closer to the action so were put in the West Stand.

I could see why Paul and Panno wanted me to get to the front wall on the Shelf, the view could not be bettered on any terrace. perched six feet above the heads of people at the back of the lower terrace, you got an uninterrupted view over the pitch.

As the ground filled, I thought if we can get around 20,000 it would show the support had stayed loyal. At kick off 27,000 watched us beat Sheff Utd 4-2 in an entertaining match. It was good to be able to show my joy when scoring instead of fearing for my safety. The Spurs crowd were good, especially The Shelf, the most fervent part of the ground.

As I left the ground that bright August afternoon, snorkel parka over my arm, I was sad to leave, delighted to have won but wondering when I would be back. I boarded the thronging train at White Hart Lane Station, not getting a seat but making sure I could see the floodlight pylons fade into the distance. I had made my mind up I would be back before Christmas.

I retraced my steps after leaving Liverpool Street Station and walked along the Thames Embankment, after all my coach didn't leave until 10.30p.m that evening, so I had plenty of time to kill. Passing a large group of Charlton Athletic fans on their way back from Fulham, like me wanting to take in the evening sunshine. I arrived back at Victoria at around

8p.m. and made my way into the busy café that earlier that day had felt so menacing. I read the programme reliving the day in my head. It had been eventful.

6a.m. on a cold Sunday morning I disembarked from the coach, back in my hometown, pleased I had my snorkel parka to keep me warm on the ten-minute walk home. I let myself in and got into bed planning to sleep until lunch time.

The Sunday Mirror newspaper did not mention our result now we were in Division Two, even less news about Tottenham in the Northeast papers.

Five weeks later, September 24th, I was back at White Hart Lane, Spurs 2 Luton 0, same routine. Christmas couldn't come quick enough for my desire for Spurs, I had to get back.

I didn't get down to the Lane again until November 5th, against Burnley. The only change I made to my routine was that I decided against the walk from Victoria to Liverpool Street mainly because it was Autumn and dark when I arrived in London. My new route was to take the tube from Victoria to Liverpool Street on the Circle Line, so just missing the walk. It meant I was up to Tottenham an hour earlier, but I was getting used to my surroundings in North London. The match, my first under the lights at the Lane would take on that extra atmosphere, that first glimmer of a blue haze that emanates from the lamps casting their shadows onto the players. It gives the crowd that little bit of a buzz. Spurs won easily 3-0, not quite as easy as the 9-0 when Spurs had beaten Bristol Rovers a few weeks earlier, but good enough to keep us in the promotion spots.

Towards the end of the game, I got a tap on my shoulder, it was Harry. I hadn't seen Harry since the Middlesbrough episode. I told Harry how the Middlesbrough bastards had got my scarf, him telling me how he had sorted a few of them out.

I was gullible at the time to Harry's stories. Along-side Harry was a ginger haired lad, with massive fuzzy hair.

'This is Richie from Sunderland', Harry said, 'goes to most games'.

We got chatting and I soon found out that Richie, like me, was a keen collector of Spurs programmes, so we had a common interest and got on really well. As the years have passed Richie's hair has got shorter and shorter to virtually nothing, but his eating habits haven't changed. Richie is one of the reasons why fish and chips will remain a British institution. It's a common joke now with all the lads that Richie will frequent a chip shop at every opportunity. We head to the pub, Richie heads to the chip shop, getting his fix. Richie has never drank much at games, whereas I didn't drink much in the early years but soon caught up with the rest of the lads in later years. If Richie had two pints you knew he was on a bender.

Another thing about Richie is when he sets his heart to do something, he does a top job. In the late 70's Richie decided to build a model of White Hart Lane, approximately three feet by two feet, made of wood. He would always be taking photos of the ground inside and out. I would often ask how it was going, until one day he brought in some photos of the finished ground, it was magnificent. He had even used match sticks for roof supports. It was so good he got it published in the 'Sunderland Echo' as the mad keen Spurs fan from Sunderland.

His other interests are hill walking, which ended up with Richie going on an expedition to Everest base camp. Tropical Fish is another, fish tanks all around his house. He then got into model railways which go between rooms in his house, surely the two could be linked to provide a channel tunnel. Overall though Richie is one of my closest friends and one we all like and respect for his dedication. We sometimes take the piss, but it's all in good heart. Stay as you are Richie 'Chippie' Addison.

Still getting to watch Darlington regularly in 1977-1978 they drew Chester away in the F.A. Cup first round. Gary, Mulley and I decided to go. Mulley was another close friend, and he introduced me to The Electric Light Orchestra a couple of years earlier. Mulley was a big fan of the band and thought the world of Jeff Lynne, the lead singer. Mulley had bright ginger hair, a proper copper top, quite long, about shoulder length. He decided to change his image and go for a Jeff Lynne perm. He was the first person I knew who got a perm, it was becoming fashionable for footballers, but I wasn't sure how it would go down with the working class Shildon folk. Anyway, Mulley went through with it, his thick ginger hair came out a treat, the perm was massive. Think of Motown music of the 70's, like a young Michael Jackson, big afro style. Mulley's would rival any of those, it was unbelievable. Gary soon followed suit, his turned out more Richard Beckinsale from TVs Rising Damp. Mulley's love of E.L.O. rubbed off onto all my friends, a band I still love today, they are different with their rock, string filled arrangements, and brilliant live.

The three of us set off to Chester on one of the three coaches Darlington had laid on. Of course I would still have one eye on how Spurs would fare in their promotion clash at Bolton.

The journey was ordinary. We pulled up right outside the ground shortly before 1.30p.m.

We alight, the vast majority of the near 150 heading to the nearest pub, but as we were fifteen- and sixteen-year old's this didn't come into our conversation. A burger and a programme were more us. We entered the recently opened turnstiles and surveyed the ground from the open end we had opted for, it was a neat ground, this the old Chester stadium, Sealand Road. We all agreed it was superior to Feethams, Darlington's home. The ground filled slowly. The large open bank we stood on was fairly spartan. What we did notice were a group of Chester boys congregating behind us, they didn't say anything, but they knew we were Darlington. It made the atmosphere tense. A few other Darlington fans were dotted around, but it's strange how a couple of hundred away fans can become invisible when not housed in one section, even in a crowd of only 3,330 that were present at this match.

The score went against Darlington, a 4-1 defeat. The Chester boys didn't do anything apart from a few verbal's. Leaving the ground and straight onto the waiting coaches, pleased that we were unscathed. The coaches pulled away, and within two hundred metres we were hit with a barrage of stones and bricks, most hitting the sides of the coaches, a few bouncing off the windows. Everyone ducked down on the coach, the driver kept on going. Then a stone came through the window, luckily missing everyone, but a gaping hole halfway up the coach had to be addressed, after all it was November. The coach stopped to check everyone was alright, and a jacket was put over the hole to keep the elements out. A blowy return journey was to follow. To make the journey worse a 1-0 defeat for Spurs in the top of the table clash with Bolton.

The season was going well for Spurs, apart from the blip at Bolton. My next game in early December, was for me the short thirty or so miles to Sunderland, a fixture we needed to win to keep us in the top three. Sunderland were mid-table.

I took the train from Darlington which at that time went all the way to Sunderland, so no changing. Travelling on my own my thoughts went to where to stand. I had stood on the Roker End the season before but decided to go in The Clock Stand Paddock, where away fans would be housed for a couple of years in the early 80's. As the train approached the stations nearing Sunderland, the Sunderland fans, most of them wearing three or four scarves, hats, rosettes, reminding me of the Leeds fans.

'They wear everything but the Kitchen sink', a man next to me commented.

I got to the ground at 2.00p.m. and stood in the paddock over the halfway line. A couple of middle-aged Sunderland fans began talking to me asking how Sunderland were going to do today. I didn't have the heart to say I hope you get beat. To my right in the Roker End a section of terrace was left empty, I didn't know why. By kick off there were no Spurs fans evident in the ground which was a surprise as the away support had been good on Spurs away days, over 3,000 had travelled to the recent match at Bolton.

The game kicked off and it seemed like I was the only Spurs fan in the ground. The atmosphere was good, it was always good at Roker Park, the 30,000 certainly made a din when they attacked. I looked to my right, it was now twenty minutes since the match had started, when I noticed a police escort pushing its way through the Roker End with around 4/500 Spurs supporters trailing behind. The Spurs fans were put in the empty away section which was a strange segregation, Sunderland fans surrounded the Spurs fans on both sides and above.

The atmosphere in the Roker End wasn't good, there was hatred in the air. By all accounts Sunderland fans had had a rough time at White Hart Lane the previous season and now it was time for revenge. Sunderland fans began to encroach the Spurs section, and once the first few fists were flung

Sunderland yobs moved in, in strength. I stood transfixed from my safe area as I watched my fellow supporters take a good kicking. The game carried on, the police didn't seem interested, as much as to say, 'Fuck you, you Cockney bastards, that's what you did to our fans last season, see how it feels'. There was only one escape route, as hundreds of fans clambered onto the pitch, the game was stopped. Around 300 Spurs fans started walking towards where I was standing. I saw many were blood splattered, the police trying to round them up. They were now on the touchline passing me, getting dogs abuse from the Wearsiders. One of the two blokes I had been talking to shouted.

'Feed them to the Fulwell End'.

Those six words have always stayed with me. What seemed a decent bloke to me, was condoning more mindless violence on people who are only trying to avoid a savage beating. The Spurs fans were finally led back into the Roker End and order was restored.

Two goals from my then hero John Duncan gave Spurs the win they deserved, as each goal goes in, I jumped arms aloft punching the air, the two blokes looked at me, they must have been thinking, 'He's Tottenham', nothing was said, the look summed it up.

A couple of years after that game I was in the Spurs Supporters Club for my usual pint and got talking to a lad, he was asking where I was from, when I told him the Northeast, he said he would never go to Sunderland again. His nose was to one side, he had a scar from his nose and down across both lips. He couldn't remember much about what happened, but had been knocked to the ground and then been stamped on. He'd only been in the ground five minutes. Next thing he was waking up in Sunderland General Hospital. Nobody needs that after travelling the best part of three hundred miles to watch their team.

Early 1978 was a special night for hormonal teenagers when 'Top of the Pops' first showed the video by Blondie featuring Debbie Harry singing their first hit record Denis (Denee). The blonde bombshell had made an impression on me. Her image was instrumental in her selling 'Parallel Lines', Blondie's second album by the bucket load, me being one of the purchasers. The album had numerous punchy New Wave anthems but also had the classic 'Heart of Glass' which would fill the dance floors up and down the country. Her poster would adorn my bedroom wall alongside Kate Bush, another who had her first hit 'Wuthering Heights' at the same time as Blondie. I had my Blonde and Brunette alongside the Spurs team group which still had its pride and place on my wall.

I got down to my Aunts over the New Year of 77, so I could take in Spurs beating Blackburn 4-0 but didn't get to another game until the Spring of 1978 due to bad weather. Although games were going ahead there were many postponed, so I couldn't take the chance of booking travel and losing out, especially on my small wage.

I had recently finished my Six-Month training and was taken on full time at the printers on a four-year apprenticeship. My first full-time wage had gone from sixteen to twenty-three quid, the rise was beneficial, although my mam took another pound, so I had thirteen quid for myself.

On the 8th April Spurs had their biggest game of the season at home to Bolton, first versus second, Spurs just a few points below Bolton. I couldn't miss this trip to White Hart Lane. On arrival the difference was evident, even early that Saturday morning there was a buzz around the streets. I made

55

my way earlier than usual to meet Paul and Panno, they were there near the front of the queue for The Shelf, they told me a full house was expected. In those days 'all ticket' games were quite rare, It was a case of first come first served. At 2.30p.m. the ground was heaving, I hadn't seen it like this on my previous four visits, but strangely there were very few Bolton fans present.

At kick off 50,097 supporters crammed onto the terraces. The noise surpassed anything I had ever heard at any ground which I had been to, especially the roar of, 'Come on you Spurs' which echoed around the stands, it was like the old days, like what the souvenir seller told me in the café on my first visit.

The game ebbed and flowed, but one goal from Don McAllister gave Spurs the points and put us top of the table. It looked like it would be a formality that we would go up now, but Spurs being Spurs we got into a bad run, and by the last two games of the season we needed three points. (two points for a win). I had travelled down two weeks after the Bolton game to see us lose to Sunderland, my first defeat at the Lane. The last game of the season against Southampton would be a win or bust game for both clubs. Spurs had beaten relegated Hull with a late winner from skipper Steve Perryman to set up the dramatic finale.

Spurs and Southampton both needed a point to go up, Bolton were champions, Brighton were waiting for either of the other two to slip up. A Brighton win and a Spurs or Saints loss would give the Seagulls their first ever season in the topflight.

Sitting in my bedroom for the final game of the season I was even more nervous than three years earlier when avoiding relegation by beating Leeds in the final game. The radio was switched on, our game would be the featured game.

Nottingham Forest had already won the Division One Title, which was totally unexpected after only just been promoted the season before. Under the management of Clough and Taylor more glory would follow over the next few years.

The game kicked off at a jam-packed Dell, the 6,000 Spurs fans who were lucky enough to get tickets probably as nervous as myself. All I wanted was the game over. Nil-Nil would be good all round for both clubs. Just keep it in the middle I was thinking, but no, Spurs cleared off the line, with near misses and most of it was in the Spurs goalmouth. It was torture trying to picture the game from the commentary, I just wished it was over! At 4.45p.m. Nil-Nil, and the final whistle, Spurs fans were on the pitch either climbing or pulling down the fence that held them in. I was drained but so happy, then I thought what if? I'm sure if that result had gone against us it would have been a disaster. Keith Burkinshaw our manager had faith in the team that had been relegated, and they responded by playing flowing football that had the Spurs crowd purring. Ask any Spurs fan who watched Spurs in the Second Division and most would say it was one of their favourite seasons. Of course, that's because it had a wonderful outcome. If they hadn't come back at the first attempt the manager would have left or been sacked, and the team would have been dismantled. Who knows what the future could have been, possibly going in the direction of some of the great clubs of the past, Blackpool, Preston etc. The first attempt is a clubs' best chance to come back, and Tottenham had cemented their return.

1978-79 would have two special players joining the ranks of the Lilywhites.

Argentina

During the early summer of 1978 I would stay up until 2a.m. watching the World Cup from Argentina. England weren't even there, but Scotland were. To see them and their manager Ally MacLeod, with head in hands, losing to lesser teams brought me some relief to England not being there. What I do remember of that World Cup is the power and skill of the Argentina side. They fully deserved their World Cup win, playing in front of a passionate support which gave their team a ticker tape welcome before every match, it looked fantastic, streamers and paper would flutter around the stadiums that Argentina played in. Star players were Mario Kempes, a powerful forward, Daniel Passarella, a dominant central defender and captain, and in the midfield a small but beautifully balanced player called Osvaldo Ardiles, who would skip past the opposition.

A few weeks after the tournament I was watching the news and saw that Tottenham had signed two Argentines, Ricardo Villa being one. He had made a few appearances in the World Cup and looked a powerful midfielder. Then the camera focused on his compatriot, I couldn't believe it, Osvaldo Ardiles had signed for Spurs. He would go on to become a legend at White Hart Lane. Ossie and Ricky as they would be better known hit all the back pages, even the ones in the Northeast. They were the first two high-profile footballers to come from overseas, and the outlay of three quarters of a million pounds for the two would be money well spent. Everyone would want to see them play. We would retrieve the outlay from gate receipts.

That summer seemed to go so slow. In early July the fixtures came out. I had never looked forward to seeing them as much as that year, back in the topflight. The first game on the list was Nottingham Forest away, it couldn't have been any harder, the Champions at the City Ground.

As the weeks passed towards the August kick off I had been in touch with Paul from London. He had told me the interest in North London was crazy for the two Argentines with season ticket sales at their highest in the clubs' history. You must remember pre–Premier League days, season tickets were usually only a small percentage of a ground's capacity, in Tottenham's case usually around 10,000 in a 52,000 capacity. It was great for the casual supporter who only went to a few games a season. If you wanted to go to a game, you turned up and paid at the turnstile. Paul told me that Tottenham had laid on eight special trains for the Forest match, plus a fleet of coaches, then the addition of people making their own way by car and others like myself from other parts of the country Spurs were going to have a huge following and I couldn't wait for the day.

August 19th had arrived. I left home on that bright Saturday morning to get the train from Shildon to Darlington, a short wait and then onto the train to the East Midlands. With another pay rise, up to twenty-seven quid, the near eight quid return ticket to Nottingham wasn't too bad. I boarded and soon bumped into Harry, Richie and John. It was good to travel with my fellow Spurs fans. Also, another lad called Colin Graham, I hadn't seen him before. Colin was from the Stockton area of Teesside. He was only about 18 months older than me but looked older as his hair was already thinning. Colin was easy to get on with and has become a good mate. I have been fortunate to have met people that are still close friends, the type you are always comfortable with while in their presence. Nowadays I might not see them from one year to the next, but when I see them it's as if I saw them yesterday.

We pulled into York Station and John shouted,

'Phil and Pete are getting on'.

Two more I had never met. Phil Pattinson a tall, bearded twenty-year-old from York. He was a Pete Townsend (The Who) lookalike, but like Colin looked older, Pete Wheeler was the same age as me from Harrogate. You would always see the two together, always boarding the trains with beers in hand, another two special friends. Phil would later become my best man and godfather to my second son Adam. So this was the Northern Spurs crew of 1978. The journey passed quickly, the banter was funny. John was constantly taking the piss out of Phil and Pete for being tight Yorkshire bastards. But I didn't escape the piss taking either.

When getting on the train at Darlington, I sat with Richie, John and Harry, the table was littered with beer cans, so when I put my four pack of ginger beer down which was non-alcoholic, basically pop, John looked at it.

'What the fucks that?' he said, thinking it might be a new type of lager.

'Ginger beer', I said.

'Fuckan What?'

His Sunderland accent was almost a shrill.

'Idris ginger beer', I said. 'It's brewed in Tottenham'. I proudly added, it stated it on the can, this got the approval from the others.

Phil soon clocked the ginger beer when he came aboard.

'What's that?'

Phil and Pete were so easy to get on with, that between York and Nottingham it was like I had known them years. I handed him the freshly opened can.

'Try it', I said.

Phil took a slurp.

'Wow, I couldn't drink that it burns your throat'.

As I still wasn't drinking, the Idris ginger beer would be drunk for a while longer. Alcohol would come later.

Arriving in Nottingham at mid-day we headed towards the ground, soon passing a pub with a large Spurs following inside, the chance of being served in the next half hour would be slim, but it didn't stop Phil, Pete, John and Harry from trying. The rest of us stayed outside. Although the temperature was in the mid-twenties, scarves were still adorned by supporters, many of which were now spilling onto the forecourt of the pub. A group of thirty Forest fans were spotted walking down the road, and it wasn't long before an equal number of Spurs fans were chasing them back to where they came from. You could imagine the same scene would be happening all over Nottingham that day, that's what it was like in these times of the late 1970's.

Richie and I set off to the ground at about 1p.m. and were met by a long queue snaking away from the turnstiles allocated for away fans. Spurs fans were allocated along the side, a deep paddock, for which we received half of the approximate 12,000 capacity. From what I was told from Paul in London this was not going to meet requirements.

We entered the ground at 1.45p.m. It soon filled, and by 2.30p.m. the section was full. We heard the gates were now locked in the away section, with thousands of Spurs fans locked out, but this didn't stop them. The gates were smashed and more and more piled in, pushing from the back to try and get in, the crush was now dangerous. My coat sleeve began to tear off in the crush, hanging on by a few threads, everyone pushing to-and-fro. Spurs fans were now in the open end to our left. The gates finally closed all around, an official crowd of 41,000, but there must have been a few thousand extra who had gate-crashed there way in.

Many of our supporters were busy ripping newspapers so the team would come out to a ticker tape welcome from the estimated 10,000 Spurs fans.

Lead out by Stevie Perryman, paper fluttered in the summer haze, we hoped it would mean something to Ricky and Ossie, a welcome from the Tottenham supporters. We would do this throughout the season on our travels, a section at every ground littered with paper, it must have been a nightmare for the terrace cleaners after every match.

No cameras were allowed at Forest that day, the club had banned them from the country's biggest match of the day, even though everyone wanted to see the two Argies play their first game, it would only be the paying patrons that day.

Spurs took the lead, Ricky Villa notching, our support so packed you could hardly jump for joy. Ossie had a quiet game, but his time would come in later games. Forest equalised before half time and this is how it ended. We were delighted to get an away point from the Champions. 'Tottenham are back, Tottenham are back, hello, hello, Tottenham are back' rang around the City Ground at the final whistle, sung to the tune of the much-maligned Gary Glitter hit of the early 70's.

I spent the next week in London at my Aunt's who was always so welcoming, but as much as I liked to see her and my Uncle it was the opportunity to take in two home games.

The Wednesday couldn't come quick enough, I was even more excited to welcome Ossie and Ricky on their new home patch more than I had at their debut the previous Saturday. This being my first mid-week game at the Lane just added to my anticipation.

Taking the twenty-minute train ride into Victoria, then a tube to Liverpool Street and a train up to White Hart Lane, I arrived at around 5p.m. leaving the packed train carriages of suited businessmen, but mainly scarf wearing football supporters, some of whom still wore the less than fashionable butcher's coats. This was a white coat made of cotton that supporters would decorate with their favourite players, parts of the ground they stood, and the cockerel badge. These coats were more popular in the late 60's and early 1970's, but I liked nostalgia, so they were good to see.

A quick bite to eat, I was around The Shelf turnstiles by 5.30p.m. to meet Paul and Panno, both had gone to Nottingham, so we discussed the match and the crush. The gates soon opened, and we ran up onto The Shelf to get our usual spot. The ground looked immaculate and filled quickly. The floodlights flickered on one at a time, the crowd already anticipating the action soon to follow.

At 7.25p.m, kick off at the old traditional 7.30p.m. the Spurs team came out of the tunnel to a wave of noise and tickertape, it wouldn't be the last tickertape welcome, but this was the best one. Paper emanated from all corners of White Hart Lane, the floodlights making the spectacle an even greater sight, Ossie and Ricky said later it made them feel at home. There was a crescendo of noise as the whistle blew to start. Aston Villa the visitors were making a game of it in front of 48,000 and took the lead to quieten the expectant crowd. Spurs just couldn't get into it and eventually lost 4-1, it would be Villa who were crowing, and it wouldn't be Ricky. It was disappointing but it was early days. As I traipsed out of the ground at least I had the comfort that I would be back on the Saturday against rivals Chelsea, a team that even I knew Spurs fans had a hatred for.

That Saturday I set off early following the same route as on the Wednesday. I took defeats quite badly when I was young so it was good to get another game in quickly to erase the festering feeling that can stay with you, I'd had this feeling too long over recent years with the team struggling with relegation. After promotion I was hoping to see a new dawn.

Arriving at Liverpool Street at around 11a.m. I boarded the train to White Hart Lane. The trains at that time had carriages sectioned off into small compartments each holding around twelve people, the full width of the carriage, so you had an exit door on either side, no passage to walk the length of the carriage. Once you were in, that's where you remained. I was the only one in my section as the train pulled out of Liverpool Street Station. I looked at my surroundings and it dawned on me how dangerous and threatening these compartments were. If there was an incident you couldn't leave it, you were trapped.

We pulled into Stoke Newington about the half-way point of the journey, a lad a bit older than me entered the compartment, and I immediately felt threatened, paranoia setting in. He sat opposite me, so there's now just the two of us. I catch him out of the corner of my eye looking at me.

'Going to the game?', his thick cockney accent cutting through the clickety click of the tracks.

'Yes', I replied.

I thought back to 1975 and the vicious fighting that took place the last time Spurs met Chelsea. Now I'm thinking could he be Chelsea coming up early to take it out on some poor Spurs fan just to gain revenge. I thought quick and planned what to do next. The fateful question was soon asked.

'Are you Spurs or Chelsea?' he asked.

It was like a million-pound question, but in my circumstances get it right, then have a chat with him, get it wrong and who knows, a knife attack. Remember these two sets of fans hate each other. Looking back older and wiser, of course he was Spurs, very few Chelsea fans would be travelling to North London that early. My answer to his question was quick and diplomatic.

'I follow neither, I'm from the Northeast on holiday and I'm taking in a game'. My accent was enough for him to believe me.

'I'm Tottenham', he said.

He chatted about Spurs, stuff I already knew, and to be honest I could have probably told him more about Spurs, such was my interest in Tottenham's past halcyon days.

The train pulled into White Hart Lane Station, he wished me well, I responded my telling him I hope Spurs win, he nodded his approval, and we went our separate way. I headed to the Spurs Supporters Club, Warmington House, which was next to the ground, an old Victorian three storey house, their primary objective was to give supporters the chance to book tickets for away travel, but it had a bar and food, which was basically burgers, hotdogs and sandwiches. It was somewhere to go before the game.

As usual I took my place on The Shelf, the difference today was that the whole of the Park Lane End had been given over to Chelsea. The ground filled, you could sense the animosity between the two factions, which seemed to have started in the early to mid-1960s when skirmishes were happening, not only at White Hart Lane but also Stamford Bridge.

By 2.30p.m the ground was a cauldron of verbal abuse from the two sets of fans. In those days fans would enter the ground much earlier than the present day. Now you have a seat, you know where you're sitting, and you're guaranteed that position in the ground. Also, there wasn't the thunderous music you have today over the P.A. system, more a sedate record request from the D.J. Fans would make the pre-match entertainment by shouting obscenities.

The atmosphere was really building inside, but you could also hear it outside the ground as trouble was escalating behind the Park Lane End. You could hear the roar of running battles, it was mad, but it was exciting. I hadn't seen this before, this was football hooliganism on another level. At kick-off, the crowd of just over 40,000, disappointing really, considering Chelsea had around 6,000 present, not quite filling the Park Lane terrace and seats. The atmosphere crackled, the large away following really made a difference. Spurs took the lead, John Duncan swivelling to hammer home. His joy as he ran towards the Shelf was only surpassed by the Spurs faithful. Our gloating towards the Park lane was short lived as Swain equalised within a minute. Chelsea's fans explode. Within seconds Spurs fans give out the regular chant of the time, 'Your goner get your fucking heads kicked in'.

The game settled, many of the fans just eyeballing each other, only looking at the on-field action when it gets into the penalty areas. Another goal each and a very good game ends 2-2.

Afterwards, with the Park Lane End closed off to stop Spurs fans heading down that way, I walked around the back of Paxton Road and onto the High Road towards the Supporters Club. I stood outside listening and watching the chaos as battles commenced down the Tottenham High Road towards Seven Sisters Tube almost two miles away. The infamous chant by Spurs fans to the tune of 'It's a long way to Tipperary'! It's a long way to Seven Sisters it's a long way to run' seemed apt. After half an hour of letting the crowd stream away I made my way back to my Aunts. It had been an interesting holiday.

The North West, Leeds and Anti-Semitism

After the a tough opening fixture against the Champions of England, Nottingham Forest, our next away fixture would be against the eventual Champions Liverpool at Anfield, a daunting prospect for Spurs. The usual headline in the papers were 'Spurs have not won on Liverpool's turf since the Titanic went down in 1912', but after the encouraging display at the City Ground, I would travel in hope. My best mate Gary had decided to make his Anfield debut and travel with me. Gary like me had seen his initial Liverpool games around the North-east grounds, so was excited to be making his first visit to Liverpool. Along with Gary, was his mate from work, Col Norman, who was one of those lads full of himself, another Liverpool fan. He liked to make his mouth runaway, but he was ok in moderation. I only mention Col because seven years later he died of cancer, still in his early twenties. Things like that show how vulnerable life can be, a tragedy for his family as his brother Tony died aged eleven, when falling from a chimney he had climbed up.

Travelling to Liverpool was another first for me, as was everywhere else I went that season. It was exciting to visit stadiums you had only seen on 'Match of the day'. We arrived at Liverpool Lime Street at around 11a.m., the three of us got a bus to Anfield.

On arriving at the ground, the queues were already evident at the Kop End, even at this early hour. Spurs were going to be a big draw this season, many clubs getting their biggest or near biggest gate, mainly down to fans wanting to see Ossie and Ricky, it was a novelty at the time. Gary and Col decided to go in the Anfield Road End, I was surprised they didn't fancy the Kop. I left the two of them and decided to stand in the Main Stand Paddock near the player's tunnel, not sure why I didn't go in the Anfield Road corner where the 2,000 Spurs fans were housed. Anfield was one of the best stadiums, but like our own looked smaller than it did on TV, but it was dominated by the huge Kop End which at the time could hold 24,000. I did feel some envy for grounds that had a large bank behind the goal, which White Hart Lane didn't have.

Five minutes before kick-off Gerry and the Pacemakers burst into life over the tannoy, the Liverpool anthem 'You'll never walk alone', the red and white scarfs thrust above everyone's head, but not mine, or the pocket of blue and white in the corner, it sounded magnificent and like the bloke next to me had said,

'No one sings it like us'.

He was right, no one did sing it like them, its strange to think now how many fans copied this chant back in the 60s and 70s, even Man Utd fans could be heard singing it! I've been to Anfield many times since and still get a tingle when I hear it, one of the great football anthems.

The game kicked off, it was one-way traffic as Liverpool constantly put pressure on. We were soon a goal behind and it's not long before the next goes in. I'm thinking game over, let's keep the score down. This Liverpool team would win the league by a canter, only letting in sixteen goals in a forty-two-game season, only four of them at Anfield. Nineteen home wins, two draws, no defeats, many Liverpool supporters say this was the best ever Liverpool team, and I couldn't argue. Three down at half-time, we just had to tighten it at the back. Second-half, four, five, six, seven, we were annihilated. You could only admire Liverpool as Spurs suffered their record defeat. I will not see a team take us apart like that again, they were brilliant.

I left the ground, I could have cried especially hearing the exuberant scousers not only praising their team but ripping into my team.

'They were fucking shite, Ardiles, Villa, World Cup winners, fucking shite'.

These were the sort of comments I heard as I left Anfield. It was true Ossie and Ricky were finding the English league tough.

I met Gary and Col at our pre-planned meeting point. Gary didn't say a word, he knew how I felt and strangely I was pleased in a way that he had seen his team win on his first visit, maybe not by seven though, a victory would mean a lot to him. I've always remembered Gary's respect for my feelings that day and I never mock other supporters in defeat, they don't need to hear it. Col on the other hand, taunting me on the bus back to Lime Street Station. I met up with the Northern Spurs lads John, Harry, Richie, Phil, Pete and Colin, who told Col the Liverpool fan to shut the fuck up.

We had a quiet train ride back, drowning our sorrows, in my case over a nice cold ginger beer.

Arriving in York I said my farewell to Pete and Phil. John, Harry and Colin decided to get off and go for a couple of beers in York, Richie just tagged along. I told them I would see them at Leeds in two weeks. It left Gary, Col and myself to change trains for the last part of the journey to Darlington.

The 125 train entered the station bound for Edinburgh, as passengers spilled from the train it would still remain packed, the three of us stood inbetween carriages. Another Liverpool fan was stood next to us. We didn't know him, he wore a Liverpool shirt and scarf and we soon got talking to him. Col quick to point out I was Spurs, so feel free to mock him. He looked a similar age to us, sixteen or seventeen, he didn't give me any stick. The conversation was interrupted when three Newcastle fans walked through the compartments where we stood, older than us by a few years and quite drunk.

69

Newcastle had been playing at Cambridge in the old Second Division.

'Ye been tha match?' one said.

'Yes', the four of us replied.

'Fuckan seven noot wonnit?', another said noticing our new friend's Liverpool shirt.

'Yes', I said reluctantly.

The third Geordie piped up,

'A fuckan divn't like Scousers me like'.

Suddenly the lights went out, the carriage thrust into near darkness, we were jostled and heard a commotion and shouting from the Geordies and from the Liverpool fan. The lights were out for a good minute, I was nearly knocked over, so I knew there was a fight ensuing, I kept out the way, but it was hard to see except for a slight silhouette. The lights kicked back into life, I looked round and saw the Liverpool fan with a bust lip and his Liverpool shirt was now adorned by one of the Geordies, a little tight I may add but it's on. The Liverpool fan now shirtless, looked shocked, we said nothing, the laughing Geordies moved on with a final quip.

'As I say I divn't like Scousers'.

Luckily, the lad had a coat to cover his shirtless torso. This would be the first of several run-ins with the Geordies.

As planned, I met up with John, Harry, Richie and Colin on the train to Leeds two weeks after the Liverpool debacle. Spurs had won the previous week against Bristol City to pull away from the bottom of the table, so travelled looking to get a result against Leeds. I chatted to the lads about the previous time I had been to Leeds and the trouble in the park. Some of the lads had been in the away end that day but said they had kept out of the way of the scuffles, but I still travelled with some trepidation. Phil and Pete got on at York, so we were up to our full quota of Northern Spurs as we travelled the next fifteen miles or so to Leeds, with scarves either hidden or not brought.

Arriving, I immediately saw the sign again, 'Welcome to Leeds'. It was only just after 11a.m. so there were only a few Leeds about, still clad in scarves. We left the station.

'There's a pub at the bottom of slope near the taxi rank', Phil said.

He was right, a small bar which was quiet, only a few people in and no Leeds fans. Beers were bought, Richie and I didn't bother. After several drinks the pub began to fill with Leeds fans, having spilt from their trains as they converged on the nearest pub. Having Phil from York and Pete from Harrogate gave us the confidence to stay longer, their Yorkshire accents some help. More Leeds fans came in, their colours clearly emblazed, they looked at the table where we were are sat, as we had no colours on our attire it was time to go. I didn't say anything to the rest, after all I was the new kid on the block, it wasn't for me to say it's time to go, but I was looking around, faces peering over at our table, paranoia was setting in.

John shouted over to the rest of us,

'Let's fuck off out of here'.

The beers were swilled down, we left, heading back to the railway station, staying in the buffet bar until we heard the roar of 'Tottenham, Tottenham', echoing around the station. It was the Tottenham special, the train laid on by the Supporters Club. British rail had been loaning their most decrepit rolling stock to football clubs for quite a few years, taking supporters around the country at a cheaper rate to stop fans using their mainline trains to avoid them being damaged. It seemed to work to some degree. The specials could hold up to 700 fans and Tottenham would always have a train on. Many supporters though preferred to use the normal service trains, paying a bit more but avoiding being pushed around by the local plod, which is what invariably happened as you alighted the special.

The Spurs support poured out of the station to the waiting double decker buses, which were included in the price of their ticket. This was our signal to leave the buffet and join the throng. We were all members of the Supporters' Club, so we flashed our cards to the Supporters' Club committee member and jumped on the bus, they didn't have time to check your card properly which would be stamped with that particular game. It was a good way to get to the ground and avoid any trouble, especially at Leeds who seemed to have a dislike for London clubs and their supporters.

Once in the ground you felt safe, we were housed in the corner of the Lowfield's Road Stand, with Leeds fans ten yards further along. The South Stand, where the Spurs supporters stood the previous time I was there had now been seated. Leeds fans who were in there were pushed to the far half of the stand. The verbal's soon started.

'We hate the cockneys, Leeds sang.

'Who the fucking hell are you', Spurs replied.

I listened and joined in. It became so apparent how football and music collide, when the tune of Mary Hopkins 'Those were the days' was sung by Leeds.

'We'll see you all outside, we'll see you all outside'.

Within an instance we reply.

'We've heard it all before, We've heard it all before'.

The teams came out, many of us had been ripping up newspapers to give the team a tickertape welcome. We threw it in the air in unison, a flutter of paper drifts in the air as the 2,000 Spurs applaud their heroes. What riles the Leeds fans is that the Spurs team came right down to the corner in a line, giving us a wave, like the Leeds team used to do under Don Revie.

'Who the fucking hell are you, who the fucking hell are you', their grimaced faces yelled.

Spurs go on to win 2-1, this leaves the Leeds fans irate, which wouldn't help our exit from the ground. Leeds police kept us locked in while they cleared the streets, after half an hour we were let out, the double decker's were in front of us for those who had come on the 'special'. The Spurs fans who had come on coaches and in cars made their way out too.

The area around the ground had changed a lot, the park had been replaced by a ring road, but it wouldn't stop the skirmishes starting, as the Leeds hangers on tried get at the fans going to their cars. The police got us on the buses, a quick flash of our membership cards and we're on. Cans and bottles clattered the windows, everyone kept their heads low as the buses pulled away. Around thirty spurs were left behind when they tried getting on the buses, but are turned away, they not having membership cards, they would have to stick together as the large mob of Leeds fans were baying for blood. I could only hope they got away safely. Getting back to the station and back on the train home, it had been a fun day.

'Jingle bells, jingle bells, jingle all the way, oh what fun it is to see, Tottenham win away'.

Coming back from a match in 1978, having left York Station for the last leg of the journey North, up the carriage walked the Northern Chelsea fans who we knew slightly. They like us, were from Teesside, Hartlepool, Darlington, and one other from Easington near to where Harry and John lived. Harry had no time for him, the rest of them we all got on fine with. The lad from Easington came up the carriage chanting.

73

'Gassing time at White Hart Lane'.

I didn't know what he meant, I asked Richie.

'What's he singing?'.

'He's on about our Jewish fans', Richie said.

I knew little about our Jewish support, other than I recognised we did have some supporters who had a different ethnic look other than white British. But we are all Spurs supporters and follow one thing, and that is Tottenham Hotspur. It did make me think though, Arsenal, West Ham, Chelsea, and for that matter any club could have Jewish supporters, especially in London which is so multi-cultural. Maybe Tottenham have more, but this Chelsea fan was so ignorant he could well be slagging off his own fans. He soon picked on Harry.

'Fucking yid'.

Another term I hadn't heard. Richie said it was another term for a Jew. The wording in the dictionary states, 'A derogatory word for Jew'.

Harry was getting annoyed, muttering.

'I'll smack that mouthy cunt'.

Things calmed as we chatted to the rest of the Chelsea lads, Easington boy fell asleep, half pissed.

Chelsea fans have had this antisemitism thing with Spurs for years now, chanting about the Holocaust of Auschwitz, it would get the back up of our fans, especially our Jewish followers who may well have lost family members to the Nazis during the Second World War. Chelsea were not alone, the two Manchester clubs were just as guilty in giving the same abuse.

Things would change though as 1979 approached. Street vendors around White Hart Lane who peddled their unofficial merchandise, like Tee shirts/sweatshirts had now emblazed the word 'Yids' on the front of their garments, but in a positive way. Tottenham fans were going to turn this derogative word full circle and take it for themselves, to deflect it from the minority. It didn't go down well with all though. The club were opposed to it, and many of our Jewish support were horrified. But there was a bigger support for it, and many of the Spurs Jewish community agreed it was better this way and showed solidarity with the Spurs crowd.

To the present day (2021) the debate goes on, the cry from the terraces of 'Yid army, Yid army' from Spurs fans still rings around all grounds we play at. Chelsea are still giving the same abuse, as the hatred grows between the two sets of fans. There seems little anyone can do, although the football authorities are trying to bring people to court for using this obscenity. But how can you take a Chelsea fan to court and not a Tottenham fan for basically singing the same thing, only time will tell.

Two football specials rolled into Manchester Piccadilly Station for our visit to Maine Road, the home of Man City. Seven of us had made the trip, us crossing over from Manchester Victoria to Piccadilly, a quick drink in a pub across the road, then back to the railway buffet, a few other Spurs were in there too. Outside the buffet, faces were glaring at us through the window, 'The City boys'.

The police moved them on as the first special rolled in. 'We are Tottenham, Super Tottenham from the Lane' to the tune of Rod Stewart's 'We are Sailing'. A new chant I hadn't heard before, its noise echoed around the station alongside numerous Alsatian dogs barking in unison. We joined the crowd, showing our supporters cards, and were on the buses to Maine Road.

I hadn't been to Manchester before so to go to Moss Side, one of the most deprived areas of Manchester was not what I was expecting. If you haven't been to Maine Road, think of TVs Coronation Street, street after street of terraced houses and cobbled back lanes, not an area you would want to get lost in. We got dropped off, leaving the buses about half a mile from the ground, and walked there with the large police presence keeping us in order, hitting anyone who left the pavement. Once at the ground it was straight in, it wasn't the place to loiter around. Spurs fans had been allocated a section of the 'Kippax Terrace', a large terrace with a shed above. The terrace was vast and stretched the full side of the pitch and could hold around 25,000. We had a section holding about 5,000. Once inside and under the dark pitched roof, which was strewn with supporting girders, the noise you could make was incredible.

By kick-off there were around 3,000 Spurs in our section, not full but more than enough to make a fantastic din. The two sets of supporters were divided by a four feet high metal railing fence, the sort you might see in an ornate garden which ran from the front to back of the terrace and looked inappropriate for 1970's feuding fans. The City fans began hissing at us to replicate the noise from the gas chambers of the concentration camps where millions of Jews were exterminated during the Second World War. This had the Spurs support racing to the fence, shaking it violently, no stewards in those days, it was down to Manchester's plod, wielding battens.

'City, City, City' The Kippax cry.

'We hate the Cockneys'.

'You're the shit of Manchester', in quick reply.

'You're gonner get your fuckin heads kicked in'.

'We'll see you all outside'.

Many of these old chants have now been put into football folklore.

The abuse was incessant aimed at each other across the divide, the game which had started, appeared only a side show.

City fans started throwing coins, then bottles came over, no CCTV cameras then. It was mayhem as bottles were aimed at the roof supporting girders, smashing for maximum impact. You ended up watching for missiles rather than the game. It did settle though, and I do recall we played brilliantly, it was the best performance of the season so far, but we lost 2-0, which at least meant we didn't have as many City fans hiding down the alley's ready to ambush us. We were frog marched back to our buses and homeward bound.

The Bull Ring, Merchandise and Manchester again

I had given up going on the overnight coach to London for home matches. I found out Richie, Harry, John and Colin were now travelling on the morning coach. I checked out times and found that the 8a.m. from Darlington would get to Hendon in North London at around 2p.m. The coach stopped at Woodall Services near Sheffield where I would change coaches and join the coach which had come from Sunderland and Teesside, which would have the other lads on.

I never enjoyed the journey, I felt the pressure that we wouldn't get to London on time. Any later than a 2.15p.m. arrival at Hendon would make it a struggle to make Kick-off. Once at Hendon it was onto the tube to Kings Cross, change onto the Northern Line to Seven Sisters, then the train up to White Hart Lane, and run to the ground. If all went to plan, we would get in the ground as the players came out. It was obvious why I enjoyed the away games far more when using the train.

Heading to Birmingham for the away game at West Brom, I boarded the train, the lads had got a couple of tables in the buffet car adjacent to each other. The buffet cars had around a dozen tables. They weren't the most comfortable seats on the train, hard orange plastic, but it meant they weren't often used so we could nearly always guarantee two tables, handy for the card school and especially the buffet as the beer the lads would bring onboard was soon dispensed of.

Phil and Pete boarded at York, four cans in hand, along with a young gangly lad with a distinct haircut who I'd never seen before. This was Dave Jacklyn from Boston Spa, sporting a skinhead haircut with lines cut into it. For a short while he was known as Tennis Ball, which summed up his hair style perfectly. Dave was sixteen, four cans in his hand which were covered in soil.

John soon piped up,

'What's with the fucking mud on your cans?'.

'I bury them in the garden so my dad can't find them'. Dave replied.

This brought a laugh from us and breaks the ice. Dave becomes one of the crew, a good lad we all liked, but a bit misled. He would often bring a newspaper on the train called The Bulldog, a paper dispersed amongst The National Front. The paper was sold around many London grounds in the 70's and early 80's. No doubt trying to recruit the hooligan element that seemed so prevalent with the 'Far Right'. We never thought of Dave being a Nazi, in fact we'd often see Dave chatting to our black supporters, so I don't think he was a threat to anyone.

The train journeys would fly by, cards being played across the two tables. Only Richie wouldn't join in, which was beneficial for me as I would often ask Richie if he could lend me ten quid if I was on a losing streak. Richie would always be kind enough to oblige. The next match, Richie would always get his money back from me, and on occasions I would ask for it back two hours later if having another bad day at cards.

We pulled into Birmingham New Street Station, noticing straight away that it was underground. As soon as I left the train I found it a dark almost intimidating place. We climbed the stairs up to the next level seeing quite few other fans about, Villa were at home to Man City, other Spurs fans were coming off other trains. Wolves, Walsall and the Blues of Birmingham City who were renowned for trouble, were all hanging about. It wasn't a place to stay around. We looked around to get our bearings, I could sense the lads were itching to find a pub, Richie a chip shop.

A lad approached us.

'Yow Spurs?' his Birmingham drawl apparent.

'Yes', Col replied.

'Am ifter one a yow lot', the Brummie said.

'What you mean?', all of us now interested.

'Got done off Spurs tow years ago, I remember his face, so Im ifter im'.

Needle in a haystack I'm thinking. Col tells him we can't help him and wished him well.

We had a quick look up to the famous Bull Ring shopping complex, possibly one of the first indoor shopping complexes in the U.K. We make it short and sweet, after all shops weren't of interest.

Leaving the Bull Ring we came out onto a back street, the cry soon went up, 'Pub over the road', (The Shakespeare). It didn't matter what it was like, if it sold ale it was good enough. Entering the pub you were met firstly by the carpet sticking to your feet, like suckers on the bottom of your trainers. The pub was quite large with a high yellow nicotine-

79

stained ceiling and a tired interior. About twenty old men sat around reading their racing papers, playing dominoes and cards. They glanced up at the eight newcomers entering their domain and then their heads dropped back to what they were doing. We stayed for an hour or so, getting info on which bus to get up to the Hawthorns, the home of the Albion. We left the pub with some of the lads now looking pissed, none more so than Harry.

Onto the bus for the twenty-minute ride, Harry was throwing up all over the back seat. We got to the ground before 2p.m., the lads couldn't find a pub other than the one behind the main stand, which was only open to members. We reluctantly decided to go in the ground.

In the 70's it was well known that some away supporters would go into the home end to try and take it, Spurs were no different. Just before Kick-off a surge could be seen from our view in the opposite end, arms and legs flailing into each other. Around fifty Spurs fans were led by the Old Bill down the perimeter and put into our end to swell our numbers, some of our support were even applauding them. The now large Spurs support were in full voice, the police having to push the Albion fans across the terrace to give space to the thousands of Spurs still trying to get into the away section.

The game kicked off and we were under the cosh for the entire game. Albion at the time were one of the best teams in the league, but Barry Daines the Spurs keeper had a blinder saving everything, then Peter Taylor broke away and slipped a shot past Godden in the Albion goal to win it for Spurs.

The fans gave the team fantastic backing all game and the celebrations lasted long after the match, so much so that we missed the 6.00p.m. train out of Birmingham.

The lads descended into the railway buffet, I told them I was off to the phone box to let my mam know I'm going to be late. I got to the phone and just as I was opening the door there was a tap on my shoulder, two lads of similar age were looking at me.

'Yow Spurs?'. Just like earlier that day, of course they knew I was, my Spurs scarf gave it away.

'Yes' I said, 'Just give me a couple of minutes lads I'm just phoning my mam'.

I entered the box and phoned home telling my mam I would be late getting back. The two Albion lads waited. I don't know if I thought they wouldn't try anything, or I was feeling brave with so many people about. I talked to my mam, while looking at the two lads still waiting. A couple of amateurs I thought, if they were going to do anything they would have dragged me out of the phone box. I put the phone down and opened the door.

'What do you want', I asked them.

'Where yow from?'.

I told them Darlington. I think they were surprised I wasn't from London.

'Yow too good a supporter, following Spurs from Darlington', and walked off.

I was surprised nothing came of it. I told the rest of the lads, and we boarded the 7.00p.m. train, cards in full swing and a 1-0 under our belts. Harry slept most of the journey.

As we entered November, we all agreed that the coach to home games was spoiling the match day experience, so we decided to bite the bullet and pay British Rail the exorbitant seventeen quid for a day return to Kings Cross, even more for the lads from Sunderland. This was double the coach fare, but worth it to get to London for 10.45a.m., having only set off at 8.10a.m. from Darlington.

Once up to Seven Sisters it was a case of hitting the High Road pubs. The Swan public house was always omitted as we were told it was for Blacks only, of course it wasn't, but being young we took it as gospel. Nottingham Forest, the Champions was our first match travelling in our new format. A full house was expected, and a game I remember well, not only for being a fantastic match which Spurs lost 3-1, but the first game that White Hart Lane had a perimeter fence around three sides of the pitch, the West Stand being given a reprieve. It gave the ground an ugly look. The match programme stated that due to some mindless fans encroaching the pitch the club was left with no alternative. The fact was the only Spurs fans who ran on the pitch were a few youngsters who would run on at the end of a match to pat the backs of their heroes. We did have the mass pitch invasion in 1975 versus Chelsea, but nothing since, so it seemed a knee jerk reaction.

The game itself against Forest was played in a wonderful atmosphere, 50,000 packed into the Lane, the floodlights glowing through the slight mist made thicker by a smoking generation, with an ever-darkening sky it made White Hart Lane look special. The game ebbed and flowed, the noise incessant, the result went against us, but when you watch an occasion like that you almost feel the result irrelevant.

A few weeks later, early December, I watched the most mind numbing 1-0 win over Ipswich, the game forgetful apart from the raucous West Stand Enclosure singing 'Man U, Man U, here we come, Man U, here we come'. This a game I really looked forward to!

With football there is the merchandise that goes with it. In the early days you could only get scarves, most likely knitted by your gran, but as the 60's approached clubs would sell scarves, pens, pennants and the like, but the replica kit was still in its infancy. Tottenham sold a white shirt, which you then had to buy a separate cockerel badge that your mam or gran would have to sew on. Tottenham didn't bring out a replica kit until 1977 when we were in the Second Division, they sold well.

Clubs at the time knew there was a marketplace for merchandise. By the mid to late 70's anything you could emblazon the clubs name on was sold, mugs, towels, watches, tee-shirts, jumpers, the list was endless. But if money is to be made, then the unofficial vendors will soon latch onto the possibility of easy money, and football wasn't going to be an exception.

On Tottenham High Road by 1978 stalls would be springing up selling all sorts of unofficial merchandise. Tottenham would often write in the club programme 'Do not buy unofficial merchandise, as it is an inferior product and the club gains no revenue from it to invest in the team'. Part of this statement was true, but fans wanted something different, and that's what they got! Slogans on shirts which were derogative to other clubs were seen on many fans attire. One top I remember seeing was a shirt which had a row of ships anchors on it and read 'West Ham are a bunch of - and in front of the anchors was a well-placed W. The producers of this shirt would be selling the exact same one at Upton Park, slating Spurs, that's how it works. Another item that always springs to mind were the large button badges that came out, lasting only a couple of years and then seen no more, a two-inch diameter badge, which at first were naïve and innocuous, with innocent slogans like 'Spurs are magic'. Within months they became more inflammatory, with comments like 'We hate Arsenal' and 'Stick your poxy Arsenal up your arse'. A badge I did see being sold at Old Trafford read, 'Joe Jordan fucks Alsatians'. I'm still unsure if it depicts how hard Joe was, or his sexual preference. These badges must have sold by the barrow load at grounds all over the country. Clubs couldn't sell items like these, so knew the money they produced wasn't going into their coffers. It must have hurt the hierarchy.

As Christmas approached, we made the trip to Old Trafford, the home of Man Utd. They had the most notorious fans in England. Throughout the 70's they ran amok through towns and cities across the country. The red army was vast, with supporters from all parts of England converging on grounds in huge numbers causing mayhem. Tottenham saw it at the Lane the previous year, fights breaking out around the terraces, and streets outside. Old Trafford was a feared place and clubs other than Man City, the Mersey clubs and Leeds wouldn't go in any great numbers, Tottenham included, but this was different, and as the cry at the Ipswich game of 'Man U hear we come' rang out, Spurs fans would travel.

Phil and Pete boarded at York to bring us up to our usual crew, another lad sat with us, a United fan that Phil knew. Alan was from York and followed United home and away, his distinct black teeth noticeable. We soon nicknamed him 'The Dentist', although other United fans who boarded knew Alan as 'Virgin', possibly down to his teeth letting him down with the girls.

We trundled through West Yorkshire and into Lancashire picking up more and more United fans, it made you realise how big their club was. We had no issues from any of them, a couple of glares towards the two tables of Spurs fans playing cards was about it.

Pulling into Victoria Station, Alan 'The Dentist' said he would take us to a pub that was safe, but no Spurs scarves. The pub was fine, we kept quiet, but John wanted to move on.

'Fancy fucking off, see if we can get in our end?', he asked Richie and myself.

Tottenham had sold tickets for the Scoreboard End which none of us had, so we hoped there might be a turnstile open to pay on the day, If not we would of had to of stood with United fans. John, Richie and I walked up to Oxford Road station where you could get a train up to Old Trafford, once there we had a twenty-minute wait. John fancied another pint, so we headed to the pub next to the station. The pub was packed with United, we hadn't even been served when a group of United fans came over to us.

'Yer Tottenham aren't yer?'. You feel that knot in your stomach.

John quickly answered.

'We United'.

'Yer awright lads, you can have a drink with us, and we'll take you up to the ground'.

'Let's go', John said.

We followed him out the pub, John pulled an empty Brown Ale bottle out of his pocket.

'Just in case it was needed'.

Back on the platform I told John they were probably decent lads, John said he couldn't trust them, and to be honest the reputation they had he might have been right.

We got the train without any more problems and were up to the ground by 2.15p.m. One turnstile was open for Spurs fans, the three of us were ecstatic. They didn't let many more in before it was locked. The rest of the lads would of had to of stood with the United fans.

I was looking forward to seeing Old Trafford in the flesh, I had seen it many times on TV. I paid my entrance money and walked into what we would now call the concourse, it was drab, dark breeze blocks, very dim lights, a small urinal, two small hatches, one to get a Bovril or pie, the other a programme. No alcohol served! Unlike now, where supporters chat, have a pint, a selection of food 'admittedly at exorbitant prices' in well-lit comfort and don't go to their seats until ten minutes before kick-off. Here at Old Trafford in 78 there was hardly anyone about, it was a case of have a piss, get your pie, and enter the arena. We walked up the tunnel, coming out almost by the corner flag to a thunderous noise, floodlights beaming down, their bright glow on a cold but dry mid-December afternoon. I made my way from the tunnel along the back of the scoreboard paddock behind the goal. I looked across to see how far our allocation was along the terrace, which was already full.

'To the far goal post, good turnout', I said to Richie.
He agreed, 3,000 at Man Utd was a good following, the United fans on our right in the side paddock were very vocal.

'Who the fucking hell are you', they screamed.

'We are Tottenham, We are Tottenham, super Tottenham from the Lane', we sing with gusto. The thing I do remember is that this chant was originally sung slow, the same speed as Rod Stewart sang his 'Sailing' song, but it has speeded up over the years. The players came out and the volume goes up. The Stretford End, which I assumed was where all their chants came from, was just a part of the wall of sound. The side paddock, the adjacent other half of the Scoreboard End and seats behind us, made the whole atmosphere frightening, I had not heard a crescendo of noise like this. The whistle blows and we feel like it's a non-stop onslaught on our goal, the ball pinging around our penalty area. It wasn't like United were top of the league, they were only a couple of places above us in mid-table, you could see why they did well at home if they received this backing. You go to Old Trafford now and it's a pale shadow of that day, even though they get 20,000 more fans inside.

It proved a less than fruitful day and we go on to lose 2-0 but play well. Ossie was now settling in well and showing the skills which took him to the World Cup Final. When the final whistle blew, as usual the players came down towards us applauding, thanking us for our backing, whether they heard it was another matter. United fans launched a few missiles from the seats above us, but it wasn't as brutal as their Manchester counterparts. But we now had to face the Red Army outside.

A month earlier I had been talking to a lad called Eggy from York, a big Man City and England fan who said,

'Watch it when you come out at Old Trafford, City had a rough time the season before last, when the police let us out in small numbers, we were battered'.

Over the tannoy a voice says.

'To all Tottenham fans - we are holding you back for ten minutes for safety reasons'.

This started a chorus of 'We don't need an escort, we don't need an escort, na na na – na na na '.

Forty-five minutes later the gates were opened, and we hit the Manchester darkness, not a sole in sight. Walking towards the station past the Old Trafford Cricket Ground we got a few bricks thrown from kids down the side roads, but we got back to Victoria Station safe and sound. The rest of the lads met us in the buffet. They had stood in the Stretford End keeping their mouths firmly shut. When we got to our platform, two United fans were stood, one had a large two-inch button badge on his scarf which said, 'We hate Tottenham'. John walked over, ripped it off his scarf and threw it onto the track. I told you these badges were popular.

The North London Derby

Anyone who says the North London Derby, Spurs v Arsenal is less passionate than its counterparts, the Manchester, Mersey or Tyne & Wear Derby is talking rubbish, and is often said by Northern writers and footballers who haven't played in one. I can remember Paul Walsh, ex-Liverpool, Man City and Spurs player being asked which he thought was the biggest Derby, he said, 'They all generate fantastic atmospheres in the stadiums, but the Spurs v Arsenal match has a sinister feel to it, like they really do hate each other'. As I'm from the North-East, I know the passion of a Newcastle v Sunderland derby, but like all derbies you will see the opposing fans at work the next day, the friendly banter will be given out, the losers of the derby taking the brunt of the stick.

At the Ipswich home game on December 9th vouchers were handed out to Spurs fans when entering the ground, these could then be exchanged for a ground ticket for the North London Derby, along with one pound, the price of admission.

Attendances would dip alarmingly in all divisions the week or two before Christmas as people would do their Christmas shopping, that is unless you had a big derby or a top of the table fixture.

People wouldn't even dream of doing Christmas shopping in October like they do today, tinsel and baubles were not seen until mid-December. As it turned out the gate versus Ipswich was a healthy 33,000 so the club were delighted to give out so many vouchers.

My voucher was sent back to Tottenham with a one-pound Postal Order, well that was my intention, but on a walk to the post box, not more than three hundred metres from home I managed to lose it. I looked everywhere, I walked back and forth numerous times to no avail, I gave up and went home. I couldn't get it out of my head how I could lose a letter. I moped around the house for the rest of that Sunday until later that evening my mam came up to my room and said there's a man at the door asking for you. I went to the door to see who it was.

'Are you Ian? I found a voucher in a letter with your name and address on it, it was in a bush'.

I could have kissed him, what an omen, we had to beat Arsenal now.

The day after my eighteenth birthday, I travelled to London to stay at my Aunts for Christmas, taking in the Arsenal home match, and Q.P.R. away on Boxing Day.

Meeting the lads in the Supporters Club before the Arsenal game you could feel the rivalry in the air. Arsenal had been allocated the Park Lane End, like Chelsea had, but Arsenal would fill it, 8,000 would pack the seats and terrace.

Still meeting up with Paul and Panno I arrived early as I wanted to feel the passion of this one. The ground filled early with the Shelf Side taunting the Gunners fans in the Park Lane, them giving it back. Half an hour before kick-off some of the Arsenal players came onto the pitch, still in their suits presumably to get a feel of the turf. Target number one was Willie Young, the ginger haired centre half who fled White Hart Lane. Terry Neil signing him up during our relegation season. The Spurs support tore into him 'Willie, Willie, Willie, Young, Willie Young (repeat) oh Wank, Wank, Wank, Wank (Numerous more times). Willie Young smiled at the Shelf Side, there was no forgiveness for a deserter going to the enemy, unless your name happened to be Pat Jennings, he was given a fantastic welcome back. Jennings never wanted to leave Spurs but the hierarchy at Tottenham thought he was too old, and Arsenal made a good offer. He was only thirty-three, he would prove how good he was at Arsenal in his seven years there.

The atmosphere grew with the chants back and forth, totally drowning out the basic sound system playing songs of the day. The teams came out, tickertape flutters in the already darkening sky.

'Kick-off', It's a brutal start, boots fly in, no fairy football today, it means too much. Arsenal score, an explosion of writhing bodies to my left in the Park Lane end.
The cry of 'You're goner get your fucking heads kicked in' rings around the Shelf directed at the red and white foe. Half-time, only one in it.

Last time they played at the Lane, Spurs were two-down but got back to draw, all was not lost.

'Second-half' Every Spurs fan who was there in the 42,000, a disappointing gate even if it was just before Christmas, would like to erase it. The goals would fly in, and all in our net, 5-0, capped by an Alan Sunderland hat-trick and a classic Liam Brady goal which would arc into the top corner, repeated on the BBC far too often, but which I could only admire. It was a drubbing, and before the final whistle the Arsenal fans would taunt us with Rod Stewart's song 'Sailing'.

'We've won five nil, we've won five nil, we've won five nil at the Lane'. A song they would chant for the next five-years until we gained revenge with the same score line.

I left White Hart Lane along with the rest of the Spurs fans, although many had gone long before the end, the torture of watching the celebrating Gunners fans too much to take.

It was a subdued walk back to Seven Sisters. I passed hundreds of Spurs fans lining the High Road waiting for the Arsenal fans to emerge from their sanctuary, I wasn't interested and carried on. I could at least see Spurs again in three days' time at Loftus Road, the home of Q.P.R. I would enjoy Xmas and move on.

Boxing day and an early start, even though I was only in Croydon I still had to get across London on limited train services. Q.P.R. wasn't all ticket, this one of the things I really liked about football at the time, you could just turn up if you fancied going to a game. Today it's a major operation, booking a train early to get cheap travel, the possibility of the date changing due to TV demands, then trying to get a match ticket to be sat next to a total stranger. You want to be with your mates, that's why I hope the terraces come back in some form.

Although Q.P.R. was a London derby it was just another game, the fact both clubs were from London was immaterial. Spurs have only one derby and that was against the team who crushed us three days previous. Only Chelsea and West Ham have any other importance, although the Chelsea game has grown significantly as has the hatred as the years have passed, it's fair to say some Spurs fans are happier beating them than the old foe from London N5, four miles down the Seven Sisters Road.

I met Phil at White City Tube Station, Phil was the only one of the Northern Spurs who could get down on the limited train service. We headed to a pub which was full of Spurs, as was the whole surrounding area around Shepherds Bush. I had managed to get to the ground by 1p.m. and hardly saw a Q.P.R. fan. Already Spurs fans were queuing for the Loft End, which was the Q.P.R. end, so we thought that was best avoided. The other end had been allocated to Spurs, but it was apparent Spurs fans would be all over the ground. Phil and I went into the away end, which was already quite full, the home end opposite also filling with mainly Spurs fans.

Q.P.R. supporters were already over to one side to avoid the sporadic fights that were breaking out. Boxing day it was!

The ground at kick-off was attended 50/50 in the near 25,000 crowd. The Rangers' fans were mainly in the two sides that were seated.

Spurs dominated the early part of the game and took the lead, it looked like we would hammer them. Rangers would be relegated by the seasons end, but one player I was pleased to see was the Rangers favourite Stan Bowles a player I wished Spurs had bought. A true maverick. He had issues in his life, none more so than his gambling, his addiction so strong that on occasions he would sneak out of the ground at half-time and go to the bookies in his Rangers kit to have a bet on the horses. Can you imagine that nowadays?

As I watched the game my attention was drawn to the over-zealous nature of the London Metropolitan Police. One copper in particular must have had a bad Christmas or was it he had to work Boxing Day. I doubt that, with double time wages and the chance to give some unfortunate a slap. Let's face it there will be a lot of coppers who volunteer to work on match day just so they can let off a bit of steam and get away with it. This copper and his colleagues were shouting at the Spurs fans 'Anyone jumping around or clapping will be ejected from the ground or nicked'. He'd hardly got the words out of his mouth when the popular Cockney song 'Knees up Mother Brown' was chanted, accompanied with the traditional bobbing up and down, like a pogo dance. The Old Bill enraged steamed in, pulling anyone out, it was ridiculous as scuffles began which could have resulted in a major disturbance.

Rangers equalised, I had almost forgotten there was a game on due to the chaos in our end. The Loft End opposite saw a spike of violence as the Spurs support surged towards the Rangers following in the corner. Soon after we let in another, typical Spurs complacency. Although some supporters were giving the team stick, we started to really get behind them and with a minute to go we equalised. The whole end goes mental, not only because of the goal, but also a big 'fuck you' to the police.

On the 30th December Spurs were due to play at Everton, it was the first day of what would become the worst winter for twenty-six years and would decimate the football season. I had already bought a terrace ticket for the match. I looked out of my bedroom window that morning and saw at least six inches of snow and a blizzard increasing the depth by the minute. I wondered if the game would be played, I asked my dad.

'Don't be so bloody stupid', he said.

I reluctantly decided not to bother going. The game, to my annoyance went ahead. The Goodison Park undersoil heating did its job. It didn't matter in those days what the surrounding streets were like, safety for spectators didn't matter as long as the club coffers were filled. Some of the lads managed to get there. Richie said it was so cold in the ground the Spurs fans lit a bonfire on the old wooden terrace which was still present in the Park End. These were removed at the end of the season when the terrace was halved in size.

Altrincham in the cup the following week was postponed but played the following mid-week. A miserable 1-1 draw at the Lane against the plucky non-leaguers meant a replay. Altrincham decided not to play at their small home ground, instead moving it to nearby Maine Road, the home of Man City in the hope of a big crowd and a financial bonus. John had got in touch with Richie to see who fancied going, Richie asking John about his new wheels.

'What sort of a car have you got?'.

'It's not a car, I've just bought a van', John said.

'What type, like a transit van?', Richie asked, thinking great, a van for away games.

'Aye, something like it', John replied.

I couldn't make the match, so I backed out.

On the day of the replay John turned up in his new van, a three-wheeler Reliant Regal, the very same type that Del Boy would make famous in 'Only Fools and Horses'.

As Col said later,

I couldn't fucking believe it, squeezing in the back of a three-wheeler'.

Spurs won 3-0 in front of a healthy 27,000, the majority being City fans. After the match, the lads were chased around the back streets and alleys of Moss Side until they found their speedy getaway vehicle! John had the piss taken out of him for weeks, especially the furry dice that hung from the mirror. John's image was shot to pieces, he soon sold it.

The freezing weather continued into February. Spurs managed to fulfil most of their fixtures, a surprise considering few clubs had undersoil heating, today most of those games wouldn't be played for the safety of players.

During the week leading up to the away game at Coventry I would check out the weather to see the likelihood of the game going ahead. The forecast for the day of the game said the Midlands would be 4c, that was good enough for me, irrelevant that the temperature had been as low as minus 10c overnight. I set off on that freezing morning from Shildon to Darlington to meet the 8.10 train to Birmingham. The train was on time, the old diesel trains generally were.

Phil, Pete and Dave got on at York. Phil asked if I thought the game would be on.

'Definitely', I replied.

'Why you so confident', Phil asked.

'I've been in my back garden this morning and the ground was quite soft', I told Phil.

I was being serious. I had gone into the garden and jumped up and down on the turf, and dug my heel in, it felt okay. In reality it was absolutely ridiculous that a piece of grass two hundred miles away from Coventry would have a bearing on what the pitch would be like there. Phil found it funny, but the game went ahead, played on a rock-hard surface that was white with frost. I don't know if the ref was pressured to play the game due to clubs having a fixture pile up. It shouldn't have gone ahead but we were pleased it did, with a good performance and a 3-1 win.

Some days stay with you for life, our away trip to Birmingham City holds that for me. It was the next away game after Coventry, so a similar Saturday trip, the same scheduled train but the weather had picked up.

When Phil got on at York he still wanted to know if I had been in my back garden to see if the game would go ahead. It became a standing joke, any bad weather, Ian the weatherman would put your minds at rest. My garden exploits were now well known.

On the trip to Birmingham, Gary the Liverpool supporter joined us for part of the journey, he on his way to see the Reds at Derby. Although having only met my Spurs mates during the September trip to Anfield, Gary got on well with them and probably appreciated what we had, six or seven close mates travelling to see their club. As well as Richie and Col travelling there were a few other lads from Teesside with us. Duffy who had gone to Forest, then another a big lad, and I mean big, named Sinka, about six foot and at least twenty stone, admittedly overweight but you wouldn't want a punch off him. Alongside Sinka was his cousin known as baby Sinka, younger and smaller, the last lad was Pete Emblade, just known as Sherpa. His name was apt, when Sinka said 'Pete get to the bar for four cans of Foster's Lager' Peter didn't question it. Pete would be a regular at the bar as Sinka could drink. Pete (Sherpa) was a really good lad and would go to quite a few games with us over the coming years.

Arriving at New Street Station we headed out the side entrance to the 'Shakespeare', the pub we had gone in at the West Brom game. The same sticky carpet welcomed us, looking around the pub it was like Groundhog Day, the same characters sat in the same seats, doing the same thing as four months earlier. A quick look to see who had come in, the odd nod, as much as to say we remember you from last time. We stayed in the pub until around 2p.m. before making our way to the taxi rank where we got three taxi's. As well as the lads mentioned, Pete and Dave had joined us at York, so we had our biggest turnout from the Northern Spurs.

Birmingham City had a reputation for being one of the clubs with a hooligan problem, so when we approached the Small Heath area of the city where 'The Blues' played you could see this part of Birmingham had seen better days. Now the area is well known for the TV programme, 'Peaky Blinders', the often-brutal drama set in the early 20th century depicting the life and times of a gangster family. A lot of which is based on the truth.

Dropping us off near the ground we looked at our surrounds, it wasn't long before one of the lads piped up 'Shit hole'. The ground appeared to be circled by mass demolition, not the place to hang around, so made our way to the away section. The back of the stand was a mass of rubble and house bricks, you only thought of one thing, 'ammunition'. We entered a large corner terrace partly covered by an end shed.

The ground swept around to the huge side terrace, bigger than any I had seen, it must have looked impressive in its halcyon days when full, but today only 20,000 were present, and a healthy away following buoyed by the mid-week cup win away at Wrexham.

As Spurs often did, a good win was followed by a distinctly poor result. That was Spurs, you just didn't know which team would show up. The game came to an end with the 'Brummies' giving a final rendition of their 'Keep right on to the end of the road' chant, which is a unique and uplifting song when sung by the whole ground.

Spurs lose 1-0. We left the ground, a minority having running battles amongst the rubble. We walk the near three miles back to the city centre, luckily I had kept an eye on which way the taxis had brought us.

We make the train out of Birmingham with minutes to spare, then looked to find a few seats with tables for a game of cards but only managing to get seats here and there, we watched at each station seeing who got off, so we could get seats together, but to no avail. Col, Sinka, Sherpa, Duffy and baby Sinka had already gone up the train to the first-class eight-seater compartments.

As the train rolled into Derby, I saw Gary out of the window and gave him a wave, so he knew where we were sat. A lot of other Liverpool fans got on as well, all in a good mood having seen another Liverpool win. They headed to the buffet. It was another normal away trip back home, but that would soon change.

Phil, Pete and Dave got off at York, leaving Richie, Gary and myself sat together, the Teesside lads still up the train in first class. Gary was wearing his Liverpool scarf, me my Spurs, Richie had removed his. Down the train walked three

Liverpool fans looking pissed and loud, all early twenties. One said

'Hey, we've got a Spurs fan here'.

Richie looked at me, we knew where this was going. Gary looking uncomfortable, caught in the middle, people he might see on future Liverpool trips, so he was reluctant to say anything. I could understand his predicament.

'Give us your scarf?' one said aggressively, his gaze focusing on my navy and white scarf.

'No' I said, I wasn't going to give another scarf up like at Middlesbrough two years earlier.

'Just give me it you cunt'.

'No' I replied.

The scouser became more and more irate, grabbing the scarf and trying to pull it off, but it was knotted around my neck. Even if I wanted to fight back, I was fastened in by the table in front of me, so couldn't even stand. I was expecting the first fist, but a voice behind him just shouted,

'Just get your knife out and fucking stab him'.

We weren't yet in the knife culture of today (2021) but the words send a shiver through my body, my resistance subsiding immediately.

'Ok', I said.

He let go of the scarf, I unknotted it and reluctantly handed him his prize, they wandered off, pleased with themselves heading back to the rest of their mob in the buffet. Richie and I had the same thought, to go and see Col and his mates, especially Sinka. Gary said he couldn't get involved as he would have to travel with them in future games, that was ok…

Sliding the first-class compartment door open, I told the Teesside Spurs what had happened.

'We'll have a look', Sinka said.

Sinka, accompanied by his younger cousin, set off up the train, coming back a few minutes later.

'We'll have to leave it', Sinka said, 'Too many of them, about fifteen, we've only got seven'.

The numbers were too much. We would have to leave it. I sat down next to the sliding door, Richie opposite, Sinka alongside me. Suddenly the door is swept open, a small stocky lad stood in the doorway.

'I hear you want trouble', his Glaswegian accent evident.

Sinka speaks up knowing the numbers are not in our favour.

'No, we don't want any trouble, just we weren't happy that you took this lads scarf", glancing down at me.

'So, what?'. the Jock says.

I felt the tension, I knew this was not going to end well. Sinka stood up dwarfing the jock in the doorway.

'Just shut it', Sinka said in an annoyed tone, his patience wearing thin.

'Ay what you ganner dee about it?' I could see a line of bodies behind the jock in the aisle.

'I'll tell you what I'll do to you, you little Scotch bastard', Sinka shouted.

'Yeah'. The jock makes the first move, almost diving at Sinka.

I saw Sinka's punch hammer into the jock, and in that split second a boot catches me in the head. I put my arms over my head. I'm pinned to the seat as I'm constantly stamped and kicked. As I'm next to the door each body that runs in is raining a blow in my direction, I can hear the punches and jostling in the background but can't get up as the violence is thrown at me, the pain wasn't too bad, each kick was more of a thud on my body, the wonder of adrenalin shutting out the inevitable pain which would follow later. I heard a couple of the train guards shouting they would stop the train and get the police. The mob retreated. I rose up from my almost foetal position, I looked across at Richie he was rising like me, an almost mirror image. I looked in my hand seeing a large clump of hair which I had unknowingly pulled from my scalp but hadn't felt a thing. I also noticed a small chip in one of my teeth, something else I hadn't been aware of. Sinka had a bloody nose, the rest looked fairly unscathed.

Col was laughing, he had been against the carriage window.

'I couldn't move, there must have been nearly twenty of them in the compartment, I couldn't get a good punch in, there wasn't room to get a swing'.

A guard walked in, we told him what had happened.

'Well looking at the state of some of them they came off worse', he said, which was some comfort for the pain that was starting to hit home.

Pulling into Darlington, I got off at the opposite end from the Liverpool supporters, some of them also getting off. I got onto the Shildon train, Gary oblivious of what had happened. I arrived home, my mam asking how we got on, and if there had been any trouble.

'Lost and no bother,' I told her, no point worrying her.

I lay in bed that night with my bruised head, it had dawned on me that I had been involved in my first hooligan episode, and like most fans of that time who went to watch a football match, met violence they couldn't avoid. I was now one of those statistics.

The North London Derby at Highbury

The season was drawing towards its end, but there was one big game still to play, Arsenal away. I'd enjoyed the season, it was a season of mediocrity, but I had been to many new grounds and for our first season back we had held our own, apart from the Anfield debacle. Losing in the Sixth-Round of the F.A. Cup to Man Utd after a thrilling game at The Lane, which ended up all square, then a trip to Old Trafford in the replay losing 2-0.

I recently watched the highlights of the game at The Lane on 'YouTube' and the thing I noticed was the atmosphere, although good, it didn't transfer through the TV like it did being there. Almost 52,000, including over 10,000 United fans, created some noise. Of course in those days there weren't the microphones around the pitch like today's Sky extravaganza picking up every sound.

As the matches passed at The Lane, and getting closer to the Highbury derby, the fans would count down with regular chants of 'six weeks to Arsenal, there's only six weeks to Arsenal'. Two weeks later the cry would go up 'four weeks to Arsenal' and so on, until the midweek game arrived. Other chants would ring out 'We're going to take the North Bank Highbury'.

I'd heard from lads in London, that Spurs for many years would go in Arsenal's North Bank, the home of their most vociferous fans.

Col, Richie, Harry and I travelled by National Coach to London arriving at Victoria at 2.00p.m. It was a lovely warm April afternoon, Richie had guided us to a fish and chip shop, followed by Col leading the way to a pub. Phil and Pete were coming down by train.

After a couple of pints around Victoria we walked up to the Houses of Parliament, the route still fresh in my mind, part of my walk on my first visit to the Lane. Arriving, we stood chatting, looking up at Big Ben admiring its beauty. There appeared to be quite a large police presence across the road around the Parliament Buildings. We waited, along with a few Japanese tourists, their camera's in hand, them like us thinking there might be a celebrity due. As our gaze looked across the road we heard the screech of a speeding police van mounting the pavement within ten yards of us. The back doors are swung open, the crash-helmeted heavily armed police with semi-automatic machine guns leaped out of the back. They ran towards us, swept us off our feet and slammed us against the wall of the building behind us. We were moved apart from each other, one copper asked my name,

'Ian Stones, what's going on?' I asked.

He wasn't interested in answering my question.

'What are you doing here?' his voice still aggressive.

'We're going to the Arsenal v Spurs match, what's happening?'. We would have all given him the same answer.

'Stand there and don't move'.

I wasn't going to, with the barrel of a gun looking at me. He quickly says he thought we were I.R.A. terrorists, tells us to stop loitering and get out the area. They got in the van and speed off. The Japanese have stop looking at Big Ben and we are the focus of their cameras. No apologies from the police for slamming us against the wall, luckily no injuries, we head down the road laughing at our thirty seconds of fame.

We had heard that the I.R.A. were plotting to do something, possibly a bombing, maybe the recent instalment of Margaret Thatcher as Prime Minister made her their prime target, but little Harry masterminding another Guy Fawkes explosion was a funny thought.

The four of us made our way up to Highbury, a ground Col and myself hadn't visited. Richie and Harry had been there the previous season to see the Arsenal v Walsall cup tie. Our game the same day had been postponed. Harry got locked up for being drunk and abusive to the Arsenal fans.

The derby wasn't all ticket, but a near full house was expected. We made our way to the Clock End where we had been allocated a section for 6,000, but there were Spurs fans all over the ground, in the Paddocks, the seats and definitely in The North Bank.

Fifteen minutes before kick-off a huge roar went up from the corner of The North Bank, to the left as we looked from the opposite end. There was a huge surge of thousands of bodies, with punches and kicks raining into the fleeing Arsenal fans. Arsenal regrouped and slowed the surge, it was like watching Braveheart when the Scots rushed into the English, it was brutal, the 6,000 in our section were roaring their approval. Arsenal are barely clinging on to their end as Spurs keep moving forward, the Old Bill finally get a foot hold and force a gap.

The game kicked-off with the cry from the North Bank 'We took the North Bank, we took the North Bank, we took the North Bank Highbury'. No one could argue, they had almost got to the middle of the end.

The match was hard fought and looked like a 0-0, when Arsenal scored in the last minute. Another surge, just as it had started, the game would end with a battle. We left disappointed, but knew the hype was true of the brutality that would take place on Arsenal's patch.

Down on a Tube Station

The last game of the season at home to West Brom was a meaningless match, my twenty-ninth match of the season, but would end up being remembered for the wrong reason.

At the previous match, Spurs last away game of the season at Bolton, I'd travelled to York to meet Phil who said we could get a lift off a bloke he knew called Peter, who would later be known as 'Pete Yellow Coat', more of that later. Peter was about fifteen-years older than me, a nice bloke, originally from Cambridge but had moved to York to work on the railways. He had arranged to pick us up at 5.30p.m. at York Station. At 6p.m. we were still waiting, when he finally pulled up in his Renault 4 ten minutes later we got in and he flogged it to Bolton for the 7.30p.m. kick-off, only hampered by commuter traffic and the torrential rain. This didn't bode well for the open away end we would be allocated.

Parking up on a grass verge at 7.25p.m. Phil and I ran to the ground, Peter said he was standing with the Bolton fans under cover.

Phil and I got in the ground, missing the first ten minutes, already soaked as we made our way onto the vast terrace to add two more bodies to the small band of no more than 400 Spurs fans. Maybe there were more like Peter dotted about keeping dry, but as the Gene Kelly song goes 'We're singing in the rain' and that's what we did. We may have been small in number and wet through, but we created a great noise especially in an open end where the acoustics were zero.

The Bolton fans were quiet, content in the knowledge they would play another season in the topflight. Our team played like we sang and rewarded us with a 3-1 win, our soaking bodies forgotten as we applauded our team from the field, and likewise them doing the same to us.

The following Wednesday our last home game against West Brom. Walking up Tottenham High Road on a gloriously warm early May evening, I picked up the match programme and read the manager's comment.

'Firstly, I would like to say a big thank you to the vociferous band of Spurs followers who travelled to Bolton in the torrential rain last Thursday evening'.

I read it proudly, not only being part of that vociferous band, but because the programme rarely passed comment on the away following that we would take around the country. It was nice to get recognition and know we were appreciated by the club.

Only Richie and I had travelled by coach for the game, the coach home not leaving Victoria until 11.30p.m., so a leisurely evening lay ahead. The game went the way I hoped, a 1-0 win and a terrific goal by Ricky Villa capped the season off. Two wins on the spin had us finishing exactly halfway in the table. The Spurs faithful were boisterous considering it's a nothing game, many of the near 25,000 stayed behind to applaud the team in a lap of honour, Richie and I stayed, we weren't in any rush to get the coach at Victoria.

Leaving The Lane for the final time, we walked steadily down Tottenham High Road amongst the thinning crowd, jumped on the tube for Victoria, chatting about the highs and lows of the season. The stations passed quickly until the tannoy on the train blared out, 'This train will terminate at Victoria'. We emerged from the tunnel, I looked out of the window and to my horror I see a platform packed with red and white scarves, the two of us had totally forgotten Arsenal were playing Chelsea at Stamford Bridge. We were the only two remaining in the carriage. Richie didn't hesitate, he began running through the other carriages towards the back of the train, but for me, instead of following Richie I'm transfixed, looking at the sea of faces, my executioners, there was no escape for me, for that moment the menacing faces looking at me weren't interested in going home, not when they had an unfortunate Spurs shirt glaring back at them.

The train came to a halt. You have that couple of seconds where you wait for the doors to slide open, I looked at the faces, some had likely been in the North Bank a month earlier fleeing as Spurs took their end. Well now they could have a little bit retribution. No face stood out, there were too many, I could almost see the saliva dripping from their mouths, their prey almost in sight. Strangely I wasn't scared, I knew I could be in for the best hiding of my eighteen years, but what I did know was I had to make this damage limitation.

The doors slid open, the tannoy loud in the background 'This train terminates here', but these people were getting on. Like a fly in a spider's web, my fate was sealed. The doors hadn't fully opened when the first body and boot headed in my direction. I backed off, it was futile to even think of fighting back. I backed into a corner, so I had some protection, the first blow has me reeling, I go down managing to get into the corner, a stamp to the head followed by kicks all over my body. The adrenalin working well, like it had three months earlier. The kicks kept raining in, I'm conscious throughout hoping that they will soon stop. I can't tell how many are booting me, but it feels like three or four by the number of kicks I'm getting from difference directions. It was as if Paul Weller, had written part of his song 'Down on a tube station at midnight', about me.

First felt a fist, and then a kick,
I could now smell their breath,
They smelt of pubs and wormwood scrubs,
And too many right-wing meetings,
My life swam around me,
It took a look and drowned me, in its own existence,

106

The smell of brown leather,
It blended in with the weather,
Filled my eyes, ears, nose and mouth,
It blocked all my senses,
Couldn't see, hear, speak any longer,
I'm down on a tube station at midnight.
Lyrics Paul Weller 1978

I hear a voice, the voice I wanted to hear. 'Leave him he's had enough' never was a truer word said. They left me motionless. I waited for what appeared to be a minute, then I had the courage to lift my head, the carriage was empty. I lifted myself from the ground, I was shook up but coherent, no blood, my hands a bit scuffed where the boots had reined in.

The pain hadn't yet set in, I was still filled with adrenalin, and yet to find my way off the train. Looking out of the door the platform was empty like it had been a dream, from a full platform only moments ago to nothing, had I lost consciousness after all. I could hear the Arsenal fans, it sounded like they were coming down the escalator.

I jumped off the train and headed for the North bound line, a train pulled in, I saw Richie. He was ok, he had managed to escape. He'd thought I was right behind him when he ran. This is what I should have done. We got on the train and headed one stop up the line to Green Park. We were now a good mile from Victoria so had to run to get the coach, I was struggling from the pain around my ribs, my adrenalin friend was exiting my body. Making the coach with minutes to spare I sat with only one thought, not that I had been beaten up, but how much worse it could have been. The next week or two my bruised body healed as I looked forward to going to watch England at Wembley against the Scots.

Cartoon Capers

Although John my brother made his visits from Leeds infrequently, it didn't stop the arguments at home between my mam and dad, they would go hammer and tong, and one such incident has always stayed fresh in my mind. My dad had been to the Workingmen's Club for his traditional Sunday lunch time drink. The club would only open between Noon and 2p.m. so with only two hours to drink, it would be get down what you can in a limited time.

Coming home a little worse for wear, with the Sunday lunch in the oven staying hot, it wasn't long before an argument reared its ugly head. The shouting would start, which was annoying as I was trying to watch 'Shoot', the equivalent of the 'Big Match', highlights of the previous days matches for the local area. My dad was in his favourite armchair and me on the settee. The constant quips were going back and forth from living room to kitchen, the volume of the two of them escalating to the point where it was impossible to hear the TV. When out of the corner of my eye I saw my mam running into the living room with a large frying pan, without a thought she struck my dad over the back of his head with such force it would have laid out many a man. My mother had one thought, get the hell out of here, so like how she would have played rounders at school, she threw the pan down and ran into the twenty-metre length of our back garden to first base.

My dad gave one of those Tom and Jerry quick head shakes, I was surprised I couldn't see those little stars above his head. My dad rose from his chair and in the same movement picked up the poker, 'his weapon of choice' and sped out of the living room, the poker above his head. My mother was now screaming, running around the garden possibly looking for second base, me in pursuit as referee, my dad shouting.

'I'll kill you, I'll kill you'.

With no frying pan my mam didn't have a shield, so my dad had the upper hand. The screams from mam were piercing which was fortunate as Mrs Woodward from next door came running out and with a yell of.

'George, stop it'.

The incident came to an end, just like 'Shoot', the whistle had blown.

Braveheart (it wasn't)

During the early 70's I began taking a strong interest in how the England national team were doing. The game I looked forward to the most was against Scotland In the Home Internationals.

I began having a deep-rooted disdain for anything Scottish, I think it came from when the Scots would come to Wembley and take over the place, I didn't like it, taking over your home ground was embarrassing. What would other countries think if they watched it? 'Shameful English fans selling on tickets to make a few quid profit', probably.

In May 1979 I was offered four tickets for Wembley, no chance of me handing them over to the Scots. I had delighted in the 1975 game when we beat them 5-1, then it turned to despair when two years later they beat us in that infamous game when the Scots almost destroyed Wembley. Who can forget the tens of thousands of marauding Scots in their tartan clothing, like a Bay City Rollers concert on acid!

The following year in Glasgow, they sang 'We're on the march with Ally's army', as they beat us again on their way to the Argentine World Cup, at least that ended in joy as they were eliminated early.

The four tickets went to Gary, Phil, Pete, and me.

Boarding the usual 7.50p.m. the train was packed with Scottish accents, not a seat in sight. It was up to the buffet, which was packed with more, I shouldn't have been surprised.

Pulling into York, Phil and Pete got on along with Alan (the dentist), Eggy the Man City fan and the Kent brothers, big Leeds and England followers. A couple of others joined us until there was around a dozen of us.

Arriving at Kings Cross in heavy rain we promptly headed out the station towards Euston, some of the lads knew a quiet pub they used for league match outings. Finding the narrow road, the quaint fronted pub looked inviting on a cold wet morning. Opening the door to a pub full of Scots was not what we bargained for. The cry from them instant.

'Oh, spot the loonies, spot the spot the spot the loonies',

'Come in Boys', the kilted reveller said. 'You'll give us something to take the piss out of'.

'Can you hear the English sing, no no, can you hear the English sing, I can't hear fecking thing'. they sang.

We respond with a tame chant of 'England'. I think they were happy to see us just for the piss take, to be fair they were a decent bunch. Staying for a couple of drinks we made our way to Wembley, the Tube was heaving with them, it seemed like there were no English about. Then a rendition of 'Flower of Scotland', a fantastic anthem and so uplifting, it puts ours to shame. The beer swilling Tartan Army, many in kilts were giving us good natured abuse, they knew we were English even though none of us had any scarves or badges on our attire, but we had no tartan either.

Pulling into stations, if there happened to be women on the platform, a Scotsmen would lift up his kilt to show his manhood, Some women would smile, some would shake their heads in embarrassment.

Reaching Wembley, we alight, another group of England join us, our numbers double. The main road down Wembley way forks off with barriers, but we decide to go down the middle unpermitted road shouting for England, striding on getting dogs abuse from the thousands of Scots, strangely not one bottle or can was aimed at us, well not with any beer in, they're not that stupid.

Once up at the stadium we said our farewells, the tickets are for different parts of the stadium, we also wished everyone a safe afternoon. Phil, Gary and my ticket are for the lower standing at the opposite end to the tunnel. Inside you get a realisation of the level of Scottish support there is in all areas of the stadium. Both ends are Scottish strongholds, no English evident or at least none physically showing it, the two sides seated are about two-thirds Scottish, so approx. 80 - 90,000 to 10,000 of ours. The level of drunkenness is unbelievable, and the abuse towards anything English is scary. A quick word to Phil.

'If we score, we do nothing', he nodded, it isn't the place to be a hero, in fact we hardly speak to each other in case we are sussed out.

The game kicked off, the atmosphere special, England play wonderfully in the wet conditions, especially Keegan's goal after Brooking puts him through. The ball hits the net, it should be joy, I bend down as though fastening a lace, but really I'm screaming 'Get in'. A quick look at Phil, a sly wink said it all.   An Englishmen raises his hands in delight a couple of metres from where we stood, a drunken Scot pushes past us and plants a whisky bottle over his head, his head opens up, blood is pouring out, he stumbles but keeps on his feet. Another Scot says to the lunatic.

'What ye de that for?'

'He's a fecking Sassenach', the loony said.

The decent Jock nods, 'ah yeah your right'.

The English lad is led out to the awaiting St. Johns ambulancemen. I wondered how many others had the same treatment. 3-1, a satisfying win. We made it home safely along with the rest of the lads we had travelled with.

As the years have passed the English have taken more pride in this game, and English numbers grew significantly, until we soon outnumbered the Scots in the ground.

To date I have not seen England play again in the flesh. Spurs mean far more to me and I don't mind the Scottish people.

Born as the King

There has never been any doubt in my mind, or my fellow Spurs supporters from my generation that Glenn Hoddle was, and is, the greatest Spurs player of all time. I would even say fans from the 60's who drooled over watching the goal machine that was Jimmy Greaves would still put Hoddle top of the list. He had almost everything, goals, passing, balance, and skills that had the fans crowing like the cockerel he wore on his shirt with pride and loyalty. I'm so thankful that my regular visits watching Spurs ran parallel with Hoddle's Spurs career. The 79/80 season was when Hoddle went to the next level, he knew he had Ardiles and Villa to play off him, which released Glenn to push further forward knowing he had the ammunition to score. His goal record of twenty-two goals was phenomenal for a midfielder considering the team ended up finishing in the bottom half of the table. Hoddle was given his first England cap in October 79, the first of little over fifty caps in his career. The England team should have been built around him, but it was said he couldn't defend, which was true to a degree, but did Cruyff defend much when playing for the great Dutch team of the 70's.

One of the difficulties about playing for England are the supporters, they are loyal to their clubs.

England at that time seemed to have a large following from Chelsea and West Ham, who despised Tottenham, so one wrong pass from Hoddle and they would jump on his back leading to the tabloids writing 'Is Hoddle good enough'.

Gary, my mate loved Hoddle, he couldn't understand why he was regularly omitted, but that's why we love football, it's all about opinions.

The new season had started disastrously with three straight defeats. Things then picked up with a League Cup win at the Lane against Man Utd, and Hoddle was at his imperious best scoring one of the best Spurs goals ever, a free kick taken by recent signing Terry Yorath, flicked on by Ossie and Glenn hits a volley from the angle of the eighteen-yard box, both feet off the ground. The ball arrows in the far corner with such power it rebounds off the back stanchion as quickly as it entered. The Shelf Side half jumped, we didn't know if it has gone in because of the power, but also at the audacity of what he had done. The ref points to the centre circle for a goal. The ground is buzzing with what they had seen. The remarkable thing is, he hits an almost identical shot three months later against Nottingham Forest to seal a 1-0 win. A true Spurs legend deserving the regular chant of 'Hoddle, Hoddle, born as the king of White Hart Lane'.

Ant Music

I would be paid on a Friday, give mam her board, the rest was spent mainly on football, apart from now and again buying a pair of Levi's or trainers and occasionally a Harrington jacket which were really common at the time, black with a red tartan lining and seen on many football terraces of the late 70's. It was a look that was seen around the country post punk, the beginning of the New Wave scene and Ska, bands like The Jam, The Specials and Selector, vibrant music that carried the story through lyrics of the despair from the youth of the nation. No prospects and mass unemployment growing by the year.

 I felt lucky not to be one of those statistics, and had disposable income to spend, or as my dad would say, 'Wasting it watching that team'.

By October that team were going along nicely, especially after such a poor start, another trip to Leeds beckoned. All the regular Northern lads were going. We all met on the train and decided to go for a drink in the railway buffet, the environment around the station was still hostile and wasn't going to change in the year since we were last there. In fact even today it's still one of the grounds that lives in the past regarding the safety of away fans, not as bad as then, but still has a sinister feel especially after games.

Once in the buffet, which had the feel of a pub, we settled around a couple of tables. Across from us were a group of leather clad punks, although punk music was in decline it still had a good following for live music.

Pete who was into punk and new wave music, The Ruts being one of his favourite bands walked over to the group of around twenty spikey haired lads, along with a couple of girls who sported their distinct punk haircut, shaved hair with a fringe and longer hair at the back. Though their leather jackets had names of various bands adorning them we weren't sure who they were going to see or where they were going to. Pete asked one of them.

'Who are you seeing?'

'Adam and the Ants', the punk replied.

I was listening, I hadn't heard of them at the time.

'Playing in Leeds tonight', he said.

Adam and the Ants had begun as a punk band which morphed into the band everyone had heard of by the early 80s, dressed up on their play of the highwayman Dick Turpin, videos transporting them into the almost Teeny bop pop culture. It must have been hard to take for their loyal following of punks who now had little kids of five and six singing 'Stand and Deliver.'

The Leeds hooligan element had clocked us in the buffet, banging on the buffet doors and there was a lot more than the eight of us. They were gesticulating with the knife across the throat threat.

'Who the fuck are they', one punk asked.

'Leeds, we said, we all follow Tottenham'.

The punks glare at the Leeds yobs who are not moving, but aren't coming in either, the only people coming in are commuters. Every time the door opens a shout could be heard.

'We hate the Cockneys'.

'If they come in here, we will give you a hand if it kicks off, one says'. All the punks nod in agreement.

It was good to know we would be backed if anything went off. The next hour passed well as we mingled with them until we knew the 'special' was arriving.

A large assembly of the local plod turned up with the constant dog barking accompanying them, any Leeds hanging around were pushed out of the station. We wished the punks a good night and thanked them for the backup if it had been needed. We left, as the Spurs boys in their hordes stream out the station onto the awaiting buses, a flash of our cards a repeat of last season and were on our way.

Entering the away section, access was only from the back, it soon dawned on me that Leeds had put another fence into the away pen, to split it up which would reduce its capacity by around 500 from the previous season, it would now hold around 1500 max. These were the days before the capacity restrictions, this same section now would hold about 800. I was thinking results have picked up, we'll bring a couple of thousand, so this section isn't going to be adequate.

The Leeds fans were a good thirty yards further along the side, with two two empty pens next to us. The Yorkshire police had no intention of giving us more space, with more and more coming in pushing from the back the crush was getting dangerous.

John was just down from us, almost folded over a barrier not able to push back with the weight of bodies pushing on him. At the front of the terrace against the fence bodies were crushed against the mesh, people were shouting to get the gate open at the front, some were trying to scale the fences but were forced back by the police.

By kick-off many couldn't watch the game because they were trying to escape the madness, it was ridiculous there was only 25,000 at the game in a ground that could hold in excess of 45,000, and our 2,000 were getting the life squeezed out of them. Eventually after many at the front, some girls and young kids pleaded with the police to let them out, the gate was opened. A couple of hundred were let out at the front,

116

John being one of them saying his ribs were hurting. The police put them in the seats next to us in the stand behind the goal. The crush still excessive and the two goals we scored were met with only a little jumping around as you were lodged in, but for a win it was worth it.

Leaving the ground and onto the buses, an unlucky few were left to their own devices again as we headed to the train station. A few cans and bottles clatter the side of the bus, but we get to the station safe and sound.

Liverpool a Guided Tour

Spurs good form continued into November and our biggest test of the season came at Anfield.

The game wasn't all ticket, not many were, but Spurs were selling tickets for the away end, so we queued up after a home game to get tickets to take any stress away from getting in at Anfield.

Travelling to Liverpool, were our usual Northern quota, along with Gary and a couple of other Liverpool fans Phil knew from York, Mel and Steve, two good lads we got to know well.

We all felt confident that we wouldn't get the tanking we received the previous season. In fact, we were playing that well we thought a draw was a possibility.

The train pulled into Lime Street, we walked down the platform, a bunch of scousers were hanging around looking and listening hoping to detect a London accent so they could get a sly punch in, our northern accents were of no interest to them as we went into the buffet. Gary, Mel and Steve went their separate way.

The first of two Spurs football specials rolled in, a roar echoes around Lime Street 'Tottenham, Tottenham' just to let people know they'd arrived. The eight of us waited in the buffet, the beer too much of a pull to leave just yet. John said.

'Wait till the next one comes in'.

As well as the eight of us, a couple of new lads had joined us from Darlington, they were Brass and Beef, their names sounding like a couple characters from The Beano comic, but it was all we ever called them, never giving it a thought to ask their proper names or even how they got the nicknames. They were both sixteen and they seemed to like meeting up with us. They would be regulars with us for the next three or four years.

The second special came in and like the first the doors are flung open, the train still moving. The same roar goes up, we were all out the buffet now waiting for our chance to mingle in to get onto the waiting buses. But the scousers were hanging around as well. Plenty of verbal's are exchanged. The Mersey police with their long canes, were either prodding or waving them around to seize order. We all managed to get in the mob, many still wearing donkey jackets, but some of the skinheads now having green bomber type jackets which were to become popular.

We boarded the buses, Spurs fans banging on the windows at the snarling scousers. Arriving near the ground the police on horseback are wading in trying to keep us in order. The scousers are baying for blood, a few skirmishes were kicking off around us, but we get in the corner of the Anfield Road.

With hundreds of Spurs still outside with no tickets and our section already full the police take the decision to drive the Liverpool fans across the Anfield Road End to create our fans another section, it was a decision that didn't go down well with the Liverpool fans. Batons were drawn as police and locals clashed. The push continued, Spurs take the space over to swell the Spurs support up to 4,000. The atmosphere hostile to say the least, coins are raining down on us, picked up and thrown back. Richie gets a coin into his fuzzy hair, he puts it in his pocket. Spurs fans then turn their attention to the unfortunate seated Liverpool fans in the Kemlyn Road on our left, raining coins on them, which was out of order. I was thinking if this happened every game you would need hard hats, its madness.

The game settles everyone. Spurs play a high line and catch Liverpool off-side time and time again which has the Liverpool fans howling their derision. Spurs fans singing 'Off-side, off-side, off-side, off-side'. It wasn't pretty, but after the 7-0 last season we would do anything to thwart them, we still lose 2-1, but we cheered the team off as if they had won the game.

We were locked in for thirty minutes, which meant we were going to struggle to catch the 6p.m. train home, we had to try and get out of the police cordon once out. The police are lined up blocking anyone who wants to get out the escort, some managed to see gaps but are stopped and pushed back. It was risky leaving the safety of your mob in case you were sussed, but we often tried to do it. We gave up, so on a dark November night we were marched what seemed miles around the streets of Liverpool, the drudgery only livened up when we were walking down a dual carriageway that had a footbridge above, we are pelted by bricks and stones off little scallies, this has us spreading out to avoid being hit, the police still shouting, 'get on the pavement'. I said to Richie.

'If the train is late getting away, we might catch it, we'll leave the escort at Lime Street'.

It's 6p.m. when we get there. I made the move to get out the escort, it's not like we were going to London, I'd only gone five yards.

'Hey where you're going?', a copper shouted.

'I'm going for my train'.

'No, you're not, get back in the line'.

I still made the move, the copper comes running over gets hold of me, virtually lifting me off my feet, slams me against a police van and says in no uncertain terms.

'Get the fuck into that fucking line, you've come this far with us, you are going all the fucking way'.

'I'm not going to London', I tell him.

'I don't give a fuck where you're going, but you're going in that line, or in the back of that van'.

He pushes me into the line, Harry cheers. We miss the train, it's the 7.00p.m. train for us.

Birthday Snow and Ardiles Delight

The F.A. Cup draw was made, Man Utd again. Having had two games with the Reds the previous season in the cup it was a mouth-watering draw, but a strain on the wallet. My twenty-seven pounds a week pay minus my mams cut was making it a struggle to get to the up-and-coming games in the South but having missed few games I was determined to keep going to as many as I could afford. Spurs were becoming an obsession, going to work to make money, my life seemed to be all about waiting for a Saturday. Richie was no better and hadn't missed a match.

Going into the Boxing Day game away at Arsenal, Richie wanted to fly to the game as it was a morning kick off, but the cost was too great, he would have to miss it. The game itself went off with very little trouble after Arsenal had handed out vouchers at a previous match, no voucher no access to The North Bank, so Spurs fans couldn't get in. Compared to the season before it was a tame affair on the terraces.

Before the Arsenal game we'd had a trip to Ipswich on a Friday night, my nineteenth birthday. Four or five of us made the trip to Kings Cross, over to Liverpool Street Station and a train to Ipswich. It was going well until we got about twenty miles from Ipswich then the snow came down and it was heavy.

Leaving the train in a blizzard we made our way to Portman Road, the match still on as we entered the ground, the pitch already covered in snow with ground staff clearing the lines, nowadays it would have been off in the blink of an eye. Most fans want games to go ahead even if they are a farce. People spend a lot of time and money to see a game and for clubs to say its off, but your ticket will be valid for the rearranged game seems a very hollow gesture especially for the away contingent.

Once in the ground, our section behind the goal had a huge mesh fence which went from floor to roof to stop missile throwing into the Ipswich section on our left, but in between the two factions lay an empty pen. The Ipswich choir were giving our fans a bit of lip, it wasn't long before Spurs fans were shaking the mesh to try and tear it down to get to the lippy antagonises, it rocked to-and-fro, the local plod didn't seem bothered, more interested in keeping out of the blizzard.

At kick-off, the snow must have been six inches deep but the game continued, our fans now making a large hole in the mesh, Spurs fans were leaping through from our crushed section into the empty pen. More and more went through until the police decided to open the gate, the Ipswich fans began backing off as the Spurs boys began shaking the next fence to get to their foe, the mesh violently shaking. The team were losing in a farce of a game, each goal we let in encouraged more to shake the fence, but the game ended before they broke through, defeat on both fronts.

Defeat in the North London Derby focused our attention on the F.A. Cup. The Cup at the time still held huge prestige where clubs playing at home would get one of their best attendances of the season. Teams would be at full strength, unlike now with its watered-down apathy where its only taken seriously in its latter stages. To be fair the Cup still holds strong in Tottenham hearts to this day and it's our tradition to have a good go at it each season. But in 1980 a home game with Man Utd couldn't be taken anything but seriously.

At the start of the season Spurs made the West Stand enclosure a season ticket only section, Richie asked if I fancied standing there for a change from our usual Shelf position. I agreed, we hadn't stood there before so we went to the ticket office to see if we could get in. The old ticket office was a small brick building behind the West Stand not much bigger than a large garden shed, a far cry from today's state of the art office. We received two complimentary tickets, the ticket office manager asked where we were from having heard our accents and was kind enough to give us them for free for our loyalty.

The enclosure was a shallow terrace, no crush barriers, noisy and really tight to the pitch, you could touch a player if he was taking a throw in.

The game ended in a 1-1 draw which was a fair result. It meant another game, but a game I couldn't miss, Old Trafford was one of my favourite away days. I loved the banter and the fact we were a small section of fans in a mass of noise giving our best to be heard.

I was in my second-year print apprenticeship, going to Middlesbrough Art and Print College on day release each week. I enjoyed going, great set of lads from Darlington and Teesside and got on well with all of them, but that day I would have to skip off at lunch time, the pull of Old Trafford too great. I didn't tell my boss Alan at work that I would be bailing out of college, but I'm sure he would have guessed.

I met up with Richie, Col and Brass at Darlington station for the 3p.m. to Manchester. I always wondered why it cost seventeen quid to London and yet you only paid a little over a five quid to Manchester, admittedly half the distance but I thought a reasonable fare.

At York, the Man Utd boys got on, Alan the dentist, Mick Watson, Spaz Cooper, lads who we had met on countless away days, decent lads, although the latter two were a bit mouthy. You know the type, Man Utd this, Man Utd that, we the biggest, we the best. Biggest yes, but a long way from being the best.

'Don't know why you're bothered coming tonight, we going to fucking slaughter you lot tonight' Mick Watson said.

His arrogance just short of being big headed. He may have been right, but you go hoping that you might win.

Pulling into Manchester Victoria we walked up to Oxford Road, calling in a quiet pub on the way, then got the train up to the ground. We all had tickets for the away section. Through the turnstiles at 7.00 p.m., down the tunnel to emerge into the floodlit arena, the noise seemed louder than last seasons' Cup replay. The Paddock along the side was in full voice, abusing us, the hissing of gas is blatantly obvious, the antisemitism meant nothing to the local plod, it was only abuse to us, but of course to some of the near 2,000 Spurs followers who were present it would have cut deep with their Jewish heritage. 'You're the shit of Manchester,' we chanted.

The game kicked off, it wasn't long before the ball was pinging around our eighteen-yard area, Spurs clearing. We were doing ok though and had a share of the game, but we thought that was about to change when Aleksic, our keeper fell heavily and was taken off, no substitute goalkeepers then, so it was whoever fancied taking over in goal. Glenn Hoddle accepts the responsibility, saying to a reporter after the game that he quite liked playing in goal, just like he did as a kid. Hoddle put the green jersey on. We expected an onslaught from United now, especially from crosses. The United crowd were urging them forward, but United players almost over did things instead of playing their normal game, they were rushing things. Hoddle had a few minor saves and dealt with crosses, but he wasn't really tested.

The game ended nil-nil and went into extra time.

I saw Pete yellow coat, the guy who took Phil and me to Bolton. This is the game where he got his name. He was wearing the brightest yellow coat I had ever seen, the sort security stewards wear at matches nowadays, but this was before stewards wore them, the floodlights were making the coat even brighter. I could see a scenario at the end of the match of Pete coming out the ground and some unsavoury Mancs shouting 'There's that fucker with the coat'. Talk about making yourself obvious.

Extra time started, Glenn in the goal we are behind, we gave him a huge reception.

'Born as the King of White Hart Lane' we sang. Everything he touched is cheered. The United crowd is quieter, our voices were now being heard.

We went into the second period of extra time with only minutes left, Ardiles picked the ball up just outside the area and curled a dipping shot past Bailey in the United goal. The ball hits the net, and 2,000 bodies explode with joy, we can't believe it, our best player in goal, and we had won it. I've watched the goal many times on YouTube, if you look closely you might see a bright yellow coat towards the front. I always think of Peter when I recall this game, a lovely bloke who was tragically killed when knocked down in 2000.

The ground emptied quickly, we were held back, but not bothered, we sang to the leaving Red Army 'We're the famous Tottenham Hotspur and we're goin to Wembley, Wembley, Wembley'. It was early days, but we could dream. Those sorts of nights you never forget, they live with you all your life.

Coming out of the ground the streets were deserted as we made our way to Piccadilly station to get the mail train home, which appeared to stop everywhere. Pulling into Darlington at 5.30a.m. I got the Shildon train and was home for 6.30a.m. and went to bed. An hour later my alarm was sounding, I got up for work. I told Alan my boss that I had been to Manchester and missed the afternoon at college.

'Thought you would,' he said. I think he admired my honesty.

Balaclavas and Sleepers

Three days after the cup win I was back on the train to Manchester, away at City, a sense of blind loyalty, it was only January, but the league games felt pointless, but we all met as usual on the train.

Although the games in the league didn't mean much our camaraderie was strong, and you always ended up having a laugh, non-more so than John taking the piss out of Pete for being a tight Yorkshireman. Pete had gone to the toilet on the train so John stuck a ten pence piece to the train carpet with

125

chewing gum, when Pete came out the toilet, walking down the carriage he spotted the coin and immediately went for it, but with it stuck to the carpet it didn't move, we were all laughing, John screaming at Pete 'get your hammer and chisel out you tight bastard'. I've never regretted spending almost all my wages following Spurs home and away.

We got a 1-1 draw, surprising considering we had a hard game three days earlier going to extra time, normally Spurs let you down after the euphoria of a brilliant result.

We drew Swindon away in the F.A. Cup, but before this we decided to go to the away game at Brighton. We made the trip an hour earlier than a normal home game, getting into Kings Cross by 9.45a.m., the tube to Victoria and then onto the Brighton train.

We were into Brighton not long after 11a.m. With a large Spurs following on the train with us, we knew it was going to be another away day with a strong police presence, maybe not as bad as two years earlier when thousands travelled to Brighton for the big promotion clash which resulted in numerous arrests, with trouble on the Friday night and on the day of the match.

I knew I had the expense of Swindon the following week, but I hadn't been to Brighton before so felt I needed to go in case Brighton were relegated.

Coming out the station we entered the first pub we saw, which was full of Spurs. A group of Spurs lads caught Pete's eye, they all wore balaclavas covering their faces, just two holes for eyes and slot for the mouth, they looked like they were planning a bank job.

'I like the look of them', Pete chirped up.

'What's that?', I asked.

'That look', Pete said.

126

Another couple of woolly-faced lads came into the pub, same attire as the group sat at the table. There's a theme going on here I was thinking. The pub was bustling by noon, the Spurs chants had starting up, lads stood on stools and tables, we all agreed it was time to go somewhere less boisterous.

Coming out the pub we made our way down the main street which led to the sea front, Spurs fans were everywhere.

'Here', Pete said,

Us thinking he was about to go in a pub. 'A clothes shop'!

'I'm getting a balaclava', Pete said.

Pete was in and out the shop in a few seconds.

'Don't sell them', Pete said.

'I am not surprised, the balaclava market died off in the 60s', I said.

Pete wasn't put off, going in another shop and getting a large wool hat which was so big it covered his face when he pulled it down over his head.

'This will do', Pete was happy with his purchase, his only issue now was he had no eyes or mouth holes.

'Have you got a pen Richie?', Pete asked.

Richie was the sort of lad who would always carry a pen, fortunately none of us carried knives. Pete began his work with the pen tearing at the wool to make two eye holes and a slot for a mouth.

'Done it', Pete said, pleased with his handy work.

Pete put it over his head, the two eye holes more or less in the correct position, but the mouth was on Pete's cheek area. Pete slid his balaclava around, the mouth slot was good, but the eyes had slid around, one on his ear the other over his nose. Pete decided it was best to be able to see. A muffled voice followed us around Brighton as we looked for a pub.

We stayed in the pub for an hour then set off back to the station for a train to Hove, passing the pub we first went in, it was boarded up, all the windows smashed, police vans outside, a good decision not to stay there. Getting to the ground no one was wearing balaclavas, Pete gave up on his, we saw a 2-0 win, but our thoughts were more for the cup the following week.

Swindon were in Division Three at the time or league one as it is now called. I never liked the rebranding of what divisions were called, it should just be one, two, three and four.

Swindon were a decent team pushing for promotion so we couldn't take them lightly. None of us who travelled had tickets, so we decided to travel on the overnight train to London. I boarded at Midnight, Richie, John and Harry already on. Phil, Pete and Dave were getting on at York.

The train was quiet, its journey had started in Scotland, made up of second-class carriages and sleeper compartments. It would be a long trip, not due in London until 6.00a.m.. Once the three from York were on and the general chit chat subsided we tried to get a bit of sleep, which was difficult and uncomfortable, but some of the lads dozed off.

'Phil, do you fancy at look up the train to the sleeping compartments, see if any are empty?', I asked.

Phil was happy to go, Richie half opened an eye asking what was going on, he wasn't interested.

We tried the doors of each sleeper compartment, gently squeezing the handle, we didn't want to alarm the sleeping guests. Going through the carriages, eventually my hand pushed further down on one of the handles and instead of a solid lock feel the handle pushed all the way down and the door opened. 'Bingo' I'm thinking, but still being careful opening the door, as I didn't want to see a sleeping person who'd forgot to lock the door. I looked in.

'It's empty', I whispered to Phil.

We went in and shut the door. A neatly made single bed looked at me almost beckoning me into it. Phil tried the internal door which opened into the room opposite, an identical room awaited Phil. It was like a suite for two, a dividing door which you could leave open, presumedly for a couple, or closed for privacy. In no time at all I was undressed and in bed. Phil likewise in his bed. The train motion had me asleep in a minute. It was after 2a.m. so it wouldn't be a long sleep.

It didn't feel like I had been asleep long when I heard a knock on the door, the outside door. It was 5.30a.m.

'Morning tea', a voice said, presumably the rail guard.

I couldn't open the door or say anything, I wasn't supposed to be there. I jumped out the bed, putting my clothes on in a panic, whispering to Phil at the same time.

'What we going to do?', I said.

Phil was trying to get his clothes on.

'Hello in there', the rail guard raising his voice.

I said nothing and moved into Phil's adjacent room and shut the dividing door between the two compartments. I heard the key being turned in the room I'd just left, making my bed wasn't an option. We could hear him enter the room, as he did, we left Phil's room and ran down the train corridor to where the rest of the lads were.

We sat down and pretended to be asleep, within seconds I got a push on my shoulder, I gave my best acting role of someone startled having been woken.

'Yes, what do you want?', I say to the Indian/Pakistani guard.

'You sleep up there', he says.

'What are you on about', I'm keeping up my acting role. Phil was half looking at me.

129

'You were in sleeper, you have to pay', he said.

'Been here since I got on', I said.

'No, no, you in sleeper', he said again 'You pay, or police will be called'.

He had me now, not even De Niro could act his way out of this, Phil looked like he'd got away with it. I left my seat, he asked me to follow him back to the sleeper carriage where he had a small guard's room. His receipt book came out.

'That will be sixteen pounds for a room in the sleeping car', he said, enjoying the moment of power.

'No way, I said, I was only in three hours'.

'I will call police to arrest you at Kings Cross' he said.

'Put your receipt book away, I'll give you five quid, in your pocket, no questions asked', I said, almost pleading.

'Ok, that will be fine', the guard said.

He didn't even think about it. I suppose at that time it might have been the equivalent of three hours wages, so he was happy to take it.

I walked down the train to the rest of the lads, Phil was obviously more interested than the others.

'Did you have to pay?' Phil asked.

I told Phil we had come to an arrangement of five quid, Phil handed me two pound fifty as his share, it was worthwhile to get a bit of sleep, but I still worried that when we got to Kings Cross the railway police might be waiting for me. I could imagine being led away with a guard waving a five-pound note in the distance.

On arrival at the station there was no sign of the police, I was free for Swindon.

Across from Kings Cross to Paddington Station a little after 6.30a.m. we went for breakfast at a nearby café, Richie asked if the breakfast had chips. We ate our fry ups and made our way to the Swindon bound platform where we were met by a couple of Spurs lads.

'Alright boys, all got tickets for today?'.

'No', we said.

'Well, we've got a few, how many you need?'.

'Seven', we said.

'No problem, they'll be five quid each'.

We didn't even argue about the price, though the face value was only a two quid. Extortion it was, but we were all pleased to have got tickets with relative ease, it would make the day better knowing we didn't have to look for tickets once at Swindon. I looked at the ticket, a yellow card, it looked more like a Dance ticket, very basic.

'five quid, I could have forged these easily', I said to the rest of the lads, that wasn't what they wanted to hear, especially Dave who always travelled with the minimum of money, the big outlay would of put a hole in his drinking money.

The train ride to Swindon involved the usual card games and the time passed quickly. We arrived at Swindon before mid-day. We left the station to the first pub we saw, already rammed full of Spurs, a couple of drinks later and Richie and I left and headed to the ground.

The 6,000 tickets allocated to us were in a part of the side terrace and a section in the open end, we opted for the side which filled to another crush. We heard that some of the gates had been smashed and people were getting in, there were Spurs fans all over, none more so than in the covered end behind the goal which was the Swindon End. Fights were breaking out in pockets of the ground. Spurs have a good following in the West Country area and rumour had it Spurs fans had bought tickets from Swindon and off the many touts around the ground, it was inevitable that there would be issues inside the ground.

Shortly after kick-off in the second half a fire started near the corner of the open end which housed our fans, I think it was a programme stall ablaze. A section opened up as fans moved away from the flames as thick smoke billowed all around. The game would have been abandoned nowadays, but the game carried on as the fire brigade contained it. Health and safety was not what it is today.

A poor game ended with no goals. I couldn't afford to go to the replay which Spurs won in a tight game. Our cup dreams were still on with Birmingham being the visitors to The Lane in the next round.

The following week it was back to the bread and butter, so they say, this time another two-hundred-mile trip to The Hawthorns, home of West Brom.

It was around 1980 that Richie and I began to take notice of where Newcastle were playing. We hadn't any interest how they were doing in the league, after all they were in the division below, our main concern was that the Geordies were the worst fans to travel with. They're loud, obnoxious and you can't reason with them, they think they are the best fans, and Newcastle is the best city in the country, when in 1980 it definitely wasn't. Their support had dwindled to little over 20,000 and could drop to less than 10,000 on occasions, but to be fair their away following remained strong and they would travel in numbers all over the country.

Coming back from West Brom we suffered another defeat. We knew that the Geordies were playing at Wrexham, which is one of those places that is out of the way and awkward to get back from.

We had caught the train going back north at 6p.m., the journey was going fine. The York lads got off leaving Richie,

John and myself in the front carriage. The only thing between our carriage and the diesel train pulling us was a small room which was used as a parcel van compartment.

Then we heard the dreaded noise coming up the train 'United, United' the Geordie lilt was unmistakable'.

'I don't believe it! They've managed to get back already', I said.

Geordies don't seem to like any other fans, so this would only end up with us being splattered around. We were the only three in the carriage so there were no witnesses if they started on us. Richie hid his scarf, I still hadn't replaced the one taken the year before.

'We can get in the parcel van', Richie said.

Just as Richie and I went in, they stormed into the opposite end of the carriage, the madness began.

John was still in with them, he would have to do the talking, and he would have to be good.

We heard the conversation behind the parcel door. We could also hear the Geordie tribe leaping around on the tables, luggage racks, bulbs were taken from their sockets and thrown out into the night-time gloom. We sat quietly amongst the empty mail sacks not knowing if the Geordies had seen us enter, they must have numbered at least twenty.

'Ah reet?', Geordie said.

'I', John replied.

'Are you'se Newcastle fans?', he said, sounding menacing.

'I', John said.

'What's them two dee'an up there?', our cover blown, they knew where we were.

'Just getting their heads down', John said,

Why the Geordie would think laying on a floor of a dark dirty parcel van would be better than a seat in the carriage, was beyond me, but he bought it.

'Been tha match?', Geordie said.

John was not daft enough to say he'd been to the W.B.A v Tottenham game.

'Wey I', John said.

The Geordie now thought the three of us had been to Wrexham. John and Richie have Sunderland accents and we all know the Geordies despise the Mackem's.

'Where ye from?', Geordie asked, possibly picking up on the slight discrepancy in Johns dialect of not being a Geordie.

'Boldon', John said. Boldon is between Newcastle and Sunderland and have fans of both clubs, John's accent can be forgiven. John couldn't say Murton, where he lived, as the Geordie would have known he was from a Sunderland stronghold.

'Where ya stand at tha game?', Geordie asked John.

'Down the side', John said, he didn't know which end the Geordies would be stood.

'Doon the side, aye, we wor there' Geordie said, 'See that Geordie get hoyed oot for nowt?'

John agreed, not having a clue what the Geordie was on about.

'As gannin for a sit doon. You lot stop fuckan a boot'. Geordie tells the other loonies.

I blow out a sigh of relief, we've got away with it, the Geordies commence wrecking the carriage.

At Darlington I pass through the carriage and off the train, thinking what scum.

Over the years whenever I've spoken to a Birmingham fan, they would always say the same thing 'I was there when the Blues played at Tottenham in the Cup'. It was like a Cup Final for them, they were in the Division below us, but when they had played Spurs in previous years they didn't bring many to Tottenham.

However, for the 5th round of the Cup they must have had 10,000 at The Lane. The atmosphere was noisy to say the least and with the Brummies' singing their 'Right on till the end of the road' chant, it made White Hart Lane sound like we were at St Andrews at times during the game.

The game wasn't all ticket but the near 50,000 packed inside soon had the gates locked well before kick-off, with thousands locked out, it lead to sporadic fighting outside. Sinka later told us he had got into an altercation with a Blues fan, having been one of those unlucky supporters still outside when the gates were closed.

A good game pursued with Spurs winning 3-1, the F.A. Cup dream continued with Liverpool at home next round.

Persil, But Not For Washing

At the beginning of 1980, Lever Brothers, who were a huge company that produced household cleaning products decided to promote 'two for one' rail travel. This meant you bought one rail ticket and they gave you an identical ticket for a friend to accompany you on the same journey, but you only paid for one ticket. The only thing you had to do to get this offer was to collect tokens from Persil washing powder. Once you collected enough tokens you sent your application in the post where you were then sent a voucher to trade at the railway ticket office. This news was heaven for football fans, and no more so than us, it meant our usual seventeen quid fare to London was halved as long as you had a partner to travel with.

All of us were asking our families to buy more washing powder, my clothes never smelt so fresh. I was putting them in the wash at every opportunity, I was even buying my mam washing powder just to get a token.

After the highs of the cup win it was back to the misery of the league, our form was slipping and our position was becoming a concern, but today we would be playing Derby at the Baseball Ground. They were in such poor form at home that they had brought in a of spiritualist to lift the curse that might be hanging over the ground. There wasn't any need for a spiritualist, Spurs were in town, the curse would soon lift. Derby went on to win 2-1.

The day started off well, with Richie and I pairing up with a Persil ticket, some of the others doing the same. Brass had teamed up with Sinka to share their cost. Sinka was holding the main part of the ticket, the inspectors on the trains would only accept the main ticket, the accompanying ticket was only valid with the main ticket. You couldn't travel separately, so Brass had to make sure he was with Sinka at all times on the train.

We pulled into Derby and were met by two Spurs lads from Hull, Jacko and George, lads we had got to know over the last year or two, nice lads, but unfortunately they liked to get into a few scrapes. Jacko came over to Richie and me.

'There's a couple of Derby lads outside the station, they think me and George are Derby fans, they're a bit game and are looking for a few stray Spurs, so we're going to have em'. Jacko was enthusiastic about his plan.

'You and Richie start walking to the ground, we will tell the two Derby lads you're Spurs, so they think once we've teamed up with them it will be four onto two'.

I wasn't keen on the idea and told Jacko and George we were not getting involved in any fight.

'Yes, that's ok, we will take these two mugs ourselves', Jacko confidently said.

Out of the station, we walked about half a mile towards the ground.

We could hear the four voices behind, Richie talked about the season before at Derby when Harry said he got into a fight with a police horse and was swinging on its tail. I knew Harry was small, but it did seem a little farfetched.

We entered a cut in the road, a narrow alley, it was quiet, I knew this is where it would happen, and I was right. A thud and the two Derby lads were floored, I wasn't bothered, they were going to do it to us given the chance. Jacko and George happy with their handywork walked up to the ground with us.

At half time we were two behind against Derby. The Spurs fans were giving the team torrid abuse, and to be fair it was deserved.

'Come on Brass', Sinka said.

'Where?', Brass said.

'Home. We going to get fuck all out of this game, we can get the 4.30p.m., I'll be back in the boozer in Stockton by 8.30p.m', Sinka said.

'What about the second-half?', Brass pleaded.

'Fuck that we're going'.

Sinka had the train ticket, and it was the main part of the Persil ticket. Anyway, Brass couldn't argue with Sinka, they left the ground. Spurs played slightly better in the second-half but to no avail.

Liverpool F.A. Cup 6th Round 1980

There was an air of excitement as we walked up the Tottenham High Road towards The Lane. It was the only 'All Ticket' home game of the season, such was the anticipation of getting to an F.A. Cup Semi Final, and possibly our first Cup Final in Thirteen years.

All of the lads had travelled including Gary and Colin the Liverpool supporters. They had decided to tag along with us as they hadn't been to Tottenham before. They were more than welcome as long as they didn't mouth-off they were Liverpool, it wasn't an issue with Gary, but Colin was a loose cannon.

We headed to the Supporters' Club for a couple of drinks and something to eat, and from there to the 'Bell and Hare' pub on the corner of the High Road and Park Lane. Going in the pub, it was already full, the juke box already throbbing to the music of the day, The Jam, Madness and punk anthems. It just got you in the mood, it was terrace music.

A couple of weeks earlier we had gone in a few clothes shops on Tottenham High Road so Col could buy a two-tone suit for his appreciation of the Ska scene, the music, and the messages they sung about. UB40's 'One in Ten', about unemployment and The Specials 'Ghost Town', the title summing up the state of our towns and cities at the time of the early 80's.

By 2p.m. the pub was rocking, The Bell and Hare was popular in its day with the players, they would go in for a few drinks after training. By the late 70's it was dying off, not only the players being hassled, but more the professionalism to cut out the drinking culture that footballers once shared and took for granted.

But on occasions Steve Perryman, our captain and record appearance holder for the club, would be seen having a pint with the supporters after a match, Steve being part of the latter years of the likes of Gilzean and Greaves, who would drink to excess in the pub, Steve would be the last link to that era.

As Liverpool supporters filed past the pub, the Spurs fans taunting them, hurling abuse, any Scousers who gave any verbal's back were set upon or chased. The Corner Pin pub next door was always eager to lend a hand if numbers were required.

Gary and Colin left for the ground at 2.30p.m.

We were about to go when someone broke into the juke box and took all the records out, it was chaos as they were launched Frisbee style, from one end of the pub to the other. Any that didn't break were sent back to where they were flung from, it was dangerous as up to ten records were flying in your direction at any one time.

'Time to go', I said to Rich.

We almost crawled out the door in case we were hit. If the plod had come in someone could have got a Police record!

The game was a massive disappointment, both teams lacked imagination, but Liverpool would take a 1-0 win, a goal scored by Terry McDermott which won goal of the season, a dipping volley. As soon as they scored, they toyed with us, not interested in getting anymore, just making sure they didn't let us near their goal.

I had told Gary and Colin to meet us at the Supporters' Club after the game, but when we left the ground you could feel a sinister vibe. The two of us walked from The Shelf round to the Park Lane End, the Liverpool fans hadn't been let out yet, they were still celebrating getting to the Semi-Final and rightly so.

Once onto the High Road we were met by an army of waiting Spurs hooligans and hangers-on, the type who would normally go home or to the pub after a match, but today was different, the massive anti-climax seemed to have tipped them over the edge.

We arrived at the Supporters' Club, only about fifty yards from the mob, and stood on the wall to see what would happen.

The Liverpool fans came out, they were met by a barrage of bottles, then a charge as the hooligans fought running battles, the police struggling to contain the violence, it was the worst I had seen outside the ground. I wondered if Gary and Colin had escaped unscathed.

We had a pint in the club then strolled down to Seven Sisters tube station, we had arranged to get the 7p.m. train back. It was us who were hoping to be celebrating but it wasn't meant to be.

We met with Gary at Kings Cross and listened to a Liverpool perspective of events. Gary said it had been as bad as it looked, a lot of Liverpool had taken good hiding, but many were genuine supporters not after bother, I found this sad, it had happened to me, so I knew what it's like. I didn't mind the trouble at games as long as opposing supporters wanted the same thing.

Gary had got split from Colin and jogged down the High Road kicking a can, singing the praises of Glenn Hoddle. This was Gary's way of hiding his true colours. It's a psychological thing. Gary said it was an experience at Spurs, the dodgiest place he had been to, and he wouldn't forget it in a hurry.

A New Low for Football

The game against Liverpool forgotten, it was now just the bread and butter of the league for the final two months. The derby with Arsenal was the only game left that had any meaning to us Spurs supporters, it wasn't like we were going to be relegated, just other games were fairly unimportant.

Arsenal had wanted Tottenham to call the game off as they had a Semi-Final in the European Cup Winners Cup against Juventus a couple of days later, but Tottenham would have none of it, much to the delight of Spurs fans. We didn't want to give them anything.

The usual Northern Spurs were down, along with an Arsenal fan who lived at Murton where Harry and John lived. He was called Frankie, a funny lad who always had a story. He was about 17 and said he would go in the ground with us on The Shelf, that was ok as long as he kept his mouth shut!

Arsenal's team was read out over the tannoy, Spurs fans were all pleased to hear that they had six reserves playing as they didn't want injuries ahead of their match with Juventus.

With the factions hurling abuse at each other, only the Shelf/Park Lane corner empty for segregation, this to stop the two tribes getting at each other.

Out the corner of my eye I suddenly saw a bottle thrown from the Arsenal fans housed in the Park Lane End, its aimed for The Shelf side. At first I didn't think much of it, but as it landed in the empty no man's land it exploded with a plume of smoke. 'They had thrown a petrol bomb'! How they had got it in I didn't know, but it was sickening, the thought that they wanted to maim or kill people was incomprehensible.

The same thing had happened at Newcastle the month before, when Newcastle fans had thrown a petrol bomb at the West Ham supporters' which had exploded in their section, luckily no one was severely burnt.

The flames were put out on the Lower Shelf corner by the police, Spurs fans were enraged. I'm sure 99% of Arsenal fans were disgusted at the horror they had seen, as I would have been if we had done it to them. As they say, when one does it, it will be copied. The Arsenal lunatic, copying the Newcastle counterpart.

Strangely I had bought a book in the mid-70s called 'Albion Albion' by Dick Morland, set in the near future. The back cover read, '1982 Two coach loads of Spurs fans are burned alive by Villa fans. Football is banned'. I could only hope this wasn't to become a reality in 1980.

The game was played in a hostile atmosphere, with Arsenal and their reserves looking the better team, a point to prove to their manager maybe. As if the day hadn't started badly enough, Arsenal go on to win 2-1, a win they fully deserved. Many Spurs fans left well before the end, such was the lack of pressure and urgency towards the Arsenal goal. The Arsenal fans were in full voice singing 'Arsenal Reserves, Arsenal Reserves, Hello, Hello'. For the second year running we had their fans dancing on White Hart Lane terraces.

The final whistle, we left the ground, Frankie the Arsenal fan kept to his word, he said nothing as we walked around the back of the Park Lane end, still with the din of the celebrating Gunners.

As we met the junction of the High Road, we saw the street packed with awaiting Spurs fans, I thought at the Liverpool cup match there was a big Spurs reception, but this blew it away.

Frankie commented.

'I've seen nothing like this at Highbury, what a mob'.

And he was right.

We began to walk down The High Road towards Seven Sisters and the mob was huge, the petrol bombing was not going to be forgotten. We got a good half-mile from the ground and then you could hear a huge roar go up, presumably the Arsenal fans had been let out, we didn't need to know the outcome.

The final game of the season, and my forty first Spurs match was nil- nil bore against relegated Bristol City. I think watching the peanut seller selling his 'Percy Dalton peanuts' meandering through the bodies on the Shelf Side was more interesting than the game.

The club programme front cover showed a model of the new West Stand which was to commence in the Autumn of the next season. The new stand would have seventy-two executive boxes and would be Tottenham's first big movement into commercialism.   Many clubs were looking into making money   from other things other than turnstile revenue, transfers and merchandise. Everton and Liverpool had been the first to put advertising on their shirts to gain extra income, Spurs didn't want to be left behind.

It's the start of a new decade, the eighties would eventually alienate the many working-class fans that had followed their clubs through generations.

Scotland Bound

1980-81 would be the season I would follow Spurs more often than any other season. I know I will never get to the number of games I did that year again. Forty-seven games, and still living the two hundred and sixty miles from White Hart Lane.

The first of that season would be at Tannadice, the home of Dundee United, my first ever trip north of the border. John said he was going to drive up to Dundee United for the friendly.

'You still haven't got the three-wheeler have you', I said to John, on the phone.

My mam had recently got the phone installed. It was heaven sent. I now didn't have to walk half a mile to phone people up from a phone box to arrange train times. I was always the organiser of the group, sorting train times for everyone. Then in later years I would be the ticket organiser for away games.

John said he had traded the car for a four-wheeler but didn't say what make, but it had to better having four corners on the tarmac.

Five of us, Richie, Col, Phil and me, plus John driving made the trip. Some of us made our way to Durham for the pick-up.

John turned up, we only knew it was his car from the fluffy dice adorning the driving mirror, the same ones that hung on the Del Boy Reliant he previously had. He pulled up, UB40 blasting out. I looked at it in amazement, I couldn't believe how small it was, the smallest Japanese car on the road, a Honda I think, no bigger than the old minis, and we had to get five in.

The car struggled along, up the A1 on our way to our first port of call at Berwick, the border town on the English/Scottish Border.

A couple of drinks and we were away from Berwick by 3p.m., we hit Dundee at 5p.m. parked up near the two grounds of Dundee United and Dundee, only a stone's throw between the two.

We were confident that this season would be exciting, Spurs having invested heavily on Garth Crooks and Steve Archibald. The latter would become a huge cult hero to the White Hart Lane faithful. Getting two strikers, the one department we had struggled with the previous season would make a huge difference, the two would hit it off from the word go.

We entered the almost empty pub, apart from a few familiar faces of Spurs fans, we didn't know them to talk to, but they were faces you would see on your regular away days, you know they're Spurs, and they know you are. We nodded in their direction. John walked over and was soon chatting to the London lads.

The pub filled with the sound of Scottish voices, there was no animosity between the two countries, which was good, your never sure how things will go when Scots and English meet.

John walked back over.

'We are off in their end when we go'.

We all agreed, it wasn't like we had been allocated a section of the ground.

We set off to the ground, maybe forty of us along with a group of Dundee fans, who had come along to support Spurs just to rile the Dundee United supporters.

Entering the covered end behind the goal, we stood at the back, and the first cry of 'Come on you Spurs' was met by heckles from the Scots. Steve Archibald who we had just signed was taking a lot of stick having signed from United's rivals Aberdeen.

Surrounded on three sides by the Tangerine Army, only the back of the stand stopping a complete enclosure, a gap formed around us with the Scots about eight feet away. We didn't see any police in attendance.

When we scored our small knot of 50/60 jumped up, there was a surge of Scots towards us, but it was mainly impressionable youngsters who didn't want to get too near in case they might get a slap.

United won 4-1 and to be honest the banter was good natured, there were no incidents as we left the ground. We squeezed back into the car.

'It's only 9.30p.m., we can get a drink in Edinburgh', John said.

No one was bothered about drink driving then, it wasn't uncommon for the drivers to have six or seven pints before a match.

Pulling up in Edinburgh just before 11p.m. we managed to find a pub that would serve us a couple of pints, leaving the pub thirty minutes later.

Looking around at our surroundings, a pretty much a deserted city centre square with an impressive building which looked like a City Hall, built of huge blocks of granite.

John went over to the car, opened the door, all of us thinking of getting in, when John pulled out a spray can of blue paint. As his car wasn't blue it wasn't getting a touch up tonight. John went over to the town hall and set about his work. I've never liked seeing buildings daubed with spray paint and tonight I felt no different. There was no stopping John, in large blue letters it read 'Geordie Spurs', It looked terrible, defacing a beautiful building, especially with what he had wrote. None of us were Geordies. I wondered what the morning commuters would of thought on their way to work, 'bloody Sassenachs', I would presume. John threw the can under the car seat and we all boarded. John then left the car again and went up to the wall and had a piss, probably smiling at his artwork. He was just zipping up when a policewoman shouted.

'Hey you, what ye doing?'.

'Nothing', John replied.

'You were urinating against that wall'.

I was thinking, never mind having a piss, if she sees what's above the piss-stained wall we are done for.

'I was spitting', John said.

'So, you spit with your penis, do you?', the copper's not stupid, a police van soon pulled up.

'We have reason to believe that someone has been spraying graffiti on the wall', she points to the fore mentioned wall.

'Not us', John quickly answered. I thought too right, for four of us at least.

'You don't mind us looking in the car then?'.

The can was soon found, John still denied everything.

'All you lot in the van'.

We were soon whisked off to Edinburgh Police Station and all put in a large room and left for an hour or so. We sat around a large table telling John what an idiot he was. Then we sat down to the more important Push Penny Football Tournament on the large table.

Still playing, a copper walked in and took us all out, each of us going into a separate room where we all have to write a statement and questioned about the events of the night. I confessed all, singing like a canary.

The police knew John was guilty they just wanted it down on paper. The copper told me a woman over the road had witnessed it all and had rang the police.

I was led back to the room we had been in, where I met the rest.

'What did you say?', John asked.

'I told the truth', I said.

'You fucking cunt', John said.

All the rest had said they had seen nothing. The rest of the lads were laughing. I felt bad, especially being the only one to say anything.

John was told he would get a letter in due course and to return to Edinburgh and expect to get a heavy fine.

Fortunately, that letter never arrived, so John got away with it, Scot free, but it didn't stop John calling me a grass for the next few months, and I deserved it. We were let out at 4a.m. for the journey South.

Boots the Chemist, Moving Left

The league got off to a flyer, beating Forest on the opening day. Archibald and Crooks our new signings played brilliantly, the duo hitting it off from game one. We beat Palace, then drew against Brighton setting it up nicely for the away game at Highbury against the old foe.

Keith Thompson, an Arsenal fan from near where I lived said he would drive down to the game. He picked me up at 6a.m. on a bright Saturday morning. Keith said he would be going in the North Bank, me telling him it would be at his own risk, knowing Spurs would be in that end in big numbers.

The previous season, Arsenal had used a ballot system to ensure that Spurs fans wouldn't gain entry into the North Bank. Arsenal gave vouchers out to their fans who would normally stand on the North Bank at a pre-selected game and in return this would guarantee an Arsenal fan a ticket for the aforementioned end. It was a way of ensuring no Spurs fans would be in their end. The plan worked a treat, hardly any Spurs fans were seen on the North Bank. It was such a success they scrapped it for this seasons game! Maybe it was because it was so early in the season they couldn't implement it, so once again it allowed a massive turn out of Spurs fans onto the North Bank, Arsenal's home end.

148

Keith parked up at Euston and we went our separate ways. I hoped we'd slaughter them but wished Keith a safe journey. I knew Spurs would be in their end, but I didn't realise just how many.

I took my place in our allocated away section in the Clock End, I was in a perfect position to watch what would unfold. The beautiful sunny day made it even more clear, more colourful than two years previous when it was mid-week game. Around fifteen minutes before kick-off the surge began. Spurs fans were under the North Bank roof in seconds, Arsenal fans running for safety or smashed past, Spurs fans were almost to the middle of the North Bank. The colour of it was vivid, the police appeared to be thinking, 'let them have their bit of fun, then we will get amongst it'.

With our fans whistling the Laurel and Hardy tune as the large mob of coppers moved around the perimeter to the warring factions they entered the battle zone, soon separating the madness, forcing a large gap, police either side of the fans.

I later found out that Richie had gone down the side paddock and filmed it on his cine camera for posterity.

That night on Match of the Day, Jimmy Hill presenting, said 'Our main match tonight is the North London Derby played against a backdrop of some of the ugliest football hooliganism seen at an English football ground ever. We were beaten 2-0.

After the game I met Keith at Euston Station, we went in the buffet and straightaway I recognised some of the faces in the bar from Spurs away days, a few the type not to be messed with. I quickly said to Keith 'Don't say a thing'.

I went to the bar with my programme in my hand.

'Been to the match, good result eh', one of them said.

'Only if your Arsenal', I said.

'Your Spurs then?', he said.

149

'Yes, weren't you up at Dundee a few weeks ago?' I asked.

He nodded, Keith kept quiet, the lad moved on.

The season slipped into its usual format, mid-table mediocrity, but occasionally it would throw up a result that wasn't expected.

We travelled in numbers to Nottingham Forest in November. Eight of us in our party, most of us in our Harrington jackets which were totally inadequate for the torrential rain that had fallen on the journey down, and still falling heavily as we left the railway station on our walk to the city centre pubs.

Nottingham was a good away day, good pubs and never a threat of any trouble. That continued over my many visits to Forest and County over the years.

We sat in the pub drinking and watching the weather deteriorate from our cosy place.

'We goin to get soaked today', I said, knowing that the away end was now the open end at the City Ground. There was never a thought of going in the seats or the covered home end.

'We could go to Boots the chemist', I suggested.

'What the fuck for?', John piped up.

'Carrier bags, to put on our heads', I said.

The nod of approval said it all. We left the pub and went into Boots, all eight of us, why one of us didn't go in and purchase eight bags I don't know. We went to the counter one at a time.

'Carrier bag please'.

'one pence', The assistant said.

Next person 'Carrier bag please'.

'one pence'.

All eight of us doing the same. I think the assistant thought we were taking the piss. We put two eye holes in the bags, even Pete got them in the right place. We left Boots in a line with the bags over our heads, walking to the City ground, our heads dry. The rest of our bodies soaked to the skin.

Standing together on the open terrace with a large Spurs following, we had many admiring glances and a few comments 'Wish I'd fucking thought of that, because I'm fucking soaked'.

The rain was unrelenting but the result, a 3-0 win against a Forest team that hadn't lost at home for a couple of years meant the weather was forgotten.

We got back to the station and met big Kev, a bloke we had met the year before. Kev was from Doncaster, about 10-years older than me and always dressed smartly, often in a suit or jacket and trousers, but could he moan.

'What you think of that Kev?', I said, knowing a 3-0 win at Forest could not be knocked.

'Should have scored fucking eight', Kev always sounded aggressive when ripping into Spurs.

It didn't matter how many we won by Kev was never satisfied. If we were losing during a game, you would hear a distant voice in the away section.

'You're fucking crap'.

But Kev would always be there next game, hurling abuse. We often wondered why he came to games, as it always seemed a toil for him.

Another lad we would see at games was another Peter, but we knew him as Lenses, for his thick lensed glasses. We saw Lenses this day while standing on the station platform. Lenses walked really quickly, so quick he wouldn't notice you, probably not in his peripheral vision.

'Alright Lenses', I said, him stopping immediately.

'I didn't see you there', he'd say. Me a bit embarrassed not calling him Peter.

'What you think of today?', I asked.

Peter had this droning voice that you soon got sick of hearing, and like Kev, he would moan.

'Yeah, we were ok, but we're not the team of the early 70's when I started going', he said.

Everyone thinks with rose tinted spectacles, you only remember the good games. I started watching Spurs in our worst period since the war but remembering Alfie Conn's hat-trick at Newcastle only fills me with happy feelings.

His voice was still droning on. I was thinking, why did I stop him.

Lenses stopped watching Spurs by the end of the 80's and decided to drone on to the paying patrons of his hometown club, Harrogate Town F.C.

Playing Wolves at home in November would be a sad day for me and for many Spurs fans. It was the last Saturday home game for the old West Stand before it was due to be demolished. For that match I had to stand in the standing enclosure for the last time, although I'd only stood in it once before I did like it there, and if it weren't for the Shelf Side it would have been my preferred choice to watch a game.

The West Stand enclosure being season ticket only, Richie and I had to ask very nicely at the ticket office for them to give us a complimentary ticket, telling them again how far we had travelled. The Crystal Palace game the following midweek would actually be the West Stand's last match, but I didn't go. After that it would be all change at White Hart Lane, including The Shelf.

The Enclosure supporters were to be moved to the best standing area left in the ground, that would be the centre section on the Shelf Side. The area would be sectioned off. After three years of my perfect view, I and many others would have to find an alternative area to stand. I would lose contact with Paul and Panno, I think they both bought season tickets so they could remain where they were. Richie and I did what most of the old centre section of The Shelf did and that was to move about twenty yards to the left. I would now stand between the halfway line and the eighteen-yard box. It would be my football home for the next eight years.

Tottenham said this would be the start of a new stadium rebuild on the present site, but the new West Stand would almost cripple the club with debt during the 80's. With falling attendances and poor financial decisions by the board, there could quite easily have been no Tottenham Hotspur.

The stadium by 1995 would look totally different from the ground I first visited. I will always remember the ground Archibald Leitch designed, and to many Spurs fans that was the real White Hart Lane, but times move on and now we have another new White Hart Lane (2021), which is magnificent.

West Ham and Flickheads

Our league form might have been disappointing, but the 80-81 season was all about cup runs. The League Cup at the time still held a lot of prestige, unlike now used as a second-rate cup competition to give the reserves a run out.

Spurs started with a win at Brisbane Road, the home of Orient in a two-legged tie. Even now I wonder why I went to the return leg at the Lane, a five-hundred-mile round trip on a Wednesday evening on my own, getting back home at 7a.m. the following morning and going straight to work. It's not like

Orient were a big attraction, with all due respect. Spurs strolled through the tie. My obsession for watching Spurs was like a drug. I almost felt guilty if I missed a game. However I did miss the next round at home to Crystal Palace, another win, then onto the big clash with Arsenal at The Lane. This was narrow 1-0 win, which was played to a backdrop of passion from the euphoric Spurs crowd, our first win against them at home since 1974, it felt longer than six years, but it was worth it.

The quarter-final threw us an away game at West Ham, it was a game that had both sets of fans clambering for tickets.

Make no mistake this derby is a big match for both, and maybe more so for West Ham. Although West Ham's main derby has always been the 'dockers derby' against Millwall, a fraught affair, which often ended in ugly scenes both inside and outside of the ground, but those clashes were rare due to them being in different divisions most of the time.

West Ham's other big rival has always been Tottenham, the clubs only eight miles apart and like with Arsenal, Spurs territory would overlap with the West Ham's.

West Ham were a division lower than Spurs having been relegated a couple of years earlier, but they were on their way back, gaining promotion at the end of this season. With a loyal support, both home and away, they also had some of the most feared hooligans in the country. This tie wouldn't be for the faint hearted. Tottenham's hooligan reputation through the 70's was also well documented.

On December 2nd we all made the trip to Upton Park. Getting into Kings Cross at 4p.m. we made our way over to Liverpool Street Station where we met up with a large Spurs following in the pubs in and around the Liverpool Street area. John said he was off with some London lads, which didn't surprise us.

At 6.30p.m. we headed down to the tube for the short journey to Upton Park. None of us had been to this derby before, but we all knew this could be a dodgy place to go. Once on the tube, which was made up of football fans and commuters, many of whom were well dressed suited business types, a proper mix from all walks of life.

What were distinctly missing were football scarves, this was not the night to show who you followed, not until you were in the ground.

In 1972 West Ham had an organised a mob of hooligans, they were called the I.C.F. (Inter City Firm), they would become feared around the country, a large mob who would terrorise other fans on the terraces. They were well organised and would travel to games with no scarves or badges. They didn't want to be noticed until they got to their destination to cause maximum mayhem. By the late 70s, early 80s the I.C.F. were at their height of hooliganism, but this would also see a knock-on effect with other football hooligan firms, each club having a mob of likewise troublemakers who given the chance would have a tear up before the police descended.

We all knew that the I.C.F. would be out in force that night so extra vigilance would be in order, a good adrenalin rush. We had the same problems everywhere we went, particularly Manchester, Merseyside and Leeds. The thing was, we had our own troublemakers and our big away following would bring out their mobs. It was all about keeping your wits about you, finding a quiet pub and keeping away from flash points, but I hasten to add it was still a minority, we had some great days out and good banter with many opposing fans around the country.

We got to Bow Tube Station, the train was thinning of commuters and more football fans were boarding, the majority being West Ham. The train was quiet considering

155

how many supporters were on. It was the calm before the storm!

West Ham knew we were coming over in big numbers, 8,000 to be precise. These were the days when clubs would allocate up to 25% of the capacity to away fans for a cup tie.

The train pulled into Upton Park, we headed out onto Green Street, not dissimilar to the Tottenham High Road, but a shorter distance to the ground to what Seven Sisters Tube was at Tottenham. In the near distance the bright glow around the floodlight pylons could be seen. I did like the old floodlights, it was a focal point, you knew where to walk if you were unfamiliar with the area.

Passing The Queens public house which had some dodgy looking characters hanging out the doors. We then turned left to where the Spurs fans were to be housed in the South Stand, a partially covered terrace. I had heard Upton Park was a tight football ground, and they weren't joking, you could almost touch the players on all four sides, but that made the goal we were stood behind difficult to see, unless you were tall. Phil was okay, Harry left us and went to the front of the terrace. We stood to the left of the goal, about halfway up, on our left was the old West Stand which still had a lower terrace, it would be the last year of standing on this side. Opposite that was the Chicken Run, a small terrace, where West Ham's most fervent followers were.

West Ham are known as the proper cockneys, so it wouldn't be the same without a rendition of 'Knees Up Mother Brown' which the West Terrace did, all bobbing up and down, it looked brilliant, like a giant centipede.

The Spurs fans now singing 'Chim chiminey, chim chiminey, chim chim cher-oo we hate those bastards in claret and blue' to the 'Mary Poppins tune'. Before our rendition was sung the West Ham faithful hit back with the same song

156

but a slightly different ending 'We are those bastards in claret and blue'.

Kick-off arrived with a vociferous rendition of 'I'm forever blowing bubbles'. The game was frantic, the view was shit, or at least it was when the action was at our end, I could only see the cross bar.

There was a roar, a fight had broken out in our end by the right-hand corner, but hard to see what was happening. There was a push forward from the crowd behind us. You always got it, people shouting 'come on, let's do em'. There's no chance they can get there, it's all bravado. The Old Bill piled in and pulled around fifty West Ham fans out, the Chicken Run applauding their exploits. They'd had to go in our end to show their superiority.

The game settled to a more sedate pace and then uproar again as West Ham have another go in our end. This time it was only about five yards from where we were stood, arms and legs were lashing into each other. A huge gap opened up as people tried to avoid the madness with the 'West Ham skinheads' wading in with their big boots, they all wearing green nylon flying jackets. The lads who were shouting 'let's get into them' were nowhere to be seen. The police waded in again, their truncheons hammering into anyone who looked like they were involved. The whistle blew for half-time, not only were we being outplayed, but our fans were also getting set upon, like in boxing we needed the bell to clear our heads.

The second-half was similar to the first. We weren't doing much, but it looked like we could take them to a replay. Then in the eighty second minute David Cross the West Ham forward rounded our keeper, it looked like he was going too wide but managed to get his foot around the ball and chipped it into the empty net. The ground went mental apart from our end, many of our fans left. We just didn't have the fight for

157

the battle and it seemed that many were looking for trouble outside. The final whistle blew with less than half our 8,000 still in the ground. West Ham deserved it, the home fans celebrated, we filed out past the West Ham Supporters Club, and by the noise coming from their fans it sounded like it was going to be a good night.

Onto Green Street, and with the constant din of police dogs and sirens, you knew you were in the middle of a potential kick-off with the two sets of fans.

Getting to Upton Park Tube Station we saw John for the first time since having a drink with him at Liverpool Street at 5p.m.

'Fuckan mayhem up there, Spurs have got West Ham on the run', his excited voice was shouting through the ever-growing queue to get on the tube. He might have been right but there would have been battles going on all over. Me and the rest of the lads just wanted to get back on the midnight train home. The tube was packed but like on the way to West Ham it was mixed. Spurs fans were quiet, and disappointed. West Ham were not wanting to celebrate too much. The last thing we wanted was a battle on the tube. All went well and we were back on the train going North and planning for Saturday's trip to Liverpool.

1980 would herald the start of a new football fashion that would spread across the country and would be the forerunner of the football casual. It would take over from the skinhead boot boys, although the aforementioned group would still be around keeping their culture going.

I first noticed this on my visit to Anfield. We got off at Lime Street Station and walked down the platform, the usual six or seven of us all dressed in our Harrington's, and jeans still slightly flared, but not to the extent of the ridiculous early

158

to mid-70's variety. We were met by an equal amount of similar age Scousers all in tight jeans and wearing cagoules, but the most striking thing about them was their hair. It was a sort of bob cut with a parting and a very long fringe which covered their eyes. They were constantly flicking their heads so their hair would go to one side to allow them to see. They would be labelled flick heads around the country. Liverpool was a very fashion-conscious city and many garments were introduced from there. It was said they got a lot of their ideas from their regular trips on the continent following Liverpool in Europe, many items coming back from foreign shops which had been looted by Liverpool followers, allegedly may I add.

'Ar right mate, got the time?', a Scouser said to me as we went through the ticket barrier.

Of course, it was the oldest trick in the book to see what accent you had. I looked up to the huge clock above his head and pointed, no words were required. I couldn't understand why they were at this platform anyway, the train had come from Scotland, if they were looking for Londoners it made no sense. Once they heard us talking they dismissed us as being Spurs. Looking at the Buffet area it was full of Flick Heads, we had a feeling they would be out in numbers and it proved correct, they were looking for pay back after the attacks they had received in the cup at Tottenham the season before. We didn't hang around and found a pub near the station and stayed there until around 1.30p.m. We didn't bother with the supporters buses at the station, it being too dodgy so travelled over to Anfield in a couple of taxis.

It was a miserable afternoon, raining, being in December it was dank and getting dark. I remember the journey well. I looked out of the taxi window seeing run down streets, empty shops with boarded up windows, rubbish strewn up alleyways, people shuffling along looking glum, the life taken

159

out of them. A once proud city whose people have a great sense of humour were down on their knees, unemployment was rife, the black communities being hassled constantly by the police and it was no surprise when seven months later the Toxteth Riots hit the national news. Streets, shops, and cars ablaze, as well as hundreds of people having running battles with the police. After the London Brixton riots in April many cities around Britain would follow, it was desperate times. That was Liverpool then, now Liverpool is a vibrant city and a much friendlier place for a football supporter to visit.

We lost the game at Anfield, as was usual. The welcome to our supporters was edgy to say the least, coins were thrown constantly at us and one Spurs fan was even hit with a dart, this incident made the national papers. His photo was in all the tabloids showing the dart stuck in his nose as he was led away around the perimeter to get attention. We all managed to get away in one piece, and safely back to Lime Street Station, but we had to do the 'City Tour' police escort back, but on this occasion, it was the safest bet.

Ossie's Goin to Wembley

Train journeys around the country would generally follow the same vein, playing cards and having a few beers, but the return journeys were more memorable. Richie and I would always get a programme, but wherever possible we would buy the evening paper from whatever town or city we were playing at. Buying the paper not only for the football results, but for the match report as a memento to put in the programme. The journey home would always begin well, reading the match reports, but John and Harry would usually be pissed and with more beer being consumed on the train it wouldn't be long before beer was spilt on someone. On occasions John would get up with Richie's paper and threaten to throw it out the train window. This was not a wise move, Richie was the main man when it came to papers, to lose a 'Manchester Evening News' or a 'Sheffield Green Un' out of a train window into the darkness was a risk to John's health. But on occasions John would slide open a window and hold the paper next to the window telling Richie not to move or it goes out, the rest of us almost holding our breath.

'You fucking daren't', Harry shouted.

'That paper goes out, your fucking dead', Richie said.

On a rare occasion it would be sucked from John's hand into the abyss, Richie would go mental.

'Ya fuckan twat', Richie would take John's beer off the table and throw it all over him. Beer would go astray.

'Fucking Hell Richie', John regretting his decision.

'Fucks sake Richie', Pete said, catching a few splashes. Now Pete would splash anyone with his can of beer, this would then escalate into a full-on beer fight. Beer soaking everyone. Once the beer ran out it would be a race to the toilet to fill the cans with water. By the time we had finished the rest of the carriage would be empty, every other passenger had left in disgust. How we didn't get reported I don't know.

Richie carried on getting papers well into the 1980s. He would order the Tottenham Weekly Herald from a newsagent on Tottenham High Road and collect it the next time he was at a home game. He would also order them over the summer months, so at the start of the next season he would have up to twenty papers to collect. He looked like a paper boy carrying them all, but he wouldn't leave any, by the end of the day they were all back in his Sunderland home.

As much as I wanted Spurs to win every game, I could appreciate a good game even in defeat. One such game was at St. Andrews, the home of Birmingham City. It was end to end for ninety minutes and possibly our best performance of the season, but we lost 2-1. The local evening paper said if all games were like that every ground would be full. One other thing I remember from that early winter's day was the steak pie I bought at half-time, which was so hot I still had the pie at full-time. I could have held my hands over it to keep them warm. No wonder there were St. Johns ambulance staff nearby, probably treating mouth blisters, their main role that day.

Saying goodbye to 1980 and the cup draw already made, we would go into the third round with optimism, not only buoyed by the last two seasons reaching the 6th round but the fact that we had always done well when the year ends with a one, so in 1981 we fancied our chances of winning the F.A. Cup. We had won trophies in 1901, 1921, 1951, 1961, 1971 so why not 1981! The cup run started at a packed Loftus Road, home of Q.P.R. with a 0-0 draw. I didn't make the replay, but a comfortable win gave us a Fourth-round tie against Hull City who were in financial trouble and on the brink of extinction. They must have thought they were going to get us back to their patch for a replay, but a late Archibald goal and a last minute second, saw them off. Hull were given a rapturous send off, not only from their 3,000 fans, but also from the Spurs supporters. However I doubt Spurs would have been so warm with their support if the game had ended all square.

White Hart Lane had now lost its old West Stand, bulldozed in November and gone by January. It looked strange watching games on The Shelf and seeing red London buses going down the High Road, but the atmosphere

162

remained good, and with the often-noisy older patrons from the West Stand enclosure now on The Shelf, it was a lively place to watch. Coventry City at home in the Fifth round were brushed aside easily, which gave us the relatively easy looking 6th round draw against fourth division Exeter at The Lane in front of a full house, including 8,000 from Devon. The plucky fourth division team who had beaten Newcastle 4-0 in the previous round gave Spurs a real match, roared on by their support. Spurs again left it late, with two goals from our central defenders, Paul Miller and Graham Roberts. At last, we had got to a Semi-Final where we would meet Wolves at Hillsborough.

When you think of Hillsborough you think of the disaster as much as Sheffield Wednesday. When I relive our Semi-Final back in April 81, my mind often wanders eight years forward to the Hillsborough disaster, especially the ninety-six people who died, and the countless families and friends whose lives would never be the same. So many lessons should of been learned from our visit in 81, but it seems they were forgotten about in apathy, after all we're only football fans who cause mayhem in cities and towns, who gives a shit about them. I want to give my view of our Semi-Final against Wolves on 11 April 1981.

With the game being held in Sheffield it was a lot more-handy for us to get too, we all managed to get tickets apart from Col and his girlfriend Anne.

Col, Anne and a few of Col's mates decided to go down to Sheffield on the Friday night to see if they could pick up any tickets from Sheffield Wednesday fans as they would have been allocated tickets with it being their ground. Col got lucky, tickets were obtained and they had a good night out in Sheffield.

The rest of us travelled down early Saturday morning and got taxis to the ground, bad mistake! There weren't any pubs open around the ground on police orders. The only thing we found was an off-licence, but of course hundreds of Spurs fans had also found it, which meant queuing and paying extortionate prices for cans of beer. It was the off-licence's Christmases coming all at once. Luckily it was a warm day, which meant sitting outside with a few cans wasn't an issue.

Richie and I went in the ground fairly early, through the turnstiles into the courtyard of the Leppings Lane. Ahead of you there are three entrances that take you to the terrace. You could enter by the outer entrances, which are at either end, or the tunnel in the middle, which you are drawn to, its where we went. Although it was before 2p.m. the ground was filling up quickly. Once you were in the tunnel, which is only about twenty yards long and ten feet wide you knew you couldn't go back, there are hundreds of bodies behind you, the only way is forward, driven on because everyone wants to get onto the terraces.

I can't imagine what it was like for those Liverpool fans on that fateful day who poured through the tunnel and into the two pens where the crush began, there was little or no escape as the countless bodies pushed their way through the tunnel, totally oblivious of what was happening twenty yards further forward. To put it bluntly they were killing their fellow supporters. Of course they weren't to blame, that lies with the Yorkshire Constabulary and Sheffield Wednesday Football Club who should have known that having two central pens with no gates open, so not allowing fans to escape to the side pens was an accident waiting to happen.

Richie and I popped out of the tunnel, it was almost like the old egg timers, where the sand is squeezed through the small hole into the large chamber.

The reason no Spurs fans were killed that day was that the two pens didn't exist then, the whole terrace lacked any fences apart from the large cages at the front to stop pitch invasions.

It was my first visit to Hillsborough, I was impressed with the ground and the huge open Kop End which looked fantastic, a mass of gold and black from the Wolves support. We stood at the right of the goal, but still fairly central.

We were soon met by Percy and his girlfriend Barbara. Percy was from Redcar, near Middlesbrough, about ten years older. He had wild blonde hair, a bit frizzy and a bit of a beard which didn't cover the red scars on his face. Percy had gone through a windscreen seven or eight years earlier before seat belts were compulsory, his facial injuries made him look like a right psycho, but nothing could be further from the truth, I always thought he looked like a fatter faced General Custer. We had known Percy for about a year now and he was beginning to travel with our group more and more, another great friend.

Our end kept filling, bolstered by Spurs fans taken from the Wolves end, the Police thinking better in with us than scrapping on the Wolves terrace. By 2.30p.m. the crush was becoming apparent. People at the front were beginning to climb the perimeter fences. Percy's girlfriend said she was being crushed. Percy told her to 'fuck off home, I'll see you later'. She replied, 'I'm not moving', and stayed.

Although the police were trying to stop people climbing over the fences, there was a wave of bodies going over the top.

By kick-off there were hundreds around the pitch from behind our goal up to the halfway line. The crush didn't ease, we were lucky no one was killed. There were reports of two people with broken legs, one with a broken arm and countless supporters with rib injuries, caused by being squeezed against the crush barriers. Very little newspaper coverage was mentioned about the near disaster that day.

Liverpool in their long running battle for justice for the 96 used Tottenham as an example as to why lessons were never learned. I, like many other Spurs fans who were at our Semi-Final definitely felt the loss of those lives in 1989, as that could have been us.

Spurs scored early, Wolves soon equalised. We went back in front and were virtually there, in the 'Cup Final', when Wolves stalwart Kenny Hibbitt 'took a dive', his words not mine. A penalty is given by veteran referee Clive Thomas. A decision that Spurs fans will never forgive Clive Thomas for.

Any referee from that game on who makes a bad decision in front of the Spurs crowd would get the chant 'Are you Thomas in disguise', for the next ten years.

The penalty is converted, the whistle blew almost immediately. We were that close. It would mean a replay and a short four-mile journey for the Spurs fans, the replay being played at Arsenal. For all of us, a lot further, but it was a game we couldn't miss.

We left Hillsborough feeling like it was a defeat. Our terrace emptied, only a few shoes strewn around, left by supporters who almost gave up their lives. The joyful Wolves fans were a distant din on the open Kop. The following Wednesday couldn't come quick enough.

The following Wednesday all the lads from our group travelled to the replay. We all had tickets for the match, but I can't remember how we obtained them as you could only get them from the Spurs ticket office in person. We may have got them from the Supporters Club, but we had them, and all for the North Bank. This game Tottenham would definitely take the North Bank, Highbury.

Arriving in London around 2p.m. on a beautiful afternoon, we were on the tube and heading to Islington, an Arsenal stronghold, but for tonight it would be white and navy. Spurs were expecting a massive following. Wolves expecting around 10,000 to make the trip South, they would be outnumbered four to one, and Spurs had the covered North Bank terrace which would make it feel like a home match.

Getting off the tube and wandering around we ended up in a park where a group of Spurs fans were playing football. We walked over to them, most of us in Spurs shirts.

'Fancy a game?', we asked.

'Yeah, where you lot from?', one asked

'We're Northern Spurs'.

'Ok then'.

It was Northern Spurs vs Southern Spurs, eight a side. Playing for an hour, we annihilated them with typical fast flowing football, the Spurs way. We shook hands and all headed to the nearest pub for a few pints. Richie and I headed off to Highbury to take in the atmosphere.

Around the ground we hardly saw a Wolves fan. The place was buzzing. We made our way onto the North Bank and took up our position, three-quarters of the way up, the noise already reverberating around the covered end. It made me realise how much a cover over an end gets the crowd going. White Hart Lane didn't really have any covered terrace apart from the back of The Shelf, so Spurs fans were spread around when it came to getting behind the team, but at a big game at the Lane it created a unique atmosphere few grounds could create.

The two teams walked out and were hit with a wall of noise. The North Bank roared, 'Come on you Spurs,' a noise Highbury would have seldom heard. We almost felt sorry for the Wolves supporters who had half the Clock End and a few thousand in the seats. The 40,000 Spurs support on three sides of the ground would have made it feel like a home game.

We scored early, Crooks lobbing the ball over Bradshaw at the North Bank end, delirium taking over. Crooks again making it two, Highbury was rocking. A bit of commotion broke out to our left, a gap opened up as bricks from Arsenal fans were raining into our end from outside of the ground. It soon settled down as the Old Bill moved them on. In the second half Ricky Villa hit a tremendous drive into the top corner with 'Wembley, Wembley' ringing around.

The final whistle blew. Spurs fans ran onto the pitch from all sides. Richie and I soon followed. What I really noticed when I got onto the Highbury turf was how dry the pitch was, not the lush pitches of today's premier league. Spurs fans all over the playing surface digging their heels in the ground to put divots in. If it hadn't been so dry, I'm sure the pitch would have been taken up as a souvenir.

It was a great night for Tottenham, and for me personally a night I wouldn't forget. The only downside was I was beginning to get a migraine. Beer, sun and too much excitement, but give me a migraine anytime for nights like those.

Before the Wembley Cup Final, we had a few meaningless league games. The Saturday after the Semi Final we made the journey to The Lane for the game against Norwich, which we would lose. Keith Burkinshaw our manager slating the supporters for being asleep in the sun, saying how can they support us so magnificently at Highbury and give us nothing against Norwich. He was right, we were quiet, but how can you compare the two games.

After the match we headed off to Waterloo Station, to take in the game at Southampton that coming Monday. Richie,

Phil, Pete and I were going. Dave said he would go too, although he hadn't planned to.

'How much have you got on you?', we asked.

'four quid', Dave said.

'four quid, you have to get your fare and two nights bed and breakfast', we laughed.

The four of us gave Dave five quid each so he could travel with us. We picked up our bags from Kings Cross left luggage on the way to Waterloo, Dave would have to wear the same clothes for three days. Getting to Southampton we looked for a B&B, soon finding a nice-looking street with a B&B vacancy sign in the window. We knocked on the door and an old lady answered.

'Have you got a room for five?', we asked.

'Yes, that will be ok, its five pounds a night with a full English breakfast,' the old lady said.

We went in and saw another old lady, both must have been at least seventy. They showed us to a couple of rooms, which were very clean.

'Are the rooms alright?', one asked.

'Yes, great', we all nodded our approval.

'Would you like a cup of tea?'

It was like that for the weekend, they treat us like we were their family, with brilliant breakfasts, if you wanted more you got it.

When we left, they almost appeared embarrassed to take the ten quid off each of the five of us, saying 'Was five pound a night alright?'.

It was a wonderful weekend, a good night out on the Saturday to watch a local band in a pub. The only downside was the garbage we watched on the Monday. It ended in a draw. I suppose the result was fair, the view wasn't. How Southampton could allow away supporters that view of the near goal, there was so much fencing in the way the goal vanished in the mesh. I never went to The Dell again.

We met up with big Kev and travelled back to Kings Cross with him. Kev was his usual,

'They fucking crap, we'll not win the fucking cup'.

While waiting on Kings Cross station Kev got into an altercation with this guy, which resulted in Kev taking a right hook flush in the face. Why Kev didn't smack him, I'm not sure. Kev was twice his size.

Our last league home game of the season was home to Liverpool, which was a strange affair. Not the game, but the Park Lane End which had been allocated for Liverpool fans. They only filled half of it, the other half nearest The Shelf side stayed empty, that is until fifteen minutes before kick-off when around 800 West Ham fans took it over. Their game at Luton had been called off a couple of hours before kick-off so they decided to come to Spurs to antagonise our fans by bringing up their League Cup victory earlier in the season. It was strange to hear 'You'll never walk alone' followed by 'I'm forever blowing bubbles' at the same match.

West Ham would gain promotion so another big derby would be put on the calendar for the next season.

As the season drew to a close, and another mid-table finish, my main aim was to get hold of a Cup Final ticket. For the previous couple of months Spurs had given out coloured ballot cards at random fixtures. These would usually be the less attractive games, so as to catch the more hard-core fans who had shown loyalty. Spurs had used this method of ticketing for previous cup finals and had always felt it the best way of allocating tickets, after the season ticket holders had taken their cut of course. Almost all the lads I travelled with had been given the same colour ballot ticket, apart from a couple of them. Once the draw was made, with the majority of us having the winning colour, it meant we were guaranteed a three quid terrace ticket.

Before the draw was made, I had tried to track down people who might have contacts with the Football Association at an amateur level.

Back in Shildon, I knew Kevin Stonehouse's dad. Kevin was playing at Blackburn Rovers at the time, I had got to know his dad when bumping into him when going to and from matches, him coming back from games having watched Kevin. I asked him if there was a chance of getting any tickets, he came up trumps with two tickets. I had also got another ticket from the F.A. They were all for the 'City End' at Wembley, but I didn't care. I would be there for the Centenary cup final, Tottenham vs Manchester City.

With the news of getting tickets through the ballot I could off load two of my spare tickets to my mates and try and sell the other at Wembley.

I've never liked the parasite that is known as the 'Ticket Tout'. I've used them as a last resort, but they shouldn't get their hands on the tickets in the first place. But then you think on some occasions, whether that be a big match or a concert ticket where you may have little or no chance of getting a ticket they provide a service, but of course it's at a price. I decided I would sell my spare ticket to a genuine fan at face value.

Arriving in London at 9.40a.m. on Cup Final day, a day I had watched since 1969 on TV, preferring the build-up on Grandstand, always Grandstand, I never liked the constant commercial breaks of World of Sport.

I was hoping for the sun kissed day I had dreamed of, but in truth it was like going to another match, it was even raining. But this was early morning, the day would improve.

171

Richie and I decided to go up to Wembley, the rest of the lads were trying to find a pub open. I don't know what we expected getting up to Wembley at 10.30a.m., maybe a throng of people, but it was almost deserted apart from a few hundred City fans spread around the vastness of the Wembley car parks.

'Got any spares?', a Mancunian voice said.

'Yeah', I say 'It's for the City End'.

'How much?', A look of hope on his face.

'Five quid', I say.

'Fuckin brilliant', he shouted to his mates.

He was made up and so was I, a two quid profit. Okay, I said I wouldn't make a profit, but I thought for all the leg work I had done to get the ticket, it was worth a small profit, and it did go a to genuine City fan. Everyone was happy.

We headed back on the tube to Baker Street, out onto the street and were met by hundreds of Spurs fans spilling out the pubs, already singing our songs. We stayed for an hour and then set off back again up to Wembley. I had been to Wembley twice before and on both occasions stood on the Lower Terrace. I told Richie we had to try and get up to the Upper Terrace which gave a better view of the match, at least that's what I had been told.

Although we were in the same end and both on the Lower Terrace, we were going in at different turnstiles. Once in the ground it didn't take long to find Richie, and we soon noticed that each entrance to the Upper Terrace had a steward on the gate. We watched people who had the same idea as us wanting to gain a better view being turned away by the stewards. It needed some thinking on how we could gain entrance. We both checked all the stewards on each gate, and which one looked most likely to give us the nod. Some stewards looked old school where that little bit of authority goes to their heads, so they were avoided. We ended up choosing the youngest steward, about our age. We walked over, I showed my ticket.

'That's for the Lower Terrace', he said.

'Can you let us through?', I asked.

'No, it's not allowed', he said.

'What if I give you a quid' I said.

'Ye go on then', he said, happy to gain an easy two quid off us.

We climbed the steps and entered the arena standing on the left of the Upper Terrace. It gave a great view of the Spurs fans as the terrace is curved.

Although Wembley was an iconic ground it was by then looking decrepit. The roof girders were rusting and any paint around the stadium was flaky. As for downstairs, the toilets were soon pushed to the limit, the plumbing was not able to cope, piss flowing out the entrances. It's a good job Grandstand didn't show this. All you saw on TV was the twin towers, the lush turf, the band marching back and forth, and the fans, the most important part, the thing that makes football.

Our view was excellent, the massive steps meant that even if you were a short person you would still see over the person in front of you. The occasion was full of colour, our end decked out in white and navy, with a touch of yellow from our reserve kit. Opposite was pale blue and white from the City End.

In the City End there was a large Spurs presence on the Lower Terrace either side of the tunnel. Sporadic skirmishes were breaking out.

The two teams entered the field to a crescendo of noise, our end roared 'Come on you Spurs, Come on you Spurs,' and of course a rendition of 'Ossie's Dream'. This was the song that the Spurs squad with Chas and Dave had brought out as a Cup Final song and is still sang to this day at cup matches. The obligatory flags were waved with gusto from both ends. The national anthem was sung with patriotism from all sides of the ground, kick-off beckoned.

Everyone just wanted to get on with it, Spurs were very slight favourites but there was little between the teams. The game started in wet conditions, raining on and off for most of the match, but it didn't dampen the support.

The early part of the game is not much to write home about, until City's Tommy Hutchinson flings himself to a header to put them one up.

With the huge size of Wembley, it was hard to hear the City fans. We were still optimistic, after all we had never lost a Cup Final.

The second-half started and Ricky Villa was soon taken off, his performance well below par, him Walking from the pitch and the long walk down the tunnel made him look like a broken man.

We were becoming anxious. The whole end was willing us to get an equaliser. We got a free kick, the cry of 'Hoddle, Hoddle, Hoddle' rang around our end. Hoddle could hit a ball like no other in a Spurs shirt. 'Come on Glen, curl it in the top corner' I said to myself. Our end looked on, we were around a hundred yards away from the kick. Glenn hits a poor free kick, it was going wide until their hero Tommy Hutchinson steps away from the wall, the ball catching his shoulder sending the ball arcing into the opposite corner. The giant City keeper Joe Corrigan could only look on helplessly as it nestled in the corner of the City goal. Our end erupted as one, unbridled joy, we were just happy to still be in it.

Extra time was to be played, the first time it is ever used in an F.A. Cup Final, but still it ended in a stalemate.

174

The Replay the following Thursday, would become one of the great matches in the history of the F.A. Cup.

Our group had already planned to stay the night so we could go up to Tottenham and welcome the team back, win or lose. We hadn't planned for a draw.

We all met up at the B&B we were staying at Kings Cross and decided to go up to Tottenham for a night out but planned not to stay out too late as the replay tickets were going on sale at 10a.m. on Sunday morning from the Park Lane End. We knew we had to be outside White Hart Lane for 7 or 8a.m.

We got the Tube up to Seven Sisters, then a bus up to the ground and headed to The British Queen pub, only four hundred yards from White Hart Lane and a popular haunt for the skinheads and punks. It was a decent sized place with a bit of dance floor, and always a lively place before matches. The disco was already blaring out as we entered. Punk, New Wave, Ska and a bit of Soul, it was a good mix. The place was already busy with Skinheads in boots and braces, punks with their colourful Mohicans and the New Wave and Reggae boys in Fred Perry's. Some of the black guys wearing trilby's and plenty of us in Spurs shirts. It was an eclectic mix.

It was an absolutely brilliant night, everyone on the dance floor by 10p.m., 'Ossie's Dream' getting blasted out. It was mental, but not a bit of trouble, after all we were all Tottenham.

We decided to leave just after midnight, back to the hotel a little after 1a.m. and into bed with the music still swimming in my head.

We woke bleary eyed and rushed our breakfasts, before getting back up to Tottenham. We were greeted by thousands of Spurs fans. It was only 8a.m.!

The queue, which started at the Park Lane End and then snaked down The Shelf Side around to the Paxton Road End was ten-deep. Our allocation of 35,000 looked like it might not meet demand. Wembley were also selling tickets. We headed down the Paxton Road and joined the queue. We had a near two hour wait before any movement. Just after mid-day on reaching the Park Lane End, we were told they had sold out.

'No'! A sickening feeling hit me. I had travelled to forty-six games, and the final one, the most important one, was going to be missed because of someone who probably on a whim had decided they would like to go to a Cup Final for their first game of the season. I don't know if that would be true but that's how it felt.

We all headed to the Supporter's Club for a drink. As soon as we walked in, we heard one of the stewards of the club say show your club card if you need a Cup Final ticket. We had stood for over four hours for nothing, all we had to do was go to the Club. The distraught feeling soon went, we'd all got tickets, the pint never tasted sweeter.

Ask any Spurs fan who watched Spurs from the 70's to the 2000's and I think 99% would say the Cup Final Replay would be their most memorable match. It is mine without doubt. No one could have imagined the drama that would unfold. Man City can take a lot of credit for that, it would be a pulsating ninety minutes.

We took our positions on the Upper Terrace, slightly more central than at the first game, looking down on the goal mouth.

Spurs understandably had taken the lions' share of the floating tickets, but to City's credit, they had at short notice organised travel and time off work for around 20,000 to 25,000 fans for a Thursday night. Of course we were in the same boat travelling from the North-East.

I had asked my boss Alan for time off.

'I didn't expect anything else' he said. Yet again he was giving me time off at short notice, it was 'give and take', if he wanted me to work overtime, I would oblige.

The anticipation inside Wembley was special, whether that was because it was under floodlights making it more atmospheric, or because Spurs had a massive following.

The City End had City fans in the Upper Terrace, Spurs in the Lower terrace, and of course the vast majority of the seats were Spurs.

A new terrace chant was introduced at this game, which became a huge hit with the Spurs faithful. British Airways had been running an advertising campaign on TV which had a catchy jingle, 'We'll take more care of you, lets fly the flag', so we changed it to 'We'll take more care of you Archibald, Archibald' (repeat). The chant was for our forward Steve Archibald. The song would be sung with gusto on every ground for the next three years by his adoring fans.

Ricky Villa was back in the starting line-up, when many said he didn't deserve to start after storming down the tunnel in the first match when substituted. I was pleased Ricky was given another chance. He could be absent in some games, but when on song he was a powerhouse. Tonight would be Ricky's night.

The game from the outset was nothing like the first, both teams going for a win. Spurs scored first, and it had to be Ricky, blasting in from ten yards after City failed to clear. But you knew this would not be the end of the scoring, the game was so open. City hit back with an absolute stunning goal from young midfielder Steve McKenzie, a perfectly hit volley from twenty-five yards into the top corner. City were buzzing. Kevin Reeves, the City forward made it 2-1, and we thought we had blown the cup, but Garth Crooks stabs home to level the score in the 70th minute.

The match ebbed and flowed, the atmosphere electric. It looked like extra time again as the clock ticked down. Tony Galvin picked the ball up on the left, heading down the wing towards the massed ranks of our supporters, slipping the ball to Ricky Villa who was forty yards from goal. Ricky skipped past the first challenge, got to the eighteen-yard box, went past Tommy Caton and left him on his arse, then weaved around the City defence. I screamed along with thousands of others, 'Hit it, Hit it' but he delayed the shot to beat one more. 'Hit it, Hit it' we still shouted, then Ricky slid it past the City goalkeeper Joe Corrigan. It was a brilliant solo goal. As it hit the net, the end we were in explodes, bodies lunging and falling on the large steps in joyous celebration, its chaos. We calmed to watch the closing minutes of the game. Then a rendition of 'We shall not be moved' was sung by the whole end and we bounced in unison. You could feel the end springing on its foundations.

I remember talking to fellow Shildon Spurs fan Robbie Young later that night, him saying he didn't see Steve Perryman lift the cup. He said he left the ground convinced it was going to collapse, such was the intensity of the bouncing making the ground shake. I've spoken to a few Spurs fans since and they all said the same, they could feel the end moving on its foundations!

The final whistle blew, we had won the cup. I was ecstatic, the best night ever, the joy then went to another level when it dawned on me, we were Europe bound, and I couldn't wait for that. Seeing Steve Perryman lift the cup followed by the lap of honour capped the night off.

Out of the ground I remember walking up Wembley Way and couldn't help noticing a young girl, a City fan aged about fourteen, she was distraught with the result. I told Richie to hang on and I went over to her. She looked at me, she knew I was a Spurs fan by my shirt. I told her that she could be proud of her team even though they'd lost, and Man City had played a huge part in a fantastic match that people would talk about for years to come. I hope that same girl is still watching City now, watching one of the greatest teams of all time. I left the girl thinking how much a game can fill you with such a high, but more often let you down, you have to take those highs and lock them in your memory, highs like Ricky's goal, it's always there as clear as if it just happened yesterday. I've seen it so often on TV, but it still gets me every time, that tingle up your spine, the hairs standing up on the back of your neck. But for as many times as I see it on TV, I also see it from where I was stood, Ricky bearing down on goal and sliding it home, it's a wonderful memory.

We got back to Kings Cross for the midnight train, calling at the off-licence to get a bottle of Pomagne, Champagne was out of our price range. Pete bought a four pack, which he gave to me to look after while he went for something to eat. I boarded the train, Pete followed ten minutes later. The train set off with Pete feasting on his Kentucky Fried Chicken.

'Pass a beer Ian'.

'Eh, they're still on the platform', I reluctantly answered.

'You fucking idiot', Pete said.

'Anyone for Pomagne', I said, trying to defuse the situation.

It was now party time. The songs were sung, toilet rolls were removed from every toilet on the train and are hung in our carriage like streamers, hanging from luggage racks, seats, anywhere they could go, it resembled the mummy's shroud.

We saw the guard coming into our carriage, it could have been a problem, but he just shook his head, he knew it was innocent and left us to get on with it. Finally, around 4a.m. in the morning we dozed off.

179

I got off at Newcastle, as I was at college there that Friday morning and went for an early morning coffee, reliving the previous night's news from The Daily Mirror. I went to college that day to learn about printing, but I was still on too much of a high to think or learn, the preceding night will live with me for a lifetime.

To Europe and Ireland

The following season 1981-82, would be my favourite season following Spurs around the country and abroad.

Our best team for a decade, but it didn't start too well. We won at Middlesbrough in our first game 3-1, following that our opening home game, the big mid-week derby with West Ham, with a full house on the still three-sided Lane, enhanced with 8,000 EastEnders making a tremendous din with their 'bubbles' song.

The night was an embarrassment for every Spurs fan, losing at home 4-0, to a team who had just been promoted. I left the ground along with Richie. The West Ham boys like the last time in the League Cup were in joyous mood. We hit the High Road, already the West Ham fans were coming out The Park Lane End, the atmosphere felt toxic. I had never had this feeling coming out of a home game before. We knew all about the trouble in the cup tie the season before, and this had the same sinister air. West Ham always had this thing that they were the biggest hooligan force in football and taking Tottenham on in their own back yard was something they sought.

As Richie and me walked down the High Road on the right-hand side of the road it was becoming clear that the

180

quiet almost subdued walk had a tension that was about to explode.

As we approached Bruce Grove it was becoming more noticeable that the West Ham fans were on the left, and Spurs on the right, this apparent by the occasional 'I'm forever blowing bubbles' song, which was only chanted on the left. With very few police around, Richie and I moved to the middle of the road which was quite gridlocked with traffic.

'It's going to go off', I said to Richie.

He agreed.

A large mob of West Ham moved into the middle of the road, they started shouting at passers-by.

'Come on you cunts, do you want some?'.

They turned and faced us, not twenty yards ahead of us. They knew we were Spurs. They then came tearing down the road, giving a quick look at Richie we turned and ran along with a few others. I had only ran about ten yards when I felt a hand on my jumper. I kept trying to run, my jumper stretching. It was that dream you have sometimes when you're trying to escape from the psycho with a long knife and your feet feel like they are glued to the road. It's a dream I've had several times, now its reality, as the jumper was pulled to the point of tearing. I heard this voice.

'Stop!, stand and fight them', It was the voice of a Spurs fan. It might have been a good idea to him, but not to me, my reaction was to say.

'Fuck that, I'm off'.

No one caught up with Richie or me, it was the one time I've ran at a home game. We let things calm and were back on our way to the safety of Kings Cross.

As the season entered into September results improved, but to be honest my only thoughts were on our trip to

181

Amsterdam to play Ajax. Most of the lads said they would go to the first away game in Europe, the draw had been kind in as much as we didn't have a long away trip, and Amsterdam was an attractive city to visit, so I had been told.

As the count down to the game grew closer it was apparent that only Phil and I would be making the trip on the Monday before the match, although Percy was following the next day with his mate Tony, who was only going for a piss up.

Phil had booked us on the sailing from Harwich to the Hook of Holland on the Monday evening. We travelled down to London on the afternoon and got the tube to Liverpool Street for the train to Harwich. We were in Liverpool Street for around 6p.m., already there was a large group of Spurs fans around the buffet area. Many we recognised from our regular away days. We didn't have tickets for the match, to be honest that was an afterthought, as long as we got there, we could look for tickets.

It was an exciting trip for myself, not only to see Spurs in Europe, but also it was my first trip leaving 'Blighty', so the expression goes. This was Tottenham's first game in Europe since the infamous riots in Rotterdam, so the spotlight would be on us, especially as it was in Holland again.

Arriving in Harwich, it was onto the ferry, much bigger and more luxurious than I expected. Maybe I was thinking the ship would be something like the boats that picked up British troops from Dunkirk in the 2nd World War, anyway I was impressed.

Once on board we paid an extra eight quid for a cabin and headed to the bar along with a decent amount of Spurs followers. I was having a drink and out of the corner of my eye I saw Robbie Young, the lad who had left Wembley because he thought it was going to collapse. I shouted him over and introduced him to Phil.

'Didn't think you were coming over', I said to Robbie.

'My wife recently died of cancer' he said, 'so I am going to watch Spurs more'.

Robbie had first seen Spurs in the mid-60s and would go to couple of games a season, but for the next couple of years Robbie would follow Spurs home and away regularly. I think he needed time to get over his loss, and Spurs helped him. We talked, drank and hit the sack.

Up early on arriving in Holland, we boarded a train for the one-hour journey to Amsterdam.

'Where you staying?' Robbie asked.

Phil told him he knew a place off Dam Square where he had stayed before, when at an England away game, 'we should all get in'.

The train arrived at the large, impressive Central Railway Station. We left the train and walked out the station.

Amsterdam wasn't the tourist trap it is now. I liked the look of it, trams and bicycles everywhere and impressive architecture. We walked the near mile or so to Dam Square, which was impressive, the large Royal Palace taking up one side. Just off the square Phil led us to a large town house, it would be worth a fortune nowadays. Phil rattled the door knocker, a friendly dutch guy answered.

'Hi', do you have any rooms for three nights, for three people? Phil asked.

'Ye, no problem, it will be twenty Guilders a night each', he said, the equivalent of five quid a night, which seemed reasonable.

Our room was a large bedroom with three beds. The Dutch guy said he goes out early in the morning, so use the kitchen to make your breakfasts, eggs, meats, cheese, coffee, get what you want. He passed us a large front door key to match the impressive front door and leaves. He didn't ask us any questions, who we were, where we were from, nothing at all was documented. Typical Dutch, laid back and very friendly like the many Dutch we would speak to in the bars.

We had our first breakfasts, left the house and asked someone which tram would take us to the Olympic Stadium, the home of Ajax, in the hope of getting tickets for the match.

The stadium was around four miles from the centre of Amsterdam, taking the tram we had been told to get we were soon arriving at the stadium. Instantly we saw it was an old ground, looking tired, definitely not the plush Amsterdam arena that today's Ajax play in. There was no one at the stadium, it was all closed. We asked a passing local when it would open.

'Tomorrow, hey if you want tickets the tobacconist over the road will sell you them'.

It seemed strange to call into a shop for tickets. We all walked in the shop, which was small, like a traditional corner shop in England.

'Have you got tickets for tomorrow's game?'.

'For the Spurs end?', the Dutch shop keeper asked.

He pulled off three tickets from a roll, which were like old bus tickets, costing around two quid each.

Well with that problem solved we looked for the nearest bar for a few beers. The Dutch only seemed to serve half-pint measures, a pint glass wasn't even in the equation. The barman poured the beer, its frothy head an inch above the glass, then using a sort of pallet knife he sliced the top off the head, so it was level to the top of the glass. The beer was good, mainly Heineken or Amstel, both brewed in Amsterdam. I asked the owner why he didn't sell pints.

'In the Netherlands we like our beer cold, crisp and fresh' he said.

To be fair he was right, although in a busy pub it's not really practical going to the bar twice as often, and definitely not for the beer swilling Brits. However in the Dutch bars we visited it was a chilled and a relaxed atmosphere. The barman would always say 'Pay later', recording the drinks on a tab, it was typical Dutch, and with the beers costing around thirty pence for a half it was cheaper than at home.

Heading back to the City Centre we had a quick look around the Red-Light Area, perusing the girls in the windows, many very attractive and wearing very little, but none of us took up their offers.

Later that evening we found Percy and his mate Tony by the Central Station. I had been in touch with Percy before he had set off from England and told him to go in the nearest bar to the station, the first one you see. It didn't take too long for us to find them.

Robbie liked a drink and had downed a fair quantity when we entered the bar where Percy and Tony were. They were both arseholed, sat on huge stools. The bar was really high, chest height, the stools four feet tall. I introduced Robbie to Percy, within five minutes you would think they'd known each other for years, probably there drunkenness cementing there quick friendship.

As the beers flowed Percy said he needed the toilet, instead of jumping off the front of the stool, Percy pushed himself away from the bar, the stool and Percy slowly fell backwards, he sort of floated in mid-air, the stool with him, it was like slow motion. He hit the concrete floor on his back, no hands to break the fall, he was oblivious to it even happening. We feared the worst, a 'broken back'.

'Percy, Percy, you okay? I shouted.

'Ha, ha, ha', Percy chuckled, 'get me up, I need the bog'.

We all stood laughing, shaking our heads, the night proved to be long but full of laughter.

The following morning, slightly worse for wear, as the owner had instructed we made our own breakfasts, the owner having already left to do whatever he did.

We then had a look around the city, calling in quite a few bars, having a meal, then off up to the stadium. We still weren't sure how you paid on the trams, so we didn't.

Arriving at the stadium well before kick-off, the hundreds of Spurs fans were already taking over the many bars, Union Jacks draped all over, emblazed with towns and cities showing the whereabouts of where people had travelled from. Tottenham had said officially there were 2,000 making the trip, but this was at least doubled by the likes of us, and the many who had made their own way. The club unfortunately didn't want to acknowledge those fans who didn't put money in their coffers.

We clicked through the turnstile and entered the almost dilapidated stadium, it had definitely seen better days. Its curved ends showed that at some point it would have had a running track around. The two side stands mirrored each other, and the open ends had wooden bench seats. The ground was vast and could hold around 60,000, but tonight only 21,000 would attend. We were allocated one of the open ends, half of which was closed off. No one sat, we stood on the benches, apart from a few who were laid out asleep. A heavy session on the beer and marijuana from the many Amsterdam coffee bars had taken its toll on some. To our right we saw a few skirmishes breaking out in the main stand, our end immediately chanting 'Leave it out, Leave it out' Leave it out', to try and discourage the troublemakers. We were under the microscope after what had happened seven years earlier in Rotterdam, our fans didn't want our European journey to be over before it had started, things calmed in the stands and the game commenced.

Playing some wonderful football we fully deserved the 3-1 win. We left the stadium, the mood was good and more importantly no trouble, the Dutch took the defeat well. They say that Ajax and Spurs fans get on well due to both having a large Jewish following and a dislike for Feyenoord, and that night it seemed like that was true. A couple of Dutch lads said we were the best team they had seen for a long time and were impressed with our support.

The following day was our last full day in Amsterdam, it was a day for being a tourist. Phil and I had noticed a cinema showing a film called Caligula, which was in English with Dutch subtitles. It was an epic Roman film starring the very well-respected Sir John Gielgud. The film was X-rated due to its violence and nudity.

'Do you fancy watching it?' I said to Phil.

'Yeah, why not', Phil was happy to go along with it.

After all it got us out of the bars which we were frequenting far too often.

Wow, the film was violent, but it was the sexual content that surprised us, talk about explicit, it was basically a porn film, and it was the first hard core film I had seen, none of this simulated stuff. I was shocked, especially with an old grand master of the cinema, John Gielgud, in it. He later said he didn't know there was sex in it. Yeah I bet, the dirty old bugger.

When I got back from Amsterdam, I told all my mates in Shildon about the film I had watched, and its contents.

'What's it called?' they asked inquisitively.

'Caligula', I said.

Within days they had hired the VHS tape of the film. When they next saw me, they all said the same, 'there was

187

hardly any hardcore sex in it'. Editing had cut the vast majority out of the original, they had all wasted £1 each on the video rental, I could only tell them what I had seen.

On the Friday we returned back to England, arriving in London on the Saturday morning, which gave us plenty of time to get up to see Spurs beat Everton 3-0 in convincing fashion.

The Scouse flick head hairstyle I had seen nine months earlier on my trip to Liverpool was spreading around the country, as fashion ran parallel with the new pop movement of the 'New Romantics'. This was almost the death knell of the guitar bands, for the synthesizer sounds of the likes of 'Visage, Human League, Soft Cell and Depeche Mode' to name but a few. The sound was totally electronic, even the drums. Though some of it I liked, I was more for the traditional guitar-riffs.

Around this time Phil brought a cassette tape to a match. Phil was a Prog-rock fan, liking Yes, and Pete Gabriel. However Phil did go on about a young group from Ireland, they were called U2. I played the first track 'I will follow', it blew me away, Rock, New Wave and a stadium anthem. I played the songs on that C60 tape until it couldn't be rewound anymore. 'I will follow' never came out as a single but is one of U2's most played songs, and to this day always seems to get on the set list at their concerts. I bought their album 'Boy' which the song came off, It's a fantastic debut album having some brilliant punchy songs. I still play the album regularly and to this day can't believe they wrote it as teenagers. Some people just have a natural talent for writing music, just like Kate Bush who wrote 'The man with the child in his eyes', written when she was fifteen, another unbelievable talent.

After the first riots in Brixton, London, in the April of 81 followed in July at Toxteth, Liverpool, a domino affect followed as towns and cities around the country were set ablaze. There was teenage frustration with Thatcher's government and unemployment.

In my town of Shildon there was no real issues, but after a good night out to see a band at the local Working Men's Club we began the walk home around 11p.m. when Mulley said.

'Let's start a riot'.

Mulley was the biggest drinker of all my mates in Shildon and was the most pissed of the four of us that night. A riot didn't seem right, after all we all had jobs, so it seemed to miss the point of what the riots were about. Also I didn't want to damage anything and especially hurt anyone, but Mulley in his lager fuelled state shouted, 'The Rajah'.

Mulley had his eye on the local Indian restaurant, the very same one we would frequent, having some very tasty meals there may I add. We stood outside 'The Rajah'. The restaurant was on the first floor, access was by a normal staircase where doors led into the restaurant. Mulley climbed the stairs, we stayed at the bottom. Mulley began to pull the stair carpet up. The rods that lay on each tread were pinging off as he pulled the carpet up until he got to the bottom step, where the last rod left its moorings. The sound of diners and Indian music was playing in the background. No one heard a thing as Mulley walked up the road with twenty odd feet of carpet in his hands, which he then abandoned a hundred yards further on by the side of the road. I hadn't taken part in any of it, but if we had been caught I would have been as guilty as the rest. It was hardly Brixton or Toxteth, but it was the nearest I got to a riot. I could imagine next morning an Indian gentleman saying, 'Where did our carpet go to?', but after all, not only was it a restaurant it was a 'take-away' too!

189

Spurs beat Ajax in the return match and were drawn to play Dundalk from Ireland, the first leg being away. Again, Phil and I decided to go, Percy was also going, but travelling with the Spurs Travel Club.

Before the trip to Ireland we had a match at Man City. It would be our first game against City since the epic cup final replay. As usual we stood on the Kippax alongside our large following. What stands out most that day was the constant abuse of our Jewish fan base, not only the hissing but they even changed the words of our cup final song 'Ossie's Dream'. Using the same tune but singing 'Spurs are on their way to Auschwitz, Hitler's goin to gas them again, we can stop em, the yids from Tottenham, the yids from White Hart Lane'. It really hit home to some of our fans, this vile abuse. To me and the 3,000 who stood with me the only song that would hit them hard was 'One Ricky Villa, there's only one Ricky Villa'. It incensed them that we sang the name of the man who ended their cup final dreams. It was a hostile atmosphere, but I liked the 'them and us' feel, it could be dangerous following Spurs in the North, but it had your senses on full alert.

Phil and I had set off on the Tuesday afternoon for the trip to Dundalk, getting the train to Holyhead. As usual we didn't have match tickets but thought we would get them fairly easily once in Ireland, even though the game was all ticket. Spurs had sold around 1500 tickets, but these were mainly bought by the Irish Spurs fans, only around 500 would travel from England.

We had got talking to a few Spurs lads on the train, they asked if the two of us had tickets.

'No', we replied.

'We've got a few spare', one said.

We paid five quid each for another ticket I could have forged easily, it was as basic as the Swindon cup ticket, but again it took away any worry of not getting into the ground.

Arriving in the small port of Holyhead we went for a meal and a few beers. Then, about to board the ferry we got the news it was being delayed for a few hours with mechanical problems. It meant another few hours' in the pub.

While in the pub we met up with the Spurs lads who we got the tickets off.

'Do you know where Dundalk is', one asked.

I had checked it out in the atlas and knew it was about fifty miles north of Dublin.

'Yeah, North of Dublin', I said

'Yeah, it's right on the border with Northern Ireland, it's a mining town and its full of fucking Catholics, they not going to like us English on their patch', the Londoner said.

Great news we thought. Ireland was in the height of its Catholic/Protestant disagreements, with the Catholic I.R.A. having a disdain for anything British, many innocent people died in 'The Troubles' on both sides of the divide. To me and to many Irish people it was insanity.

Boarding the small ferry to take us to Dun Laoghaire, the now disused port for Dublin we tried to get some sleep on the six-hour trip.

Once in Dublin we found a bed and breakfast for the night for after the match. The rest of the day was spent looking around Dublin and sampling the Guinness in its true home, which proved a lot better than the English version. At 4p.m. we boarded the express train to Belfast which stopped at Dundalk, in fact it stopped everywhere. By the time we got to Dundalk it was after 6p.m. which didn't matter as Dundalk didn't have much to offer. Walking to the ground we were met by countless police who guided us to the first checkpoint where you had to show your ticket. We were so pleased we had managed to get tickets on the train as there was no way you would get anywhere near the ground with the multiple checkpoint areas.

Finally passing the last cordon we entered the ground, which was about as good as a lower division ground, or even non-league. The end we had been given was a shallow open end, which had no terrace. It was basically a small bank of shale. It wouldn't be used today, certainly not for a European match. In front of us was a twenty-foot-high chicken wire fence. The ground soon filled to over 17,000, the atmosphere toxic.

We stood to the left of our goal, To the right of us in the side paddock towards our goal there were countless tricolour flags hanging. The unrest started. Bricks and stones began raining down on our supporters most hitting the chicken wire but the occasional rock landed amongst our support who appeared to be mainly protestant, waving Union Jack flags to antagonise the Irish Catholics. The Irish police seemed uninterested in the aggro coming down on us. Spurs fans began throwing bricks back in retaliation. Phil and I kept out of range of the missiles.

The police had had enough, and with crash helmets on, and long batons and shields they waded into our end, clubbing anyone. The Irish cheered as their foe were taking a beating, order was restored.

'Phil, when this game is over, we're out of this place', I said.

Phil agreed, it wasn't a nice place to be an Englishman. Garth Crooks scored the solitary Spurs goal to give us a 1-1 draw.

We left the ground, sporadic fights breaking out around us as we kept moving, heading for the railway station. A quiet after-match pint out of the question, we just needed to get out this town. We arrived at the station and looked at the timetable, it couldn't be right, no trains. The last train to Dublin was at 9.30p.m, ten minutes before the final whistle had gone. I couldn't believe it, we were fifty miles from Dublin but I had no intention of staying in this place, it was too dodgy to stay around. If we ended up going in the wrong area a kicking might be getting off lightly.

'We'll walk', I said to Phil.

It was mad to walk, but it seemed a better idea than staying. It was 10p.m. our ferry left at 8a.m. the next morning. To walk fifty miles would take around seventeen hours, and that was going some, so it was impossible.

We saw the sign to Dublin and off we marched. The road we were on soon lost its street lighting and we were now walking along a road only lit by the full moon, which was just enough light to see where to walk. After half an hour of hardly seeing a car, we heard the rumble of traffic. We moved onto the verge as five coaches sped past, Spurs flags in their rear windows all going back to the ferry. I thought Percy would be on one of them, totally oblivious he had just past two of his mates. We continued to walk for the next four hours, probably covering a little over ten miles.

'I've had enough' I said to Phil. It was a mild night and still lit by the moon and most importantly dry.

'Why don't we get in the hedge row and get a bit of sleep', I said.

'Go a bit further then we'll call it a night', Phil said.

We hadn't walked more than half-mile when a car pulled up, it was the first car we had seen going either way for miles.

'Where you going boys?', his thick Irish accent blending with the smell of alcohol which was obvious as he leaned out of his window.

'Dublin', we both said in unison.

'Can either of you feckin drive?' Neither of us could at the time.

'No', we said.

'Get in any way you can and keep me talking so I don't feckin fall asleep, cause I'm feckin pissed', he said.

He was obviously slurring, but we didn't care if we ended up in a ditch, it would still be a few miles nearer Dublin.

'Where the feck you's two going at two in the morning?', he said.

We've been to watch Spurs at Dundalk, and there weren't any trains back to Dublin'.

'So your feckin Spurs fans from England?'.

'Yeah', we said.

We continued weaving about on the desolate road, then suddenly we pulled over, he said nothing and got out the car and walked over to the hedge.

'Feckin busting for a piss', he muttered.

'What if he's I.R.A', I said to Phil.

Phil nodded in a manner that said, your talking shit but it could be true.

'What we going to do if he's I.R.A. We could be shot, are we legging it', the paranoia setting in.

Too late, he was back, he went to the back of the car, and opened the boot. We both look at each other in horror, I don't know what Phil's thinking but I'm thinking sawn off shot gun. He then moved to the drivers car door, we are both sat in the back seat, he opened the front door.

'Ah that's feckin better, get that feckin coat off'.

We blew our cheeks in relief, Dublin here we come.

Just before 4a.m. we were dropped off in Dublin. We thanked our Irish friend for the lift and headed off to the B&B we had booked the day before, which seemed an age ago.

I lay in bed still high on adrenaline, I had never known a night like it. I slowly drifted off, only to be woken shortly afterwards to get up, we had to get ready for sailing back to England.

The return leg we narrowly beat Dundalk 1-0, but I remember it more for Phil and John getting absolutely pissed before the game. We tended to have a few pints up Tottenham High Road, starting in the Beehive, The Ship, Red Lion, Prince of Wales, and usually ending up at The Bell and Hare.

On the night of the Dundalk game Phil and John were drinking like it was going out of fashion. John would look for any drinks left by customers who had set off to the ground, whether that be a small amount of beer, spirit, or wine left in a glass.

Richie & I left The Bell and Hare half an hour before kick-off, leaving John tottering around the pub picking any drink up. Phil wasn't much better.

After the game we met up with Phil and John at Kings Cross for the midnight train. Phil was slightly more coherent, they told us they had got into the match at some time during the first half, standing in the Park Lane End. John had then stumbled and rolled into a puddle at the front, where he remained unable to get up. I looked at John who was still wet and dirty,

'Good game John', I asked.

'Never saw a barl kicked', he replied.

Luton and a Free Bar

Harry decided to moved to Luton during the summer of 81, the shipyards of the Northeast were in decline so Harry had taken a job in the South as it would help him get to matches cheaper. Buying a little Honda 50 motorbike he would ride to the home games, but as the winter drew in Harry's attire would thicken out as more and more coats were worn, one on top of another. He looked like the Michelin Man coming to White Hart Lane

We would always meet up with Harry in the Supporters Club, so when we got the news that Harry had been involved in an accident, we decided to go and visit him in hospital. We didn't know at first if he had been knocked off his bike, but then discovered it had been a work-related incident.

Spurs were going really well in the league, playing free flowing football and nudging the top four, a thing Spurs fans hadn't seen for ten years.

Phil, Richie and I decided after the home game against West Brom we would go up to Luton to see Harry in hospital. Tottenham being Tottenham lost the match, which was so typical of us when we could go so close to the top. Brushing our disappointment away we got the train to Luton, then a taxi to the hospital, getting there nicely for visiting time. Harry was laid in his bed, the extent of his injury apparent, a cast the full length of his leg and a frame around to support it, with bolts going into his knee.

'What happened?' I asked Harry.

'It was my boss, he was trying to frighten me with his J.C.B, chasing me around with it. The next thing I knew I slipped, and he drives over my leg. He heard me scream, jumped out of the cab and saw me in agony. I was in shock, he's in shock, and can't believe what he's just done to me'.

Harry describes the rest of the day's events and especially his steel toe cap wellies.

'Doctor said I would have lost my leg if I didn't have my steel toe cap wellies on, and luckily the ground was muddy, so my leg was pushed into the soft earth'.

Harry said he would try and get as much compensation as he could get. His boss had already been to see him and had offered him cash not to take it any further, Harry had refused.

We left Harry, he had appreciated our visit. Harry would be out of work for many months and would not get to a match until February, and that would be on crutches.

The three of us had a quick pint in Luton, where we got talking to a bloke who asked if Richie and I were Phil's kids, which was funny, him only being three years older, Phil not finding it funny at all.

Football hooliganism in the early 80's was at its peak, all of us would avoid it as best we could. Home games were no problem in general, but occasionally when a visiting club brought a large following, Man Utd being one of those clubs, it could sometimes end tragically. In the November a United supporter was killed on the escalator at Seven Sisters Tube Station when someone hit the emergency stop button when there had been a bit of aggro, it sent the people on the packed escalator tumbling down the stairs. I didn't see the incident as we arrived a little later and things had been put in place to re-route passengers. I later met up with big Kev at Kings Cross who had witnessed the tragedy, he was visibly shook up with it and was very quiet on his return to Doncaster.

This was the second fan to die in less than a year, a Leeds fan had died nine-months previously in and around Tottenham, which meant our next meeting at Elland Road carried a warning for our travelling fans.

The weather was deteriorating into December and our match at Leeds was one of only a few games that went ahead that day.

I had stayed at Phil's on the Friday night in York and gone out that night for a few pints. Meeting up with Alan, the Man

Utd fan, the few pints trebled in quantity, which meant I was being sick in Phil's toilet a couple of hours after leaving the pub.

The following morning, making our way to the station I was sick again, leaving a trail of vomit along the pavement that looked like a slug trail.

Meeting Pete at York Station and Richie on the train we decided to get seats at the game. Rumours were going around that Leeds fans were going to get revenge for the death of one of their fans at Tottenham. It was always hostile at the best of times at Leeds, so with the added tension we decided it would be safer to go in the seats.

Once into Leeds we headed away from the station to a quiet pub. I was strictly on orange juice as my head was still pounding from the night before. A couple of drinks later we got a taxi to Elland Road. Tickets were purchased for the West (Main) Stand, and we made our way to the seats to mingle with the Leeds support, my head clearing, possibly from the freezing air.

We watched a drab nil-nil draw, but so far all was going well on the terraces. The 1,000 spurs fans who had risked coming with the possibility of the game being postponed were still safe, only verbal's being exchanged across the no-man's land of empty terraces, but of course we wouldn't be able to see what would go on after the game as we were on the other side of the ground.

No goals in the game meant our cover was still intact, but we decided to let the stand clear until we were practically the last four left in it. We then slowly moved to the front row of the seats, to where the exits were near by the player's tunnel. With no security around I asked the others what they thought about going down the tunnel, it was a weird question to ask but was met by total agreement, 'Yeah, let's go for it'.

Climbing onto the perimeter track we edged to the entrance of the tunnel, there was still no-one around so down we went, a place few Leeds fans will ever have been, never mind Spurs fans. Going into a long corridor, the first door on the left we open, it leads into the exercise suite, rowing machines, treadmills etc., well now we were in we might as well give a few pieces of apparatus a try. After a few minutes we come out and continue down the inner sanctum of Elland Road and bump into Graham Roberts and Steve Perryman coming out of the Spurs changing room, hair still wet, getting orders from the coaching staff to get the rest of the team together so they can get the coach back to London. It was quite surreal, I couldn't have imagined doing this at the start of the day. As we Passed the players, our idols, we carried on until we got to the next door, still not stopped by any security, four lads in jeans and trainers, it was as though no-one could see us, like a Harry Potter invisibility cloak. I opened the door and are met by a room of Leeds Club officials, all in club blazers and slacks, also a host of beautiful women dressed and made up to look their best, presumably the wives and girlfriends of the Leeds players. We soon noticed the bar, Pete took a step back, 'surely it can't be my round he must be thinking'. I go to the bar.

'Four pints of Tetley's?', I asked the well-dressed barman, looking dapper in his bow tie.

'Certainly sir', he said.

Wow, not many people have called me sir, well not at my age, but it sounded good. Four pints are put on the bar.

'How much?', I asked.

'You don't pay in here, not for officials and guests', he said, sounding shocked I'd even asked. The beers are handed out.

'How much?', Pete asked.

'They're free', I tell Pete, he's surprised, wishing he had said it was his round.

I look round at the classy looking people. The Leeds players are coming in, John Lukic, Brian Greenhoff, Kenny Burns and the like, all in club blazers. We look like four ragamuffins.

'Drink this one and we will get going, We're pushing our luck here' I said to the others.

We thank the barman and walk out the room, we didn't know where to go, it wasn't like we could go back down the tunnel. We walked the opposite way where we found the main doors with a club official standing by them, he opened the door and wished us a safe journey, totally unaware we were imposters. A taxi pulled up right on cue, we boarded and headed to the station.

I've often thought about that day, and how things have changed to today's Premier League. Let's just say it wouldn't happen now.

Footnote: The once mighty Leeds United are relegated at the end of this season.

Chelsea in the Cup

The season was progressing well, still in the F.A. Cup, European Cup Winners Cup, handily placed in the league and into the League Cup Semi-Final, where we would meet West Brom in the first leg at The Hawthorns. Most of us decided to go, even Harry, now back in the North-East but on crutches still recovering from his accident. Colin had hired a Transit van, three seats up front and a mattress in the back.

We set off early, around 10a.m in the morning. We had pick-ups in Boston Spa and York, then made our way to Sheffield. Colin our driver fancied a few pints or five. Pulling up outside a Sheffield pub we all piled in, some of us in Spurs shirts and scarves. The locals looked at us as though we were from another planet.

'Thought you lot were playing West Brom tonart, ye gone past Birmingham'.

We explained we were from the North, he shook his head.

We stayed in the pub for a couple of hours, then got back on the road, getting to Birmingham around 5p.m., and finally finding Smethwick the area where West Brom play.

Van parked up, we found a pub around a mile from the ground, which was packed with Spurs fans, in fact the whole area was covered with Spurs fans. An estimated 7,000 were expected to travel. By 6.30p.m we headed to the ground, Harry on crutches struggling to keep up, his injuries playing a part but so too the alcohol. Richie and I kept going.

Harry shouting.

'Aye, fuck off ya bastards'.

What sort of mates were we, but we wanted to see the kick-off.

Big Cyril Regis was their star player, but the abuse he received from our fans was terrible, but not from me. I liked Regis, but back then the black players were racially abused way beyond anything today's players get. It didn't matter that we had Garth Crooks and Chris Hughton playing for us, the abuse rained down on Regis, and not just from a minority. The Spurs support were singing 'Who's that up a tree, its Cyril, its Cyril', meaning he was a monkey. The abuse wasn't even frowned upon, it was wrong, but it was almost expected. Even then I knew racism should be eradicated from society, but here we are some forty years on still talking about the same thing.

The game ended in a goalless draw and was dull, as was the journey home, long, boring and uncomfortable. As we entered Shildon, my hometown, Colin said.

'There's a hitchhiker, should we pick him up?'.

'Yeah', was the overwhelming answer. We stopped.

'Lift mate?', Colin said.

'Yes please', he said.

'Jump in the back', Colin said.

He opened the doors to be met by a group looking at him. He nervously climbed on board.

'What the fuck are you doing out at 4a.m. in the morning?' said Richie.

We all smiled, the stranger said nothing.

I'm soon dropped off and walk the last half mile home. I got into a warm bed, my mam had put my electric blanket on. I was soon asleep, but soon woken by my alarm going off. Two hours after arriving home it was time for work.

The return leg was won 1-0 in front of almost 48,000, the first full house in our revamped stadium. The West Stand was now fully re-opened in its new guise.

We could look forward to the League Cup Final against Liverpool, but first we had to try to get to the F.A. Cup Semi-Final, in our way were London rivals Chelsea, who we would play at Stamford Bridge. Although Chelsea were in the division below us, the old Second Division, this was a grudge match for the fans. Chelsea hated us, fact. We hated them, fact. Well at least most of the supporters. I'm not particularly bothered about Chelsea, I don't like them, but you do get caught up in the rivalry between clubs because you know your own fans have a disdain for certain teams.

The media really played up to the possibility of trouble on the terraces. 'The Sun' the most popular tabloid, had back page headlines 'There will be Deaths', 'You're going to Die'. This was like lighting the blue touchpaper to the hooligans of both teams. The last time the two clubs met nearly four years earlier at The Bridge, had Spurs fans tearing down fences trying to get at the Chelsea hordes, with Chelsea fans hoping they would. Only the London Met Police kept them apart.

Tickets were purchased, most of our group were going, joining the 10,000 Spurs followers making their way to West London.

Travelling down to London we bumped into the Northern Chelsea. They told us we were going to get a good hiding, both on and off the pitch, which was a joke, especially on the pitch. The banter was good from most, but there were a few derogatory comments regarding the holocaust of World War II.

I had recently started seeing a girl called Alison, who I had taken out on a few dates. She wanted to go to a house party which was in Shildon, one of her work friends I think, but I had to tell Alison I was going to London, but would be back for 10p.m. I detected disappointment as she didn't know where to go to find the party. The best I could do was give her directions. Anyway, Chelsea or house party, no contest.

We arrived in London at our usual time. The Chelsea boys went their way while we hung around The York Bar on Kings Cross Station.

We had heard the week before that Spurs fans were heading over to Sloane Square for a drink, which was strictly on Chelsea's patch.

'Fancy going over to Sloane Square?' John said.

'Yeah, sounds a good idea', we all said.

None of us said 'Why do you want to go over there, it's going to be a hot spot for trouble'.

Before we knew it, we were alighting the tube at Sloane Square, no police about. Out onto the main road we all got into the first boozer we saw, luckily it was full of Spurs, and a lot of them looked the types who couldn't wait for the first 'Kick-Off'. Talk in the pub was about the back pages and the headlines about the trouble which could ensue. One headline said that Chelsea would be in our end and someone would be killed.

People talk about the scum on terraces, but what about the gutter press stirring up trouble, just to get a better story.

A few Chelsea came out the tube station and were walking past the pub. Before you could say 'Chelsea outside' Spurs fans were out the door and chasing them up the street.

It wasn't long before we left the pub, a few riot vans had parked up next to the tube station. Old Bill were now all over, the drone of a police helicopter was above us, a novelty at the time.

Back down onto the tube we travelled to Fulham Broadway the nearest tube station to Stamford Bridge, the train was quiet considering how many were on it, just like the journey to West Ham a year or so earlier.

Coming out onto the main road, we walked towards the ground, passing a couple of pubs, Chelsea faces peering out the doors and windows, all waiting for a flashpoint. We had no thoughts of going in any of these pubs, or any others for that matter.

Heading to the North Terrace, the open end of Stamford Bridge, we went in. I hadn't been to Chelsea before and looking at the ground I hadn't missed much.

As I said earlier most grounds looked smaller in the flesh than on TV, but Stamford Bridge wasn't the case, it was vast with large curved areas behind each goal showing its history as a greyhound track. It had an oddball of stands on the three sides, from the modern East Stand, which had crippled the club when built in the early 1970s, to a Shed at one end partially covering the terrace. The ground was full to its 42,000 capacity but still had sections closed off, condemned for safety reasons.

I always thought Chelsea had a lot of fickle fans, you know the sort, turning up for the big games but never seeing them for the mid-week league game in the rain against a lesser club.

The match before the Spurs cup game they played Cardiff in front of 9,000, their next home game after the cup match was against Leicester, 10,000. But I would also say that the Chelsea away following, like that of Newcastle always stayed loyal.

Reading the black programme cover before kick-off with the headline blazed across its front cover pleading for no trouble today, it was unlikely, but the majority hoped.

The West Stand to our right were giving us hatred abuse, particularly aiming antisemitic chants in our direction. I wondered what Chelsea's Jewish followers thought about it.

The game kicked off on a heavy pitch covered with sand, Chelsea get to grips with it, playing with gusto but little quality. Any time Chelsea came close to the Spurs goal a roar went up, the crowd may have been distant, but the noise was loud. Chelsea made the breakthrough, Mike Fillery their hero, the ground erupted on three sides, the Chelsea crowd roared their appreciation. The noise was still reverberating when the ref blew for half-time. To be honest the way we were playing it was a godsend, not just because we were not performing, but it would cool off the Chelsea support. If we had played another five minutes we would have let in a second so much

205

were Chelsea on top. We came out for the second half and to be fair whatever Keith Burkinshaw our manager had said, it hit home. Hoddle took over the midfield and we soon equalised, the 10,000 erupted. We then went for the throat, a second soon followed, the Chelsea crowd went from euphoria to despair. Once a third went in, the game was over. Chelsea did score in injury time but by then half their fickle fans had gone.

'Wembley, Wembley' rang out from the North Terrace.

The police had decided to let us straight out, which seemed the norm in London, unlike the rest of the country where you would be held in the ground for up to forty-five minutes. We were back onto the street, which was now barriered off into two sides, Chelsea on one side us on the other. There were the usual verbal's, bottle throwing, and the occasional running at each other, with a few blows aimed at each other's fans.

We walked in the crush to the tube station, only Phil and I were still together, we had lost the others. The queue at Fulham Broadway was massive, I was wanting to get the 6pm train back home to see Alison at the party.

'Phil, do you want to walk up the road to the next station?' I asked.

Phil agreed. Walking past Fulham Broadway we headed into the plush West London housing stock. The only problem was, neither of us knew where the next tube station was, we just thought one would eventually turn up as London was littered with tube stations. At 6p.m. more than hour after leaving the ground we stumbled across a tube station, both of us wishing we had queued at Fulham Broadway. We made the 7p.m. train out of Kings Cross. Most of the lads were on the train including the Northern Chelsea, who gave it the usual, 'lost on the pitch but won outside'.

'I smacked a yid because he was mouthing off', one of them boasted.

The days of mobile phones were still years away so I couldn't tell Alison I would be late. By the time I got home and got changed and over to the party it was well after 11p.m.

I knocked on the door.

'Hi, is Alison still here?' I asked hopefully.

'Yeah, come in'.

I explained to Alison what had happened, she was okay about it, but I knew she was far from happy. There was another knock on the door.

'Taxi for Alison?'

I went outside, asked her to come over the next day. The taxi sped off. Alison came over the following day, we had a quiet day.

'What we doing next Saturday?' she asked.

'It's the League Cup final', I said.

Alison phoned me that evening from her home.

'Ian, I don't want to see you anymore'.

'Oh', I said,

I didn't even ask why, I suppose I knew.

'Ok, I will see you about', I said.

Spurs were a millstone around my neck when it came to relationships, but Spurs were my love and girls could wait.

Frankfurt

Spurs and Wembley were a marriage made in heaven, we had never lost a final there in our previous visits, but the League Cup Final against Liverpool would be a stern test. We had all got tickets relatively easily from the Supporters Club having learnt from last seasons' Cup Final, but Richie wasn't happy that we had been given the tunnel end of Wembley, him being a little superstitious thinking after the epic against Man City he wanted the same end. I wasn't too bothered.

The League Cup had started in 1960 and was really a tournament for the lower division clubs, Spurs didn't bother with it until 1966. As the years progressed it became much more prestigious, emphasised when clubs were given a European place for winning it.

It's a shame that today it's almost classed as a Mickey Mouse cup used for blooding youngsters. But in '82 any match against Liverpool was big, they were the yardstick every club were measuring themselves against, and we were one of them. We fancied our chances against them and knew we had a team capable of beating them, but we still had to be at our best.

When Steve Archibald put us ahead we thought our love affair with Wembley would continue but Liverpool would keep going till the end. They often scored late goals and this game continued that trend, with three minutes left they equalised. Spurs wilted, they were now toying with us. We managed to get to full time but no amount of talk from the coaching staff could stop the inevitable once the extra time started. We were shot, the legs had gone, Liverpool scored twice, our Wembley love affair was over.

I returned home, the rest of the lads stayed in London until the midnight train. I wanted to save my money for Frankfurt in the Quarter Final of the Cup Winners Cup.

There's nothing better in football than watching your team on foreign soil. The excitement of going to a new country, new stadium, it's what all football fans hope their club will give them. After the misery of losing the League Cup final with only three minutes left, my second visit to continental

Europe to watch Spurs against Eintracht Frankfurt couldn't come quick enough. Having won the home leg 2-0 our chances of getting to the Semi-Finals were good. Phil, Pete and me all booked a week off work so we could get the ferry and train through Belgium and then into Germany's picturesque Rhine Valley, giving us time to stop off at Cologne for a look around.

With the tickets booked for travel we now only needed tickets for the game. This is where Brent helped us out.

Percy had two close friends in London, Brent and Alex a Glaswegian who had moved to Redcar when he was relatively young, and then later moved to London in the early '70's. Percy and Alex were old school mates, Alex was a Rangers fan from his Scottish upbringing but with Percy's love of Spurs it would soon rub off onto Alex, this firmly cemented once Alex moved to London. I really liked Alex and got on well with him. He would tell me the story of being a good footballer in his teenage years and getting the chance of a trial with Arsenal, he told them to shove it where the sun don't shine. He had picked up on the bitter rivalry between Spurs and Arsenal. Sadly, Alex passed away in early 2000 to the demon drink, a friend I fondly remember.

Brent lived in London, and was a former Public-School boy at Eton, very middle class, but with a very working-class outlook to football. His main angst at the match is towards referees, he would get very passionate when they gave a bad decision with a vitriol of abuse that would cascade from the terrace from where he was stood. I wasn't with Brent when Clive Thomas gave the decision to give Kenny Hibbitt that penalty in the F.A. Cup Semi-Final but there must have been steam coming out of Brent's ears that day.

Brent has been a godsend to us Northern Spurs by helping us to get tickets, especially when stadiums became all seater and you couldn't pay at the turnstile to get in. I would like to thank Brent for all he has done for us over the last forty years, long may it continue.

Apart from getting three tickets for the match, Brent had also sorted us with accommodation. I'm sure Brent had got a good deal with him working in The City dealing with Insurance. Frankfurt was also a city of Commerce.

The three of us met on the train to London, arriving around 5p.m. on the Monday evening. We made our way to Victoria Railway Station. Time for a couple of beers in a pub outside the station, then onto the train to Dover for the evening ferry crossing to Zeebrugge in Belgium.

Once on board the ferry we saw a few familiar faces, the usual Spurs fans we would often see on our travels, all congregating in the ferry bar. Very little sleep ensued with a night of beer and song.

We arrived in Belgium early on the Tuesday morning and then waited for the train to Frankfurt, a journey which would take around eight hours. With only a little amount of money changed into the Belgium francs it was a case of using the money sparingly, in other words a few cans of beer and a sandwich.

Making our way to Frankfurt on a train made up of compartments like the old carriages in England that could hold eight people.

Phil and I had travelled light. I had a vinyl Adidas bag that were popular at the time, a glorified shopping bag like my mam would use but with Adidas emblazoned on it, it was transformed into a fashionable item. Phil had something similar, but Pete had brought a huge bag that he could have probably got into. Talk about a 'hold all', this one could have definitely held all!

I got laid out on the seat in the carriage, and after having little sleep the previous night I was soon snoozing. The train trundled along with its warm under seat heater making it feel cosy. I must have gone into a deep sleep using my Adidas bag as a pillow. An hour or so passed when I awoke, the train pulling into a station. Phil and Pete were opposite me on the other seat.

'Good sleep?', Phil asked.

'Yeah', I said.

But it soon became apparent that I couldn't move my head off the Adidas bag, it had stuck to my face. The hot carriage had made me sweat, my skin had stuck to the vinyl.

'I'm stuck to my bag', I told the two of them.

I don't think Phil or Pete believed me, but when I tried to lift my cheek from the bag they could see I was definitely fastened. It was a case of slowly pulling away from the vinyl, a quick move wasn't in my thinking. Phil told me to carry it on my cheek to the match, yes the two of them thought it was funny. Eventually I managed to free myself, possibly with fragments of skin attached to my bag.

Pulling into Cologne in the early afternoon we decided to get off, breaking the journey to get something to eat. Now we could use our Deutschmarks to buy something.

Coming out of Cologne station you are met by Cologne Cathedral, its beauty awe inspiring. I was just looking at its immense size, I wanted to go in, and I wished I had, but Pete shouted.

'Hey, there's a bar over the road, fuck the cathedral'.

Pete's thoughts were more for the beer. We saw what looked like a bar and entered through a door, it led into a huge room full of Germans, many in suits, either having an early finish or a late lunch. It was wonderful, a proper bierkeller.

We were only in seconds when an attractive fraulein came over,

'Drie beers?'.

'Yes please', we said.

There was none of this trying to get served at the bar like in England. Within a minute three large stein glasses were brought to us, we soaked up the atmosphere with two or three hundred German men and women talking, singing, and generally having a good time. We finished our drinks and ordered more, it wouldn't be right to leave just yet.

Back on the train to Frankfurt, I left thinking, I've got to see that cathedral again one day. Pete and Phil were more interested in seeing a guard with a trolley load of beer coming down the train aisle.

We arrived in Frankfurt at around 9p.m. It was too dark to see what the city was like. What you could see were the clean lines of high-rise offices of Frankfurt's commerce district. We got a taxi which dropped us off at a high-rise tower block hotel, all sorted by Brent, two rooms, a twin and a separate room. We were too tired to argue who was getting what room, and in the end Pete got his own room. We hit the sack.

The following morning we went down for breakfast. There appeared to be areas cordoned off for decorators, they seemed to be everywhere. I thought I had better get Phil and Pete out being decorators themselves it would be like a busman's holiday. We left the hotel after a simple breakfast and headed to the railway station to meet Steve from York. Steve was a big Liverpool fan who had just lost his job at British Rail but could still use his free railway passes. His idea was to bring a load of lapel football badges to sell, he thought the Germans would like English football memorabilia and was hoping to get around two Deutschmarks' each for them, about a pound in English currency.

It was still early morning and there were plenty of commuters around the station, but to be honest they were mainly the suited type and a bedraggled Englishman didn't catch their attention, anyway they weren't Steve's target clientele. We hung around for a while as he tried his best to sell his badges, but it was tough and after only three sales we prised him away for a beer.

We offered Steve a floor to sleep on that night at the hotel, arranging to meet him after the match. He said he would continue trying to sell his badges. We went off for a walk to have a look at what Frankfurt had to offer which to be fair wasn't much. It wasn't a city that was a tourist hot spot, it was too business orientated. Having walked enough by early afternoon we entering a small bar with four stools propped against the bar, we sat down. Next to us on another stool was what we thought a German having a beer. On the wall above the optics was a large TV screen showing a hard-core porn film. Well, it wouldn't be polite to walk out without buying at least one drink. Three expensive beers were bought and very little conversation took place for the first ten minutes, too engrossed in the movie.

'You're here for the match?' the man next to us said, he was English.

'Yeah' Phil said, 'You going?'

'No, I live here at the moment with work' the stranger said.

'Didn't expect to see a porno on', I said to him.

'Well you are in the Red-Light Area' he said.

Funny how football fans seem to stumble into these areas, in our case without even trying.

'Watch yourself while you're in here', he said.

'Why?'

He had got our attention now, our eyes strayed from the sex on screen. You know that little twitch you get in your stomach as soon as he mentioned 'watch yourselves'.

'Saw a bloke in here last week, a stranger, see the curtains over there', he pointed in the direction across the room. Three cubicles, looking like photo booths with long velvet curtains touching the floor.

'He was getting pissed up, this stranger. A couple of the girls who work in here went over to him and asked him into one of the cubicles. He obliged and the girls asked what he would like, you know what I mean, and he got what he wanted from the girls'.

We were all ears now.

'Anyway, the girls said that will be two hundred deutschmarks to the stranger. He was immediately saying no, no, that's not what we agreed. The girls were saying you got extras. He was saying I haven't got that sort of money. One of the girls rang a bell and two big geysers came out from the back, dragged him outside and give him a good hiding'.

'Thanks for the info', we said.

'Hey, I'm not saying don't go with the girls but make sure you have the money, anyway lads I'm off, enjoy the match tonight', and out the door he went.

That should have been the time we should have done the same, but we had just got another beer in, and at these prices we weren't leaving it.

Back to watching the film, although it had lost its appeal.

The girl who was serving us came round from the bar and sat on the vacant stool next to me. As I watched the film her hand slid up and down my leg. It should have been pleasurable, but what the English guy had said left me a bit cold.

214

'Would you like more?' she said in her broken English, 'I show you good time'.

Quite possibly I thought, after all she was very attractive, but there was no way I was going behind the curtain, my thoughts of being dragged outside outweighed my thoughts of pleasure.

'Phil, Pete, it's time to go'.

They agreed, we headed out of the red-light area to a quiet bar and found out off a local how to get to The Wald Stadium, home of Eintracht Frankfurt.

The tram ride took us to the outskirts of Frankfurt to where the stadium was. The stadium lay in a wooded area, with kiosks lining the road. The smell of the bratwurst and other types of sausage filled the air as we walked past them, us stopping on a couple of occasions to sample the aromas, too hard to pass up. It certainly put the limp hot dogs around English football grounds to shame.

With the evening being dry and fairly mild it was good to have a drink alongside the Germans. The Spurs support were beginning to turn up now, and it was all good natured, just a few chants of 'Two World Wars and one World Cup, do, dah, do, dah' but the Germans laughed it off.

We moved on up the tree lined road to the stadium. As we approached, a line of heavily armed police funnelled the 2,500 Spurs support down an alleyway which was lined with more police holding long batons. Those who didn't have a baton had an Alsatian dog alongside them, which barked constantly.

We entered the clean lined bowl, two main stands, two open ends, not dissimilar to Ajax's Olympic Stadium, but this much more modern. Our contingent were housed in one corner of an end made up of seat bases bolted to the steps.

Considering we had an open end we were making plenty of noise. The Germans, like the Dutch would get behind their team in short bursts, but when they did it was loud, and they had plenty to make a noise about. Although we were two up from the first leg, they wiped it out with barely twenty minutes gone. It looked bad for us, but we dug in and got to half-time without conceding again. The talk amongst our fans was if we could just get an away goal they would have to score two more.

The second half was tight, we kept things quiet at the back, don't let the Germans' score!

Few chances were created, until the seventy fourth minute when Glenn Hoddle scored. Our section of support jumped for joy. We kept the Germans at bay and only give them a few half chances. The crowd were quiet, apart from our pocket of fans. The whistle blew, we celebrated like we had won the game, which of course we had over the two legs. Never have I been so happy with a loss. The team came down to us, and as we gave them our applause, they reciprocated. Then it was out of the ground, we weren't kept in which was a surprise, The night air was cool now.

Germans were passing us, one idiot was wanting us to pile into them. He was mouthing off, until he confronted a middle-aged stereotypical German, bit of a beer belly, large moustache and one of those hats Germans wear, especially in the Bavarian areas, he only needed lederhosen to finish the look off perfectly.

'Come on you German cunt', the yob shouted, 'you want a go you fat cunt'.

'Nein, nein', the German pleaded.

Other Germans scurried away not wanting to get involved, our English reputation rearing its ugly head again. A punch was swung towards the cowering German as he is pushed towards a mesh fence, not many other Spurs fans seemed interested. Three or four did join in, it was four onto one.

Were we just as bad for letting them do it, and not saying, 'Hey leave him alone he's not interested', but this is of the time. I didn't like it, but it was seen so often it washed over you.

The German dropped to the floor after taking several blows, his arms outstretched, pleading for them to stop, crying like a baby. All I was thinking was here's a man coming to support his team and this is how his night has ended, it's a football match for god's sake. He was now so traumatised he may never go back to watch Eintracht Frankfurt again, I hoped that wouldn't be the case. The hooligans, I can't call them Spurs fans made me feel ashamed because of their actions. They left the German a quivering wreck on the floor, while they were laughing at their sickening actions. This episode took all my joy away from the fantastic result and would be my lasting memory of this trip.

We got back to the station where we had left Steve to sell his badges.

'How many more badges did you sell?'

'None', came Steve's reply.

'Not to worry Steve, at least you have a warm room to sleep in tonight', I assured him.

Steve smiled, I am not sure if he remembered that he would be on the floor.

The remainder of the trip went well but the image of the German was still ingrained on my mind and would stay for a good while.

Pig

As I've said previously, the card school would always be in full swing either going or coming back from matches, but for one return journey from London, Colin said, 'we'll have a game of Pig'. We had never played the game before as we usually played Brag or Pontoon, but Colin said it was a good game, so we were all ears.

The Rules – Basically from what I remember, everyone received one card each. A nominated card would then be chosen, for example the two of spades, everyone then would pick a card in turn from the deck, which would be face down. Once someone picked the nominated card they would try and get another two of either Clubs, Diamonds or Hearts. If they got a match, they would put their finger on their nose. Everyone who saw this would then put their finger on their nose. The loser would be the slowest to put a finger to their nose. A simple game and really good when you picked up the nominated card.   Of course, there had to be a prize or in this case a forfeit. It was simple game I assure you!

Setting the scene, the 6p.m. out of London, and a home win. Everyone was in an exuberant mood, the train was packed.   Let the game begin. First, we would have a discussion about the forfeit.

As we were all sat at the end of the carriage the loser had to go to the far end of the carriage, face everyone and do a pig sound as loud as possible. A quiet and friendly start! We all agreed, no one could pull out of the forfeit. Game on.

A card each, then a nominated card was picked, we all took turns picking up from the deck hoping to get the nominated card. You're never sure who had what, it was a constant look at your fellow players. I went to pick a card and as I did I looked up and everyone had a finger on their nose, 'Shit', I shouted. There was no backing out of the forfeit. I got up and walked the length of the carriage looking at the passengers, wondering what they were going to think in about thirty seconds time, probably 'who is that nutter'. As I made

218

my walk I could hear the lads at the far end table sniggering like a group of school kids. I stopped at the sliding doors and turned around, half the people were facing me, the other half were seated the other way. At the top of my voice I shouted.

'Oink, Oink, Oink, Oink'

Everyone was now looking at me, even the ones seated the other way, they were all looking at my now blushing face, some smiled, some showed disdain, and of course one table was howling with laughter.

'Well done, Stoker', Col shouted from the far end. He often called me Stoker as he thought my surname was Stokes.

What is for sure, a precedent had been set, no one could back out of the forfeits. Another game started. The forfeit had been decided with the added bonus that the second slowest person would also have to join in. I was alert, everyone was as the second game started. I noticed very quickly a finger going onto Col's nose, I quickly followed, as did most of the others, but Richie was slow, he couldn't hide behind his fuzzy hair no more, he was guilty and would serve his sentence along with Brass who was also too slow. Richie got up from the safety of his train seat to meet his audience, he got on his hands and knees then Brass got on his back to ride him up the aisle. To add insult Richie had to oink like a pig. It reminded me of the film 'Deliverance', when the two main characters are caught by the Hillbillies. Fair play to Richie he deserved his round of applause as he returned red faced and probably red kneed.

Third round. Ideas were thrown around amongst us, it had to go up a level.

'See the bloke halfway up the carriage with The Times newspaper?' I said to the rest.

'Yeah', came an interesting nod, and what has Ian got up his sleeve.

'The loser goes up to him, takes his glasses off, removes the paper from his hands, then puts the glasses on and looks at the paper', I said.

A tough assignment, a person of strong will was needed.

The beer was flowing, the empty cans mounting on the tables, evidence of inhibitions sliding.

'Yeah, why not', came a resounding thumbs up to our next game.

The next game started slow, with a lot of twitching, people rubbing their noses in jest. We were all nervous, no one wanted to do the mission. You could almost see beads of sweat as each player picked up a card, wondering if that could be the card. A cheer went up. I looked up, all I saw was a group of faces with fingers on their noses, how was I so slow. It would be me leading my own mission. I regretted the proposed forfeit but knew I had to do it, I couldn't lose face.

I left my seat, heart pounding. I looked at my target, he was in his early forties, reading his paper, totally unaware of what was about to happen to him. I looked at John who could hardly contain himself, he was almost wetting himself with laughter.

'Here goes', I told the rest.

I wanted to abort as soon as I made my first step but carried on. I reached the man and stood next to him, before he looked up his glasses were removed, clean like a proper assassin, he looked at me, his eyes now looking small, he said nothing, possibly shock. His paper was whisked from his grip, the glasses were now on my face, the paper is quickly looked at, I then handed them back and thanked him. He nodded, either in respect or disgust. I felt high, a gush of euphoria swept through my body. I took the standing ovation that I received, mission accomplished. I've decided I'm retired, I can't go through that again.

We are nearing York, 'one last game', Col said, before we lose the York contingent.

Like a boxer wanting one last pay day I agreed to play. The people in the carriage now had a good idea what we were up to and knew anyone of the hundred or so of them could be the next target. It's like a comedian picking on someone in their audience, they don't want the attention as they are going to get the piss taken out of them. You could see people almost cowering in their seats, pleading don't pick me. A few ideas were thrown around and it was decided.

The game started and almost immediately I picked up the nominated card, I just needed the same to match it, a Club, Diamond or Heart to go alongside my Spade, and I soon picked it up. I couldn't lose now, I could have fun with the rest, make them sweat for a few rounds, then I would put my finger on my nose. A mad dash was made by everyone. Brass was slow, so very slow.

'Fucking hell', Brass shouted.

'You up for it Brass', I asked.

A nod is returned. The target, a very good looking blonde, early twenties, a couple of seats before the last man with the glasses. Brass set off, the girl eyed him.

'Gan on Brass', John howled.

She knew the score, she'd seen the last game. Brass approached her, leaned over and planted a kiss full on the lips. This could have gone horribly wrong, the police could have been involved, after all, look what happened to Paul Gascoigne in 2019 for a similar incident. The girl smiled, we're in the clear. Brass took the adulation.

We entered York. The game was never played again, it was a one off, sometimes it's better that way.

Wembley Again and The Stags Head

Spurs pulled out the plum draw in the Semi-Final of the Cup Winners Cup against Barcelona. It now seems strange that Barcelona hadn't qualified for the then European Cup. Their name though still one of the elite clubs to play, but this wasn't the free-flowing Barcelona team like now graced by Lionel Messi, this was a dirty team who would do anything to stop the opposition.

The home match at The Lane was brutal. The Spurs crowd couldn't believe they were allowed to get away with the constant hacking down of our players. We were willing Graham Roberts our hardcase to take out some of their players like he would do to Charlie Nicholas two years later in the North London Derby, his tackle so hard Nicholas ended up in the side paddock. We drew the match 1-1.

It looked like it would be a stern test at the Nou Camp, I couldn't afford to go. Richie made the trip to see us lose 1-0, our European dream was over.

Our next big match, the F.A. Cup Semi Final at Villa Park had us paired against Leicester City, at the time a division lower than ourselves.

More significantly our country had declared war on Argentina, which begged the question what would Tottenham do with our two Argentine players Ricky Villa and Ossie Ardiles, and what did they want to do. Ossie did play against Leicester and received terrible abuse from the Leicester crowd on every occasion he touched the ball, our support cheered him on, but at the post match TV interviews Tottenham broke the news that Ossie would be loaned to Paris Saint Germain to play for them until the end of the season.

As the Falklands War dragged on it would be almost a year before Ossie returned. Ricky decided to stay at Tottenham as he was injured at the time. Spurs won the

Semi-Final 2-0 to secure another return to Wembley to face Q.P.R. in the F.A. Cup Final.

The league season became so hectic due to a backlog of fixtures because of bad weather and also having three good cup runs meaning the last ten league fixtures were played in twenty-three days, killing our hopes of the league title.

Our penultimate game was at Anfield against Liverpool, yet again they took the title. Most of the lads travelled, along with Steve the Liverpool fan who came to Frankfurt, and his mate Mel, another Liverpool regular. They asked where we were going for a drink once in Liverpool, we didn't know, it wasn't the safest of places to wander around.

'We're off to The Stags Head, ten minutes from Lime Street Station if you want to come', Steve said.

'Yeah', we all agreed.

The Stags Head was on a main road, but was your traditional local boozer, small but clean, and run by Joe the landlord, who was a typical quick witted scouser. The pub was quiet, in fact once eight of us entered we had quadrupled the amount of paying drinkers.

For the next fourteen years we would use the pub every time we played Liverpool or Everton, and Joe was there for all those years. Every year we would walk in, Joe would be looking at his racing paper, look up at the door to see the regular Spurs contingent come in and say the usual.

'Ar right boys come for the usual defeat', which seemed true when playing the Reds, but when we played Everton, he would always wish us well saying.

'Hope you beat them blue noses, I fucken hate em', in his broad scouse twang.

The first time we went to The Stags I went to the toilet and on the reverse side of the door was carved 'Spurs', John I thought.

'John, have you carved Spurs on the door?'.

'I fuckan done it with me pen knife'.

Why I thought. In those next fourteen years, no matter how often that door was painted you couldn't erase the word 'Spurs'. It was like seeing something from your childhood when you saw it year after year.

Not many people would come in The Stags on match day, maybe five or six in the three hours we would stay there, Joe more than happy we were there to give him some custom.

On the odd occasion a local came in they would often use the jukebox, which was one of those old machines that would play records where you could see them going around on a turntable, but this jukebox was strange. I noticed this on one of our early visits. I told Phil to watch what happened when a local put his money in, Phil keen to see the local put his twenty pence into the machine. The local picked his two tunes and sat at the bar. The record dropped onto the turntable, it was clear to see through the glass frontage, the arm sat on the vinyl and the record played with no sound at all, like the volume was on zero. The record finished, the local's second choice dropped down and played like the first, no sound. Once finished the local walked over and put more money in and chose two more songs with the same outcome, no sound, not a murmur. We would just laugh at it, were these locals like dogs, with a different hearing frequency.

After fourteen years calling in The Stags for our pre match drink, Joe had gone, two young lads were in charge. It was disappointing, we didn't know where Joe had gone or even if he had died. We ordered a couple of pints of bitter and two pints of lager.

'We don't have any, we only have Mild', the two lads said. They must be joking, I'm thinking, a pub with no beer.

224

'We drank it all last night', they said. 'We had a bit of a stoppy back'.

We left, never to return. It wouldn't be the same without Joe anyway, a truly welcoming landlord. The Stags Head was knocked down around 2019.

The '82 Cup Final was such an anti-climax. For a start we were playing Q.P.R., a division lower and finishing mid-table. We were expected to wipe the floor with them. Tickets were again obtained from The Supporters Club, but the game itself was awful. We looked so tired and only managed to draw the game which meant another Thursday night replay.

I don't know what it is, but the better your team becomes the results almost feel less important. When we won games when we were a struggling team it was so euphoric, but this Cup Final didn't seem to mean much to me. It could never eclipse the previous year's Cup Final anyway, but I would still be there for the replay.

We left Kings Cross and took the tube to Wembley. Dave, who still had his skinhead hair style was soon talking to a similar looking character who he didn't know, this other skinhead seemed to have taken a shine to Dave, but was pissed and very noisy.

'Dave, you need to lose your mate', I discreetly said.

'He's not me mate I don't know who he is', Dave said.

We all took a backward step, but Dave couldn't shake him off. We alighted the tube at Wembley, Dave and his 'friend' were in front of us, the 'friend' shouting and swearing.

'He will be nicked soon', I said to the rest.

We left at the Tube exit, he was still shouting, when all of a sudden the long arm of the law pulled him out and threw him into a riot van. Davc looked relieved, when suddenly another arm of the law came out and grabbed Dave.

225

'Your fucking nicked' we heard the copper say.

Dave was thrown into the same van as his new associate. The two faces peered out the window.

John is cracking up with laughter and trying to shout.

'Give as your fuckan ticket and I'll sell it'.

It had made Johns night. I think most of us felt sorry for Dave, but it was funny.

Once inside Wembley it was apparent that Spurs had around three quarters of the support, Richie again not pleased we were in the Tunnel end, especially after loosing to Liverpool in the League Cup Final, but this game might dispel his theory.

Hoddle puts away an easy goal, 1-0 and Spurs win the cup. It was the least we deserved after a wonderful season for the club and supporters. A season that will forever remain my favourite while watching the club.

Everton, Northern Ireland and Wales

After what had been a memorable season in 1981-82 we went into the following season hoping for more of the same. We only bought one meaningful player to boost the squad, but what a player, a true stalwart to the club. Gary Mabbutt would become a legend for Spurs and to the fans. He went on to play over six hundred games in a distinguished sixteen-year spell with us, before retiring and becoming an ambassador to the club. Only Steve Perryman would play more games for Tottenham. Both players would regularly play that season, but Tottenham's form would fall well short of their previous years achievements.

Our trip to Everton early on in the season would yet again see terrace fashion change.

Arriving at Lime Street at the usual time, 11a.m. we went straight out the station and up to the Stags Head pub, staying there until around 2p.m. I liked going to Merseyside, but it always carried a threat of trouble. The Scousers definitely didn't like what they thought were the flashy Cockneys, especially in those deprived times on Merseyside.

We got to Goodison and bought tickets for the Main Stand seats, we had sat in a similar place the previous season, sitting towards our fans housed in The Park End terrace. Normally we would stand at all games, but Goodison Park's away section was a very shallow terrace, which we got crushed a couple of years previous and vowed not to stand there again.

Everton's Gladys Street End behind the goal was where their main singing area was, but below where we sat in the Main Stand Paddock, Everton's hooligan element would congregate to get as near as possible to the away section. The chants back and forth between the rival fans would start before kick-off.   The seats above the away section would often have Everton fans in, unless the away fans were allocated this section as well. On this occasion, there were only around ten Spurs fans sat above the 1500 Spurs fans below. I noticed further along a group of around twenty Everton fans. Just before kick-off the twenty Scousers started to run towards the ten Spurs fans, who to be honest weren't the type who wanted trouble. The ten Spurs fans ran across the bench seats to try and escape but only ended up against the end wall with no escape. The Evertonians below us were cheering on their comrades as they attacked the Spurs unfortunates. There was little resistance as they began to take a beating. The trouble was no more than twenty metres from where we were sat in the Main Stand, our seats sitting over the eighteen-yard box. The fight in the corner of the Park End seats cotinued, the Scousers below us cheered loudly, when

227

suddenly from the back of the stand around thirty Spurs fans showed up, seeing their fellow Spurs fans in trouble they ran towards the Scousers, who turned to face the Spurs cavalry, they couldn't go anywhere else. Spurs waded in, some of the original ten then joined in to get revenge. Bodies were flying over the bench seats, we were all cheering now, I didn't like trouble but what goes around comes around. The Scousers below us were now seeing their boys getting a pummelling. The Old Bill finally showed up and pulled out all the Everton fans, a lot looking bloodied and shaken up.

'Tharl be fuckan hell on when the games over', John said. Everton won 3-1, we were hoping their win would take some of the tension out of the earlier skirmish for when we left the ground.

We came out the Main Stand, passed the pub on the corner where their mob was already numbering around 300. We looked over the road to see the Spurs fans coming out the Park End which has only one way out, anyone coming out that end was an away fan. The Scousers knew exactly who was who, we'd been in the same situation in previous seasons. I'd always maintained that Everton was the dodgiest away ground I'd ever visited.

We passed the pub, keeping quiet, some of the Everton mob ran at the exiting Spurs leaving the away section, punches and kicks reined in. We kept moving and got to the bus stand and waited in the queue to get to Lime Street. We were all feeling the tension, we weren't sure if anyone had noticed us, a group of Spurs sat in the Main Stand. Would we get dropped in it!

Next to us in the queue was a black guy, young, but big. You had a feeling he was Spurs and if we thought that, the Scousers might think the same. It didn't take long when over walked a group of Scousers, still with the flick head haircuts

228

all wearing tracksuit tops, some with matching tracksuit bottoms, branded designs like Ellesse, Sergio Tacchini, names I had never heard of, but within a few months some of every clubs' supporters were wearing the same gear. The football Casual was born, As Kelly Jones, lead singer of the Stereophonics, sang many years later with their hit record 'Have a Nice Day'. 'We dress the same way, only our accents change', the lyrics seemed so apt for the football casual movement.

Pete liked the look and within weeks Pete was wearing a tracksuit top and slitting his jeans at the bottom of the legs which was also popular at the time.

'Ar right mate, you Tottenham?' the leader of the scally gang asked the black guy who was stood only a few yards from us. As soon as the black guy opened his mouth his cover was blown, an arm swung in his direction. He dodged the punch but noticed around forty scousers heading over. He turned and ran towards Stanley Park and into its vastness, he now had fifty scousers chasing him. He looked athletic and was keeping ahead. We watched as the chase came to a park gate, he went through but with it being a 'Kissing Gate' the Scousers had to go through single file. It was like a scene from the old Benny Hill shows with that fast music accompanying. I felt for the lad, hopefully he was as fit as he looked. We boarded the bus and set off for Lime Street, the road adjacent to the park. I looked across into the park and could still see the chase was on, who knew what the outcome would be, but one thing for certain, following your team away wasn't a walk in the park!

I started seeing Karen during the early summer and thought it best to let her know that Spurs were my passion and I would be away most Saturdays between August and May.

She understood and asked if she could go to a game as she hadn't been to a live game before. It wasn't a problem, so I got her a ticket for the Charity Shield at Wembley against Liverpool.

Karen had met most of the lads briefly at Colin's wedding in the summer. I say briefly, we were all booked into the same hotel for an overnight stay, but the lads were kicked out within an hour for being too loud and boisterous. Karen and I kept quiet as we had a separate room so managed to stay.

The next time Karen met the lads properly was at Wembley for the match and the night out afterwards around the West End. We trailed around pubs and then onto this seedy bar in Soho which was down a flight of stairs. One of the lads tripped and fell down the stairs, hitting the rest, sending them down like skittles. The pile of bodies at the foot of the stairs were soon turned away by the management.

At the end of the night I asked Karen what she thought of the lads, 'Erm' was Karen's answer.

I started to take Karen to most of the home games and she enjoyed the company of the lads once she got to know them. Making sure where we stood on the Shelf she could see the action, she loved the banter between The Shelf and the Park Lane End especially when there was a decent away following, just as long as it didn't spill over into violence.

Our first European away game, yet again threw up another Irish team in Coleraine, from Northern Ireland. Phil, Rich and I decided to travel. It meant getting the train to Stranraer on the Southwest coast of Scotland on the Tuesday morning, then a ferry to Belfast late afternoon. Phil and I were hoping it would be a better experience than the Dundalk trip.

We had a pleasant crossing to Larne and a short shuttle service into Belfast.

Still in the times of 'The Troubles', between Catholic and Protestants, Northern Ireland had seen some brutal violence and significant loss of life on both sides of the divide, but you have to remember it was only a minority of people who were making life miserable for the majority. We tried to put it to one side but it was brought home when the bus was stopped at a check point, suddenly we had the British Army and sniffer dogs on board. The dogs going around all of us, presumably looking for firearms and the like, possibly bombs. What was strange was that the locals of Belfast just chatted amongst themselves. The younger ones hadn't seen anything different. 'The Troubles' had gone on for generations, but to us it was strange.

Getting to the terminus in the heart of Belfast we alighted and had a walk around the busy city centre. It reminded me a little bit of Newcastle, everyone getting on with their lives,

I didn't know what to expect. You only saw Northern Ireland on TV with the image of cars ablaze, groups of hoodlums throwing bricks and petrol bombs at the police and the army who were invariably behind Perspex shields. This was not that image, it felt warm, a friendly place.

We found the railway station and took the fifty-mile journey North to Coleraine. Our objective was to get a ticket for the match, as was usual, and finding somewhere to stay. These two issues were always secondary in our thoughts when going overseas, it was just about getting there. After an hour we stopped at the relatively small station of Coleraine. We got off, crossed a bridge and saw what looked like a railway hotel.

'That one looks ok', I said.

The others agreed, we went inside the public bar.

'Alright boys, what can I do for you?' A broad Irish twang greeted us.

231

'Have you got three rooms, for three nights?', Phil asked hopefully.

'Yes, no problem boys, over for the match?'.

'Yes', we replied.

'Rooms upstairs make yourself at home, I'll open the bar if you want a drink'. Phil nodded his approval.

We took our bags to our rooms which were tidy and came down to the bar. The owner's son introduced himself and got us all a drink.

'If you want to go to any bars tonight in Coleraine don't go to the South Side of the town', he said.

'Why?' I asked.

'Because you won't come back, it's the Catholic area. If they get wind you're from the Mainland they'll, if you're lucky, give you a good kicking and if you're unlucky', he didn't need to say anymore.

The hotel door swung open, revealing three men with instruments

'Who are they?', Rich asked.

'We have entertainment on each night', he said.

Our mind was made up, the beer was good and there's music on, we didn't need to venture far, especially not to the South Side.

The following morning, feeling a bit rough after a good night of Irish jiggy music and one too many beers, we managed our fried breakfast. The landlord's son came over to us.

'Treat the place like your own, my room is at the top of the stairs if you get a bit bored, I've got hundreds of videos if you want to watch any. Right, I'm off to work'.

We appeared to be the only paying guests, so were tret like kings.

We left the hotel after breakfast, our main aim was to get three tickets. The ground wasn't far away so we walked to what was another typical lower division type of ground, mainly made up of shallow terraces, but at least it wasn't fenced like Dundalk. In fact the ground had no segregation, it would be a case of stand where you wanted, that was providing we got tickets.

We headed to the Club Ticket Office, which was a portacabin. We knocked on the door, not sure if anyone was around as the ground looked deserted, though the game was that night. We were soon greeted by a suited Irishman.

'Have you got any tickets for the match tonight?', Phil asked hopefully.

'We have boys, Tottenham fans from England?' he said.

'Yeah', we said.

'Come in boys, I'm one of the Directors of the Club, but help everywhere I'm needed, ticket office, cutting the grass, anything to help the club'.

You have to admire these type of people who are devoted to their club, it's the lifeblood to keeping a club going. He went behind the counter and produced three tickets.

'How much?', I asked.

'No, no, boys, these are complimentary for travelling over, enjoy your stay'.

We thanked him for his generosity and left the ground and headed off for a walk. It was warm so we had no coats on. Richie and I had identical Spurs jumpers on which we got from the Spurs club shop, these were adorned with our club crest. On Phil's jumper, which was an unofficial Spurs jumper, was a ridiculous looking bird which was more chicken than cockerel. Phil had suffered much piss taking ever since buying it, but he seemed quite proud of it.

233

We entered a park where two park attendants were brushing rubbish up but stopped as they saw us walking towards them. As we got closer one of them shouted at us.

'Hello there?'.

'Alright' I said.

The other one asked 'Would it be possible if you boys could sign a few autographs for us?'.

We looked at each other with a smile on our face, they thought we must be players and had obviously seen the Spurs jumpers, I don't know what they thought of Phil's jumper. Anyway who did they think we were. Phil having a beard could be Ricky Villa. Richie, ginger hair, Micky Hazard, and myself, Stevie Perryman. We could have played along but weren't so cruel.

'We only Spurs fans from England', we said.

The look on their faces was one of embarrassment, as they picked up their brushes and stared at the ground.

We left the park and headed back to the hotel, happy in the knowledge that we had tickets for the 6p.m. kick-off, the early start due to Coleraine's floodlights not up to U.E.F.A standards.

Back at the hotel we decided to take up the offer of watching a video. A quick look through the vast collection of VHS videos and I pulled out an eighteen certificate, 'S.S. Experiment Camp', I put it on play, it didn't take long for Rich to say.

'What the fuck is this?'.

It was brutal, women being raped, tortured, executed and then cut up for experiments by Nazis during the war. We continued watching in silence, but the truth was it's what the Nazi's did, especially to the Jews during the war. The film ended.

'Different', I said, 'Come on let's go for a pint'.

The bar was starting to fill with a number of Spurs fans, yet again, mainly Irish. The owner's son came in from work and was soon behind the bar to help out.

'We watched a video', I said.

'Which one?', he enquired.

'S.S. Experiment camp', I said.

'Good isn't it, just got it', he said proudly.

We stayed in the bar until about forty-five minutes to kick-off, then headed to the compact ground, full to its 12,000 capacity. The 1500 Spurs fans, two-thirds Irish, made the atmosphere carnival like, which was brilliant after the hatred of Dundalk, and no trouble ensued. We won the game comfortably, as we did the return leg.

On our final day we had a trip to the nearby 'Giant's Causeway', which was said 'A not to be missed attraction'. What a disappointment. I expected pillars of stone twenty feet high, but in reality, they were four feet. To be fair it's a beautiful area.

We returned back to another night in the hotel bar with more Irish music to end our trip. The following morning we left, with a big thankyou to the hotelier for his hospitality, it more than made up for Phil and myself's Dundalk trip, and showed what Ireland had to offer.

A couple of weeks later I made my second ever visit to Wales, when playing Swansea, the previous time was a day trip when I was ten, when on holiday in Somerset.

Quite a few of the Northern Spurs travelled, we decided to go via London instead of going through Birmingham and Bristol, it was a longer trip in mileage, but quicker. An early start was required, leaving Darlington at 7a.m., into London before 10a.m. and straight over to Paddington to get the first available train heading to Wales.

The six of us sat at two tables. Four of us at one of the tables and two of us at another table. The other two seats were soon occupied by two Spurs fans from London who we didn't know but were soon chatting with. We were eager to get them onboard with our card school and they happy to accept our offer. We taught them the game we played, and they were soon dealt in. I was the banker, and it didn't take long to realise that these two were either useless at the game or just flashy with their money. They would bet on ridiculous hands, throwing money into the pot willy nilly, but I wasn't complaining being the banker, and was up forty quid by the time we got to Swansea. It doesn't sound much today but I was only getting sixty quid a week at work, it meant the whole day would be a freebie.

As we departed the train at Swansea, I shouted to one of the Londoners.

'See you on the return journey?'.

'What to fucking fleece us some more?', one shouted down the platform.

'Yep', was my reply.

The train had been delayed so it was now after 2p.m., so it was straight off to the ground.

'We'll get a beer at the ground?' Pete said.

The lads had already drunk plenty, only Rich and I hadn't.

We got to The Vetch Field, home of Swansea City and went into the away section, which is like going into a third world sports ground. The facilities were so antiquated, the toilets couldn't cope with 200 away fans, never mind 2,000.

I heard Col shouting, 'Its fucking disgusting'.

I shouted back. 'What the toilets?'.

'No', Col says 'No fucking beer, they don't sell it, I don't fucking believe it'.

We entered the shallow banked away section, the Swansea crowd were very partisan and made it clear what they thought of the English, though saying that we were giving John Toshack the Swansea Manager abuse about what he does to his family sexually and what all Welshmen do to each other. We lost the game 2-0, which was becoming a bad habit away from home as the season went on. We never scored an away goal from mid-September to mid-January, which was strange because we scored plenty at home.

As we shuffled out of the shit tip onto the street, you had this feeling this was going to be a hairy trip to the railway station, several hundred Spurs fans were also making the walk. Heading along the High Street we were hit with a barrage of bottles from the waiting Swansea boys. The bottles were crashing around us which dispersed the Spurs mob into fragmented groups as we all tried to avoid the glass. The police were nowhere to be seen. Further up the road the Swansea boys on the other side of the road went tearing into one of the groups of Spurs, a mass brawl ensuing. We were getting backed off, Swansea didn't want us to get to the station. Small groups would eye each other up then steam into each other. Finally, the riot vans showed up, which were then targeted with another hail of bottles. The police were going mad, truncheons out, Alsatians going berserk. They were heavy-handed pushing us along, it wasn't like we wanted to stay. It was a relief to get to the station all safe, God knows what it was like when they played Cardiff in them days.

 Back on the train, the cards were out again.

'It doesn't look like the cockney lads fancy a game', I said.

They were nowhere to be seen, but just as I said it, the carriage door slid open.

'Deal us in', two battered figures sat down. Both had black eyes, fat lips and blood splattered torn shirts.

'Well, you might as well clean us out and finish our fucking day off'. one of the Londoners said.

We did! but a nice couple of lads.

Two weeks before we were due to play our F.A. Cup Fifth-Round match away at Everton, we had an away match at Man City. We drew 1-1. The thing I remember about it though was quite a few of the Spurs casuals were wearing Deer Stalker hats, which was the new craze going around the London casual scene. No other fans around the country seemed to have taken up this new look, it appeared that Londoners wanted to own an image that was different from the regular casual look that had swept the football terraces. It did look strange though seeing groups of Sherlock Holmes lookalikes in the pubs before matches.

Our F.A. Cup dream of winning the Cup on three consecutive occasions was still going strong, dispatching Southampton and West Brom in the previous rounds. But Everton away was going to be tough. They were beginning to put together the team that would be so strong in the mid-eighties, and they had already beaten us comfortably earlier in the season.

Into Liverpool at 11a.m. we headed up to The Stags Head. Joe the landlord was happy to see around ten Spurs fans giving him some welcome trade. Brent had come up with Charlie, Graham and old John, all from London, all good lads we had got to know, and of course Alex, who was eager to get a drink in. Brent had got us tickets and brought them with him. They were all for different sections of the ground as Spurs had been allocated The Park End, and blocks in the Bullens Road and the Top Balcony of The Main Stand, probably the highest seats in the country at the time. The tickets were split amongst us, most of us in the Top Balcony, with Richie opting for the one ticket in the shallow Park End terrace.

An abundance of ale had passed our lips, as we left the pub, Joe wished us well.

'Do the fuckin 'Blue Noses' lads, see you all next season'.

We made our way to the taxi rank, and then onwards to Goodison Park.

Heading high into the Top Balcony, our block of seats towards the main bulk of the Spurs support in the packed Park End. This one of our biggest away followings I had seen outside of London, almost 7,000 had made the trip. Below us the Scouse scallies were giving our support verbal's, the atmosphere was fraught and noisy. We looked down from our front row seats, some fifty feet above the packed Paddock below, Spurs fans singing 'Sign on, sign on, with a pen, in your hand, and you'll never get, a job, you'll never get a job, sign on, sign on' to the tune of Liverpool's famous anthem 'You'll never walk alone'. It is still sung today but seems less relevant than in the days of the Liverpool depression of the early eighties. The game hadn't kicked off yet but it was electric inside Goodison, coins can be seen going back and forth into each other's Paddock. Todays' CCTV would have had a field day.

The game kicked-off, we started singing in our block, the scousers below us looked up, probably just realising Spurs fans are above them. They started giving us stick, John is leaning over with his new head gear on, a deer stalker. He had liked the look of the Spurs boys in Manchester.

'Ya fuckan Scouse bastards', John screamed in between slurps from his can of Newcastle Brown Ale.

Everton scored, the Paddock below us exploded into a mass of writhing bodies, the Spurs fans in the Park End surged towards the fence. I don't think Richie would of been one of them. The Old Bill with their long batons moved in to try and quell the tense atmosphere, whacking people climbing the fences.

'Bastards', John shouted and throws his still half full can to the Everton terrace below.

'John' I shout, 'Calm down you could have killed someone'.

'Fuck em', John said, leering over and giving them abuse.

The scousers looked up giving John what for.

Everton scored the second, we knew then our glorious cup run was over.

The scousers were singing loud 'Tell me ma, me ma, I won't be home for tea, we goin to Wembley'. The whistle blew. We left the rejoicing Evertonians' and hit the street, past the pub on the corner which was packed with their mob in full force. I wondered how many had even been to the match, if they had they weren't interested in celebrating their victory, more interested in banging knuckles on heads. We stood at the bus stop, I thought back four months earlier to the black lad running through Stanley Park, wondering if he had made the return trip.

John, Phil, Pete and I waited for the bus not saying much as skirmishes went on around us. Then out of the corner of my eye I saw a mob heading in our direction. I felt the knot again in my stomach as you wonder how the next thirty seconds will pan out. They went to John, my heart sank.

'Come up from London mate?', the leader enquires. John went white with fear.

'Na I'm from Sunderland, support Everton', John said.

'Yer a fuckan Cockney, I know you are by that fuckan hat yer got on', Scouser said.

Get out of this pickle Sherlock Holmes, I was thinking.

'Anyway, you were up above us in the ground, I saw yer', the Scouser said,

'No, not me mate', John pleaded.

'Gizzes yer hat'.

'Why?', John asked.

'Look I know your Spurs so I'm having it as a souvenir'.

With that, the Scouser took the hat and smacked John in the mouth, which busted John's lip open.

The Scousers walked off, one proudly wearing his newly acquired head gear.

We had no interest of intervening into a fight. We would of all been given a good hiding as more Scousers would have joined in. John had got off lucky only getting one smack.

'Stupid fucking hat, you know the Scousers don't wear them', I said to John.

John mumbled through his ever-growing lip.

What we did know was that the season was all but done, and it was only February.

Grange Hill and The Irishman

In 1978 a kids' programme hit our screens, Grange Hill. It was set in a London Secondary School about the pupils, teachers and what went on in and out of school. Phil Redmond who devised it would later go on to have the hit soap opera 'Brookside'. What Redmond successfully did in Grange Hill was to bring notice to issues not seen on a kids' TV programme before, like alcohol and drug abuse. Though I was seventeen at the time of its launch, I became an avid viewer for the first couple of years, watching the lead, 'Tucker Jenkins' up to no good with his scams and bending school rules, but a loveable character all the same. As the years past I would dip in and out of watching Grange Hill but would see enough to know the latest characters.   In 1983 I knew the main character was now 'Zammo', who had taken over from 'Tucker'. The other leading role was 'Stewpot', the two of them up to know good. Forgive me if you haven't a clue what I'm on about, but for millions of teenage kids it was a not to be missed show.

On a sunny day on Monday April 4th Richie, Karen and I took our usual places on The Shelf. We had come up from Brighton on the morning, along with Phil, Pete and Dave, having stayed there on the Saturday and Sunday night. Now taking in the much-anticipated game against Arsenal at home on the Easter Monday.

At Brighton, Dave as usual had very little money and what he had was spent on ale, leaving him to find the cheapest digs possible. The rest of us found a decent hotel while Dave found a cheap place which cost three quid a night. After a good night out in Brighton, which covered up the shit Spurs performance of a 2-1 defeat several hours earlier against a poor Brighton team that would be relegated a month later, it was back to the hotel.

The following morning after a hearty full English we left the hotel and made our way to Dave's hotel to meet him. When we got there Dave wasn't about, so we went inside to what looked like a very basic hotel. I went to the reception and asked if a Dave Jacklyn had stayed.

'Room two', came the reply, 'You can go up if you want'.

I made my way to room two, the door was ajar, but I still knocked, walking into a large room where Dave was getting up, he surrounded by six other guys all getting up too. The room had around eight beds. The other clients looked like a good wash wouldn't have gone amiss, some already swigging from their whisky bottles.

'Thought you were meeting us outside?', I said.

'I would of, but I didn't dare sleep with all these piss heads in the room, I only nodded off an hour ago'.

No wonder it was only three quid, and even at that price he was robbed!

We were on The Shelf early for the Arsenal game, it was Karen's first big derby so I wanted to make sure she could see. You would usually get the younger fans in at this time, an hour or so before Kick-off, the older blokes still in the pubs. The Park Lane End housing the Arsenal fans were giving us the usual banter, and us giving it back.

The Park Lane section nearest The Shelf was still quite sparse, enough room for some Arsenal fans to sit on the crush barriers, all in their designer tracksuits. Suddenly a shout from the back of The Shelf went up.

'There's fucking Stewpot off Grange Hill'.

As it was still a youthful Spurs crowd on The Shelf, they all seemed to know who he was.

'He's a fucking Gooner', another shouted.

'We hate Grange Hill, we hate Grange Hill, we are the Grange Hill haters' the cry went up.

Stewpot looked up at The Shelf knowing he had been clocked.

'Stewpot, Stewpot you're a cunt, Stewpot you're a cunt. The Shelf sang.

Stewpot and his mates looked embarrassed.

'Stewpot, Stewpot you are dead, Stewpot you are dead'.

That was the final straw. Stewpot shuffled his way along into the more populated centre section of the Park Lane End.

243

In 1978 the 5-0 home defeat to Arsenal was a bitter pill to swallow, but this game went someway to erasing that memory. We murdered them 5-0.

'Glory, Glory, Hallelujah' the crowd sung. The highlight of what had been an average season up till then ended with a tremendous final month of form, winning six, drawing one, and only losing away to Birmingham, putting us on the verge of getting into one of the U.E.F.A. Cup spots. The final match at home to Stoke meant a Spurs win would give us fourth spot and qualification.

The only downside of the match was Glenn Hoddle had said that this would be his final game for Spurs as he fancied playing abroad.

After Ossie and Ricky had come to Spurs every club seemed to jump on the bandwagon, foreigners were cheaper to buy than the equivalent British players, but a lot of them were rubbish and weren't as good as some of our reserves, but Hoddle wanted to go the other way onto foreign soil to try his luck.

We beat Stoke quite comfortably 4-1 to secure our European slot, but what stood out most from the game was the support Hoddle got in the final fifteen minutes. A small group on The Shelf started chanting 'Don't Go Hoddle, Don't Go Hoddle, Don't go Hoddle, Don't Go. (to the tune of Auld Lang Syne). It was quickly picked up by the rest of The Shelf and within a minute The Park Lane and Paxton End were singing, it was reverberating around White Hart Lane. It was loud and went on for ten minutes till the final whistle.

Let's be honest, Glenn Hoddle is possibly the most gifted player to ever wear the Spurs shirt, so we weren't going to let him go without a fight. At the final whistle Hoddle waved at all four corners with tears rolling down his face and then left the field. Would we ever see him again?

A few days later on TV, the reporter said Glenn Hoddle has signed a new Spurs contract, with Hoddle adding.

'It's my club, the team I supported as a kid and have been privileged to have played for for eight years. Can I thank the Spurs crowd for helping me make my mind up with their support last Saturday'.

Of course, he undoubtedly would have received a big pay rise to have changed his mind, but I'm a football romantic and maybe that outpouring of love to one of the Spurs greats was the difference, only Hoddle knows that.

As it was the last game of the season we all headed up to the West End for a night around the bars of Piccadilly and Leicester Square, but before that we headed out of Kings Cross to a little back street pub, a pub we would often go to after a mid-week match to fill in time before the midnight train back North. As we stepped inside the pub at around 6p.m. it was already busy with mainly pissed up Irishmen already in song. We managed to get a few seats around a large table, the rest of the lads stood near the bar.

'Where ya been?', a drunken Irish voice slurred in our direction.

'To see Spurs', Phil piped up.

A drunken smile looked at us as he slowly lifted his measure of Whisky to his lips, almost missing his mouth, he was well oiled.

We talked at our table, Phil, Col, John, Harry and me. Dave and Richie looked on, us hardly being able to hear our conversation due to the noise of the Irish. Out of nowhere the same Irishman shouted across the table, his gaze directed at Phil.

'You there, you there'.

Phil looked at him, 'Me?'

'Yeah you, how about me and you have a fight?, I'll fight ya for a pound'.

'What'! Phil stunned at what he'd heard. 'I don't want to give you a fight', Phil said.

'Come on we'll fight for a pound', then have a drink together'.

The Irishman is keen, he's about sixty-five, quite slender and obviously pissed.

'A pound, we'll fight outside then have a drink'.

'Gan on Phil, you'll take him easy'. Harry laughing. Phil was still smiling but a bit embarrassed.

John puts his tenpenneth in.

'Gan on Phil are you a moth or what'. This was John's new saying. If you're a moth you weren't very good or brave, I think it was a Sunderland saying, Harry would say it, but Richie never did.

The Irishman is still waiting for his answer, his glazed eyes looking at Phil.

'I'm not interested in fighting you', Phil declared.

'Fuckan moth'. John says.

The Irishman pulled himself from his chair, teetering on his feet. 'Come on it's only a pound'. The Irishman turned round looking at his cronies saying, 'he won't fight me for a pound'.

'A pound its only a pound'. He was so unsteady you could have almost blown him off his feet.

'I'm not fucking fighting you for a pound, will you fuck off'. Phil was getting annoyed.

'Feck you then, it was only a pound'. The Irishman finally gives up.

We left the pub, heading to the West End, Phil getting the piss taken out of him.

Football on TV and Geordies

The following season would yet again be mediocre in the league for Spurs. A disappointment after finishing so well in the previous season, so same old Tottenham, building us up only to let us down.

There was something new at Tottenham though in 1983, it would be the first time we would wear shirt sponsorship, albeit not until December, Holsten would be emblazed on our kit for the next twelve years. It wasn't something I liked, but by 1983 most clubs had kit sponsorship, so it was inevitable. The upside was it would bring in the cash to buy top players. To get Gary 'Shaky' Stevens from Brighton as our main purchase was disappointing, but to be fair he did okay, without being brilliant.

Shaky did star and score in the first live TV match when Spurs played Nottingham Forest at The Lane. I didn't go to the game, it seemed stupid to do the five-hundred-mile round trip when I could sit at home. Nowadays it's the norm to travel hundreds of miles to see your team in the flesh when on TV.

I wasn't sure what to expect watching a game on TV that wasn't the Cup Final or England v Scotland, but I got comfortable on the settee in anticipation. My dad had been to the Workingmen's Club, had his Sunday lunch and was soon retiring to bed for his usual couple of hours of sleep, so it would be a quiet afternoon.

As it was the first live league match on TV I wasn't sure how many would turn up for the match, Spurs had put entertainment on in the guise of Chas and Dave with a stage built in a section of the Park Lane End.

By kick-off over 30,000 were in attendance, which would be our average gate that season. The one thing that was evident throughout the game from watching it at home was that the Spurs crowd were making themselves heard and most of the chants were aimed solely at our enemy four miles down the road. The Shelf Side could be heard loud and clear as they took full advantage of having no censorship, they could slag off Arsenal unmercifully without it being omitted.

To be fair I enjoyed my first experience of live league football, but it was no substitute for watching Spurs in the flesh. Anyone who says its better watching football on TV hasn't been to a game. You miss the banter, the noise, even the smell, everything in fact, but most of all it's when you score, you can't replicate that joy you share with your fellow supporters, people you don't know but feel what you feel, you are as one. Running around your living room isn't quite the same as being there. But I did run around my living room twice as we defeated Forest and the boy 'Shaky Stevens' did well.

The only good thing about watching a live game on TV was you couldn't bump into the Geordies, who were a law unto themselves. They were on the up soon after Kevin Keegan signed for them, which in turn gave the whole club a new lease of life and none more so than their away following.

As I said earlier Newcastle have always had a good away following but now the numbers were up dramatically. Richie and I would still plot how to hopefully avoid the marauding Magpies, but on occasions it was unavoidable.

Coming back from watching Spurs in the Midlands, Phil, Pete, Rich and I had to make a change at Sheffield onto one of those three carriage commuter trains to take us as far as York. We had boarded but there had been a delay, some technical hitch. We sat in the deserted front carriage and were joined by Mel and Steve the two Liverpool fans from York, they had been watching the Reds and had got off at Sheffield to get fish and chips and then joined us. We were the only ones in the front carriage but that would soon change when that unmistakable chant started ringing around the station platform 'Newcastle, Newcastle, Newcastle, New-cas-tle'. Our hearts sank.

' Or Shit It's the Mags', I said to the rest.

We still had another ten minutes delay.

'They going to know about this train' I said.

A minute later you could hear them boarding at the far end of the train.

'Geordie boys we are ere, shag your women and drink your beer', they sang.

Like flies to shit they had to head to our carriage, around fifteen of them. I wasn't even sure where they had been, and wasn't interested, I just wished they weren't on this train.

'Howld on a minute', one shouted. 'Ar can smell fish and chips in ere'.

Mel and Steve still eating, they turned sheepishly.

'Ere man, gizza chip?', Geordie said.

Steve held out a single chip reluctantly.

'What tha fucks that', as he looked at Steve with menace.

'Ar want a fuckan handful man', the Geordie shouted in Steve's direction. Steve handed him the remaining contents of his bag of chips.

'Have them mate'

'Hey, as not ya mate', Geordie says as he pushed the chips into his fat mouth.

Another Geordie was sat across from us, glaring.

'Where ya been?'.

'To see Liverpool' Mel piped up.

249

'And ar ye fuckan Tottenham fans?', as he looked at Phil's Supporters Club badge which lay on his Tottenham jumper with the chicken emblem. The Geordie looking at the jumper and in particular the ridiculous emblem, he must of thought he's a Spurs fan who's other interest is looking after poultry.

'Yeah we Spurs', Phil said.

'Ar fuckan hate Cockneys me, anyway this fuckan trains gannan to York, London's the other fuckan way'.

'We live in the North', Richie said.

'Where ye from?', the Geordie picked up on Richie's Sunderland accent.

'Boldon', Rich using the tried and tested Middle ground between Newcastle and Sunderland, Richie's got away with it.

'Ow, when's this fuckan train gannan, ar want to get back for fuckan last orders?', one Geordie shouted.

He then got up and walked to the front of the train, slid the door open and got into the driver's seat.

'Ow the fuck do ya start this cunt?'

'Sit down Tommy lad', another Geordie tried to get his mate out the driver's cab.

'If ar can get this fucka gannan we'll get home faster' Tommy shouted back. It was comical watching them.

'It'll not start Tommy lad, ya need one of them fuckan handles that gan on the gears, tha drivers only got them'.

'Fucking cunt', Tommy shouted.

I honestly believed if the handle or whatever you needed to get the train going was there, we would have been on our way to York slightly earlier than planned.

A few of the Geordies began to talk to us in the usual Geordie aggressive manner.

'I divn't nar why ya follow a fuckan Cockney team when ya live in the North' one remarked.

I tried to explain to him my background on how Spurs are my team, but it didn't interest him.

'Here's tha fuckan driver, bout time', Tommy shouted in an aggressive manner towards the driver.

'Howay man get the cunt gannan', Tommy pleaded.

'OK son no need for that language', the driver said.

The conductor walked through the door 'Tickets please?'.

'Aye, ye can fuck off a narl'.

The conductor turned round and hastily retreated. The train burst into life as the the cry went up, 'Newcastle, Newcastle, Newcastle, New-cas-tle'.

Phil who was sat next to me suddenly joined in with the chanting, but not singing Newcastle. He started chanting 'Sunderland, Sunderland, Sunderland'. I looked at him,

'What you doing?', shocked at what Phil was singing, had he gone mad.

The Geordies stopped singing, you could hear a pin drop, well you could have if the train wasn't moving.

'Who the fucks singing that?'.

The Geordie didn't even want to say the word Sunderland, they felt it so beneath them. All I was thinking was Phil had blown any chance of getting off this train unscathed.

'We hate Cockneys, and we hate Cockneys' the chant started.

'We'll be arriving in York in the next few minutes', the conductor shouted, he was probably as eager as us to get rid of the Geordies. The train entered the station. Phil stood up.

'I'll have that badge', Geordie said, looking at Phil's Spurs badge on his jumper.

'What?', Phil asked.

The Geordie leaned over and yanked at Phil's jumper, the badge was pulled off along with a square of Phil's chicken jumper. It would be funny if it wasn't for the circumstances, the chicken jumper's final day I thought.

Phil looked down at the three-inch square hole, not quite comprehending the scale of the damage to his beloved jumper.

The train pulled into York and came to a halt. I stood up and felt the thud of a fist into my mouth, my lip exploded. I look at the instigator, already feeling my lip starting to swell.

'What's that for?'.

'Cause you're a Cockney bastard'.

What could we do.

We jumped off the train and started to walk up the platform almost expecting to be attacked, but the Geordies saw a group of Leeds fans on the next platform who were giving them a bit of lip, so they ran up the platform in pursuit.

My ever-growing lip was sore.

I caught up to Phil and smiled in a fat lip way and looked at the jumper.

'You'll have to bin it', I said.

'I might be able to repair it' Phil said.

The jumper was never seen again, but Phil kept it for posterity of days gone by or was it in the hope his chicken jumper was maybe a one off, and could one day be worth money, not quite a 'Banksy' though.

Feyenoord

Although 1983-84 was nothing special in the league, it was more than made up for in the U.E.F.A. Cup.

Richie, John and Harry had gone to the first European away game in Drogheda, yet again another Irish team. I had decided to miss it as I totally expected us to get through and wanted to see Spurs at a more prestigious fixture in Europe.

My wishes realised, the next draw was made. I was delighted to be paired with Feyenoord.

The trip to the Netherlands lived up to expectations, it was to become my favourite away trip, but also one of the scariest. At the first leg at The Lane we outclassed the Dutch, beating them 4-2 with Hoddle at his best, the ageing Yohan Cruyff now looking on probably thinking I used to be that good. It was like one true great handing the baton to another one. Hoddle was that good that night.

Phil, Pete, Richie, Harry and I made the trip to Holland. Booked on a Monday night sailing from Felixstowe, and as usual we had no match tickets, still an after-thought. Getting tipsy and losing on the roulette table, we slumped down on any available benches or settees until we arrived in Rotterdam. We had all agreed that we wouldn't be staying in Rotterdam for the entire trip as it looked so industrialised compared to the cultural city of Amsterdam.

We left for the fifty-mile train ride up to Amsterdam, deciding to stay for two nights, Tuesday night and Thursday night, with a night planned in Rotterdam on the match day, the Wednesday.

The five of us descended on the hotel Phil and I had stayed at two years previous for the Ajax tie, there was little trouble getting us all in, three in one room, Phil and Pete in another.

I had been on holiday in the summer to Amsterdam, so I'd had a good look around the city instead of just drinking in bars. I could give the rest of the lads a good insight as to where the good bars were in the city.

Once the bags were dropped off we went for food, and yes a drink. In fact we went from bar to bar until we were magnetically drawn to the red-light area, don't ask me how!

'Do you fancy seeing a live sex show?', Phil asked the rest of us in a knowledgeable way, like he had been to one of those kind of shows before.

'How much will that cost?', Harry inquisitively asked Phil.

'We'll get a good deal', Phil said.

This emphatically convinced me that Phil had been down this route before.

We walked down a street which is adorned with ladies sat in their fluorescent lit windows trying to entice any Phil, Rich or Harry. We then saw a guy in a doorway looking like a pimp. We approached him, Phil leading the way.

'Hey guys you want to see a live show?', the pimp said. 'Only twenty-five Guilders each'. About seven quid at the time.

'Not at that price', Phil said confidently.

'OK twenty, I can't go any lower'.

The deal was struck.

We all entered what looked like a small cinema, rows of seats with a small stage which was spotlighted. We sat in a row along with about twenty others. We felt we had an excuse being there, all lads together like a stag night, but the rest were sitting sporadically around the venue looking sleazy. Harry got up from his seat, we were sat around ten rows from the front.

'Where you going?', Pete asked Harry.

'Down to the front row', Harry chirped up.

The dirty little bastard we all thought, we stayed put.

The spotlight brightened and on walked a guy and a slim looking girl who to be honest was quite plain. Their clothes were discarded in the blink of an eye, within seconds they were having sex. After a few minutes they changed positions, all very mechanical. Their positions changed several times then a voice came over the tannoy, 'The live sex show is over'. We got up.

'Harry are you coming'.

Maybe saying that was quite apt!

'Did you enjoy that H?'.

A smile from Harry said it all. We left and headed for more drinks.

By 10.30p.m. we were all pissed, maybe not Richie though. Harry left the final bar we were in, a cellar bar near to the hotel where we were staying. Harry had crawled up the stairs, got his head out the door and threw up. I had gone to check if he was ok and saw the contents of Harry's stomach on the pavement, which surprisingly looked like a pizza. His vomit was in a perfect circle. If you had walked past it you would of said 'Why has a person dropped a pizza and not picked it up', such was its authenticity.

Harry went to bed, we stayed out. I only lasted two more drinks, departed and hit the sack, an hour later with the room spinning I filled the wash basin with sick, which amazingly Harry cleaned up for me the next morning, good old Harry, what a diamond.

Waking with a thumping headache, we got up early, breakfast for some, then went back to the Central Station for the train to Rotterdam. We hadn't got match tickets so that was our next aim as well as booking a room near to the station.

My headache subsided as we entered Rotterdam, my mind skipped back to 1974 and the riots of the UEFA Cup Final at the same stadium that we were hoping to get into, providing we could get a ticket.

Leaving the station we walked up a tree lined street with large grand houses on either side, after no more than four hundred yards we saw that one of those houses was a hotel.

'This do?'.

'Yeah', came the resounding answer.

To be honest we weren't too fussed on luxury, as long as it was clean. The five of us entered and were met by the owner who soon picked up we were English.

'Hey, you're here for de match?', the hotelier asked.

I love the Dutch accent when they speak English, they talk like they are so inquisitive, like our ex-manager Martin Jol used to.

'Five of you, no problem, do you want a drink now?' he asked. Every country must think all English people are beer guzzlers.

'Might as well', Pete said.

Five beers were drunk, then we were shown to our rooms.

The hotel was just what we hoped for, clean, not pricey and an owner who was friendly and hospitable. We returned from our rooms after dropping off the bags and went back into the bar.

'We haven't got tickets', we stated.

'You haven't got tickets?

Our host seemed surprised.

'Go to one of the bars near the ground, they will sort you'.

The owner told us which tram to get to the ground which was known as 'De Kiup', which I believe translates to 'The Tub'.

'Hey when you get back tonight the bar will be open for you'.

'Thanks', we replied.

Setting off early afternoon for the stadium the tram took us about five miles from Rotterdam Central, passing the port where huge container vessels and cranes towered into the sky, it looked a very working-class area.

leaving the station near to the ground, it was quiet, no sign that there would be 45,000 fans descending on it in a matter of a few hours.

Venturing into the first bar we saw we asked for tickets just as the hotelier had advised us to do.

'Ye sure, five English tickets?', the bar owner asked.

' Are they for the Spurs end?' Phil asked.

'Ye, for sure'.

Tickets were around four quid each. With tickets purchased we left the bar and headed down a side street to another bar around half a mile from the ground. A few Feyenoord fans were in and we were soon chatting with them. They asked how many Spurs fans would be over, we weren't sure but 2,000 was an estimate. We all hoped there wouldn't be the troubles of '74.

Just after 6p.m. we said our goodbyes to the Dutch lads and headed to the ground, it was getting crowded on arrival and the English we did see seemed to be behaving, the atmosphere was good.

We moved towards our entrances at one end of the stadium, security was okay and not heavy handed. There was the usual banter from our fans ringing round 'If it wasn't for the British, you'd be Krauts.' The Dutch were taking it in their stride.

We entered the ground around forty minutes before kick-off, up a flight of stairs and into a section of terrace which was behind the goal. The Dutch end identical, both holding around 3,000 supporters in either end, the rest of the stadium was seated on three tiers, in the shape of a bowl. It was a decent stadium but open, apart from where the players came out, this had a small roof which covered the back twenty rows of seats. The overhang of the upper seats over the centre section was the only other part of the ground where you would of kept dry on a wet day. But saying that, once Feyenoord fans got behind their team it was an impressive noise, 'Feyenoord, Feyenoord' would boom out.

Our section half filled with another couple of hundred fans sat in the seats near us.

My mind once again went back to nine years previous, remembering the bodies hurtling down the steps after being battered by riot police, possibly the very same area where we were now standing.

The opposite end terrace was still quite spartan of Dutch fans, but as we watched we saw a sudden influx of supporters coming onto the Dutch terrace and then a fight broke out. It soon became apparent these were Spurs hooligans, you can't call them supporters. The chant 'Tottenham, Tottenham' could easily be heard from the far end. A union jack flag was held aloft, maybe a hundred had converged into a knot in the middle of the terrace. The Dutch stood around the Spurs fans, staying at arm's length.

Make no mistake this looked planned to try and take the Dutch end. The supporters in our section were on the whole totally against what they had seen, though there were a few who applauded the actions shouting to get stuck into them, the vast majority more concerned we might get kicked out of Europe. The riot police began to walk from our end to the Dutch end. We all thought they were going to go in heavy handed and pull out the Spurs instigators, but it didn't happen. The Dutch fans began moving into their section enmasse until the hundred Spurs were now totally outnumbered, then the Dutch waded in on all four sides. Even from our vantage point a hundred and fifty yards away you could see it was vicious, bodies were being thrown down the terraces. We later found out knives had been used from both factions, more than thirty people were stabbed. I've watched the incident again on 'You Tube' and it looked even worse than I remembered.

From our distant view point we all thought this was going to spill over to other parts of the stadium and that's exactly what happened. To our right in the lower seats in the side paddock a small group of Spurs fans who were sat amongst Feyenoord fans were attacked. Seat bases were pulled from their framework and then used as weapons, Spurs fans fled onto the perimeter around the pitch, but the Dutch followed with seats in hands, Spurs fans running towards the corner where there was an exit. I watched transfixed, the build up to the start of the match now irrelevant. The running Spurs fans now surrounded, the Dutch didn't hold back smashing the seat bases over the unfortunate Spurs fans, as they fell they were then continually clubbed. The riot police arrived, long batons in hand, wading into the already bloodied bodies of the few Spurs supporters and they continued to beat them, it was horrific.

We won the match 2-0, the team were brilliant, our section of supporters behaved impeccably and backed the team. The team came down to our support at the end, and we gave them a thunderous ovation. The team left the pitch, the Spurs flags were taken down by our fans, but now we had to face the Dutch outside.

'It's going to be dodgy outside, we need to stick together', I told the rest.

We walked down the steps to the exit, where we were let out at the same time as the Dutch, we were only delayed by our celebrating with the team.

Out onto the street we saw the scale of our welcome, above us to the right was an elevated walkway which was at a standstill. The Dutch were watching and waiting, looking down on the away fans exit.

We began our walk leaving the sanctum of the stadium, I didn't say a word to the rest, and they thought the same, don't speak, don't give the Dutch the knowledge we're English.

Some Spurs fans with scarves on were soon set upon, the Dutch like rabid dogs' teared into them, we kept walking, our aim was to get to the station. The five of us were still together, Dutch were all around us, talking behind us, we not knowing what they were saying made you paranoid that an attack was imminent, but we kept going and got to the station which was packed.

I couldn't see any Spurs fans, maybe they were like us, keeping quiet.

A train pulled in, we all squeezed on, still not a word. I looked down at Harry and noticed his jacket had a cloth badge with the club crest and 'Tottenham Hotspur' emblazed underneath. I reached for it and ripped it off, Harry didn't say a word, he knew the possible circumstances if it was spotted.

We reached Rotterdam Central and got off, a fight broke out just behind us. The Dutch police stormed in, baton wielding, as the fighting escalated. All I was thinking was 'get me out of here, we've come to see a game of football'.

The five of us entered a darkened subway, the only ones who go that way, at least we can speak to each other.

'Sorry about the badge', I said to Harry.

'If you hadn't done it, I would of.' Harry declared.

A shout went up at the far end of the subway from where we had come from, Dutch voices a hundred yards away. Are they shouting at us? We moved faster and got to the hotel.

'Five beers please', only one other person was sat in the hotel bar.

'Hey guys it was a fucking bloodbath tonight', the owner said.

260

We turned and watched the news on TV, you didn't need to understand the Dutch language, the pictures said a thousand words. The news showed the end where the trouble started. It was even worse than I thought, the look of fear, the anger, the aggression, and finally you see bodies laid with knife wounds, blood seeping uncontrollably from blood-soaked bodies. A person looking like he is giving another the kiss of life.
So sad!

We watched shocked, not saying anything until Pete shouted.

'Is it my round?'.

We looked at Pete, just as shocked at what he had said.

'Did I hear that right, Pete getting a round'. I said.

We break into laughter, maybe it was out of relief, we felt safe again, several beers and then to bed.

The following morning after a good breakfast we decided to go back to the stadium to have a look around, I don't know why, it was like we needed to see the scene of the horror we had all witnessed fifteen hours earlier. We all had the same thought we didn't want to leave Holland with negative thoughts from a country where we always felt friendliness.

We took the same route as the night before, it was a beautiful morning, late autumn sunshine, not a cloud in the sky. Passing a newsagent, Richie and I bought several Dutch papers which were emblazed with pictures of the night before, which told their own stories. I also bought the Daily Mirror which only briefly gave note to the violence, concentrating more on the excellent result, but it did mention that there were over thirty stabbings, seventeen being Spurs fans, the rest were Dutch, so how can anyone say we didn't play our part in the trouble.

The stadium was quiet when we arrived, our intention was to take a few photos, but we soon noticed a gate open,

261

possibly used by the stadium's ground staff. We entered the open gate, no one was about, within a couple of minutes we were stood on the same terrace we had stood the night before. It seemed so calm and serene. I looked to my right where the Spurs fans had been chased in the corner.

'Come on we'll go down', I said to the rest.

We went down the stairs and climbed onto the perimeter track and headed to where the Spurs fans were brutally beaten by seat bases, followed by a beating by the Dutch police. I picked up one of the broken seats that were scattered around and couldn't believe the weight of the solid oak seat. These were the old-style seats from pre-war when stadiums were being established and the materials used were made to last. I held it up and thought of the Spurs fan who was getting it smashed over his head and face. I then noticed the pool of blood where the incident took place.

We jumped over the advertising hoardings surrounding the pitch and were soon in the centre circle, perusing, thinking god we're on the very same pitch where we were watching our heroes only the night before.

The Dutch end where the violence took place was closed off, possibly even a murder scene. We were still unsure if anyone had died.

'Shame we don't have a ball', Richie said.

'We'll make do with a beer can', Pete said.

'Two aside then', I added.

'Where's Harry?'

Harry appeared with a different jumper on, gloves, and a hat, all items he had found discarded by Dutch fans.

'I'm taking them home, they're better than what I've got', Harry said.

We played our match for a full twenty minutes, two aside one in goal on Feyenoord's pitch, one of the best stadiums in

Europe at that time, how surreal did that feel. Richie filmed much of it as well on his new video camera. Eventually we left the stadium and headed back to the hotel to pack our bags. A few beers with our hotelier friend, we said our farewell to another great hotel stay, it was a Euro trip to remember, that's for sure.

Rochdale and All Seaters

Having missed the first live game, the home match versus Nottingham Forest I was determined to get to our first away live match, which just happened to be Man Utd at Old Trafford, a game I always looked forward to attending.

There were games that I always checked when the fixtures came out, Arsenal, Merseyside and Manchester were top of my list. The game at Old Trafford was a week or so before Christmas, a Friday night and an early 7.15p.m. kick-off. Col decided to drive down, so with a full car we hit the road to Manchester.

Once there we parked up at Old Trafford Cricket Ground, what was noticeable was the lack of hustle and bustle that you normally got when going to Man Utd. It was strange, it was going to be interesting to know what the gate would be. It was still too early to know if live football would affect attendances having only had a few live games so far. United were still pulling in 45,000 plus crowds, but what was certain was this game wasn't going to see that sort of figure, and we didn't know what sort of a following we would have there.

Not having time to go for a beer we walked up to the ground and entered the solitary open turnstile at the away section of the Scoreboard End. No tickets required tonight, once inside there was hardly a person under the stand. We

263

were all thinking 'Is our car load the total Spurs support'. We walked through the tunnel towards the away terrace. One copper greeted us just as we emerged into the glow of the floodlights.

'Got no fucking telly's in London?', he said sarcastically.

We smiled and kept walking to be met by the Mancs in the corner shouting 'Come in a taxi, did you come in a taxi?', meaning our support was small. But the support grew and by kick-off we had a good 800/1,000 in attendance. Man Utd fans couldn't say much as the gate figure was only 33,000, some 15,000 down on average.

Spurs wearing shirt advertising for the first time ever, 'Holsten' emblazed across their chests, the club finally succumbing to the inevitable, the famous Lilywhite shirt was being sold to the highest bidder.

Even with the quieter atmosphere we went on to lose 4-2. We got out of the ground quickly. The police hardly kept us in for more than ten minutes, it was just after 9.30p.m. and we were back in the car.

'Fancy stopping off on the way back for a couple of pints, there's a live boxing fight on TV tonight at about 10p.m.?'Col asked us.

'Yeah', we were all happy to go for it.

Once out of Manchester we drove a short distance and dropped into Rochdale, stopping at the first pub we saw. The five of us walked into the small pub. Three cowboys were sat at the bar, no one else was in the pub. We all looked at the three locals, cowboy hats, neckerchiefs, and check shirts. I'd heard about the Rochdale Cowboys, I wouldn't have believed it if I hadn't seen it for myself. They were only missing their Colt Forty-Fives.

'Yes, sir what can I get you?' The barmen asked Col.

'Where's your telly?' Col asked, even before ordering a drink.

The cowboys looked round, if they'd had guns, they would have been drawn.

'Telly lads?, I don't have one', he apologetically said.

We turned to leave.

'Hold on boys'. The owner walked over to the stairs.

'Son are you watching the telly?'

'No', came the reply.

'Well get it down here quick'.

Admittedly the picture wasn't perfect, but we couldn't leave now after he had gone to so much trouble. The British fighter won his title, we drank up and scooted out of town, with only the tumbleweed following.

As we headed towards 1984, commercialism wasn't slowing down, clubs were trying their best to rinse every fan of their spare money. On average to watch football at that time you would be paying two to three quid to stand on the terraces and about double that for a seat. With attendances dropping year on year, mainly down to hooliganism, it would be Coventry City who would go against its supporters wishes and make Highfield Road into an all-seater ground. Coventry at that time were averaging only 13,000, with the majority standing, but by making the ground all-seater they could gain more money through the turnstiles. Their attendances dropped even more, but costs were covered by the extra revenue of having seats only priced twice as much as the standing. The loyal fans of Coventry had no choice, you either paid it or didn't bother going. Coventry lost around 1,000 fans but felt it worthwhile. Ten years later every club had all-seater stadiums in the top division.

I had got to know Rob, a Spurs fan who lived in Wolverhampton but originally lived in Bishop Auckland, only three miles from where I lived. He would often come back to his Northeast roots to see his family. I would bump into him on occasions when out and about around the pubs, he said he was back at his mams for a few weeks and was going to drive down to Coventry for the Spurs match, if I wanted a lift down to give him a ring, I didn't need to call, 'put me down for two places', Karen would also travel.

With an early start, we were in Coventry for 11a.m. Rob said he knew a good pub and was meeting a dozen Midland Spurs. Once in the pub the Midland Spurs showed up soon after, all lads around there late twenties, and good lads. Quite a few I recognised from my many away days with Spurs, so the banter was good, as well as the beer.

Twenty minutes before kick-off we made our way to the away section of Highfield Road, which was ticket only and it was full! Spurs had been given 2,000 tickets in the 20,000 all seater ground, many of the seats just bolted to the old terraces. The ground held over 35,000 a couple of years earlier, but Coventry knew how to capitalise on dwindling attendances to still get a decent income.

We headed to the ticket office and purchased a group of tickets which were on the same side as where our fans were housed, but we were amongst the Coventry fans. After taking our places with the home fans, we settled and watched the game amongst many empty seats, the gate figure a little over 12,000.

The Coventry fans knew we were Spurs but nothing was said, that is until we scored, when a fight started to our right behind the goal. Around fifty Spurs fans were taken out and were lead around the perimeter. As they passed us some of the Coventry fans were giving them lip, and before we knew it some of the Spurs fans jumped into the side attacking the Coventry fans, who in turn started on our group as they knew we were Spurs. We now had a handful of Spurs wading into the Coventry fans, people were falling over seats, I was trying to keep Karen safe, pushing anyone who got close out of the way. I wasn't bothered if they ended up falling around me, it was just instinct to keep your girlfriend safe. The stewards ran in and split our group from the Coventry fans, who were now giving us stick for something that started out of nothing.

At the end of the match as we were about the leave when we were stopped by the police who said they were keeping us in as Coventry were waiting outside. I couldn't believe around fifteen of us were locked in, luckily they only held us for ten-minutes. We won 4-2 but my thoughts for all-seater stadiums which I never wanted had diminished even more, they were a danger especially in these times of trouble, getting out of the way of any flare ups was difficult compared to the terraces.

Within a couple of years though fan power at Coventry got the club to reintroduce standing and a 7,000 section of terrace was re-opened.

Whether Coventry's all-seater stadium was the instigator to the football casual beginning to use seats to watch their clubs I'm not sure, but the hooligan firms would go into a seated section of the ground and their counterparts would do the same, it was a way for fans to get at each other that the fenced terraced pens wouldn't allow.

The days of mobile phones were still years away so gangs would organise in other ways, going to England matches was one way, where rivals would discuss future dust-ups, exchange phone numbers and predetermined meet ups would happen.

Football violence was becoming sickening, blades were being used more prevalently, with West Ham's Inter City Firm being one of the most feared hooligan gangs. They had big numbers and were well organised to cause maximum mayhem. Cass Pennant, the now reformed general of the I.C.F. was someone I saw at White Hart Lane earlier that season, of course I didn't know who he was then. I was on The Shelf against the front wall looking down on the lower terrace in line with the eighteen-yard box. The Spurs mob were just below me goading the West Ham contingent in the Park Lane End. What I did notice below me were a group of really big black guys, not many, about ten of them, suddenly one of them throws his pint of beer in the air, 'a signal', all hell broke out, the black guys were piling into the Spurs fans. Some of the Spurs boys took a step back not interested. 'When the going gets tough'. Others went toe to toe, fists, kicks, go crashing into each other, I could watch in safety from my elevated view not more than twenty feet away. The Old Bill steamed in, crashing truncheons on heads, they pulled out the instigators and took them towards the Park Lane End. A huge cry of I-C-F rings out from the West Ham fans. I knew it was Pennant after reading part of his life story, and this was mentioned, just as I had watched it.

Anderlecht Away

Tottenham's league form was so erratic after Christmas, but not poor enough to get us into a relegation fight. It seemed once we had lost to Norwich in an F.A. Cup fourth round replay at Carrow Road, all our eggs were firmly into trying to win the UEFA Cup, a prestige trophy at the time, now known in its present guise of the Europa League. After

268

dispatching Feyenoord, we beat Bayern Munich, Austria Vienna and Hajduk Split in the Semi-Final. It was so enjoyable watching the European matches at The Lane under the lights. Richie always said the Semi-Final against Split was the best atmosphere he'd been in at The Lane, it was good, but I think the Final eclipsed it against Anderlecht.

The Final back then was held over two legs, the first of which we were delighted to see was away in Brussels. Only Richie and I travelled, although Percy was arriving on the Wednesday. The two of us travelled to Ostend by ferry arriving on the Monday night, soon finding a reasonable bed and breakfast.

The resort of Ostend was quiet, popular in the height Summer but in May there were few tourists. Once the bags were dropped off we went around a few bars, one to the next until we saw the red fluorescent lights around the windows, we just happened to have hit Ostend's Red-Light area. A few scantily clad girls were viewed through their windows before we made our way to a bar for what would be our last drink of the night. It was a quiet bar, maybe ten patrons including a couple of other Spurs fans.

We had seen around twenty Spurs supporters during our night out, all in high spirits but no issues with the locals. Then we heard the sirens of police cars or possibly ambulances, not being sure what the siren tones signified from the emergency services in Belgium, but what was happening sounded serious.

'Wonder what's going on?' I asked Richie.

'It will be a fight', Richie confidently said.

Just then a couple of Tottenham lads came into the bar seeing the two of us in Spurs jumpers.

'It's fucking going off down the road, some blokes been shot', he said to us.

'That's all we need', Rich said.

'If it's over football we will get kicked out of this competition', I said.

After what went on in Rotterdam six months earlier all eyes were on this match and how our near 7,000 fans were going to behave. We stayed for another drink to see if any news of the shooting came to the fore.

It wasn't long before the sad news came out that a Spurs supporter, aged twenty had been murdered by a single shot over a squabble with a local Belgium. I thought, as many other Spurs fans must of, 'Oh no here we go again'. I was worried that this could be the start of a tit for tat in wanting revenge, I hoped not.

An early rise and soon out the hotel, we headed to Ostend Railway Station to take the train to Brussels, arriving by noon, then asking for directions to the Anderlecht Stadium and soon pointed in its direction. The ground was in a really built-up area surrounded by elegant houses, it definitely looked prosperous. I bought an English paper, the headline, 'The murder of a young Spurs fan'. I read the article, it also stated no tickets would be sold on the day of the match. Being that this was the day before the match we hoped tickets could still be purchased as once again we had travelled without any.

The stadium on three sides was quite old fashioned but had a new main stand. Richie and I walked into the main entrance foyer where we were met by a suited gentleman.

'Hello, do you have any Spurs tickets left?' I asked.

'Of course, how many?' he said. It was music to our ears.

'Two', I said.

Percy had got a ticket off Brent's season ticket. The Belgian handed us our tickets, we paid, thanked him and left.

'How easy was that', I said to Rich.

At the end of the day they just wanted revenue. We wandered down the side of the new main stand and noticed a gate open. The two of us were soon inside the stadium, just like in Rotterdam. We wandered around the main stand but couldn't get on the pitch as it was being mowed, but we got a good look at where we would be stood the following evening. It was quite a traditional English style stadium. The end where the Spurs fans would be was a half-covered end with a seated section above, so we knew with 7,000 present we could make plenty of noise.

Richie had brought his video recorder with him, which was massive, but back then it was just your normal camcorder, nowadays you would film on a phone, but back then you had to lug a case around to carry it in. If you can remember an episode of 'Only Fools and Horses' where Del Boy buys a consignment of Russian DVD camcorders, that was how big it was. I wouldn't have lumped it around but I'm so pleased Richie did as he probably has the only footage of the match taken from the Spurs end during the game, Pictures, chants, the whole atmosphere of that Final, it's a unique insight of that match.

We left the stadium and looked for accommodation for two nights, but unfortunately everywhere seemed to have 'No Vacancies', Spurs supporters must have booked before arriving. We were all set to give up on Brussels to look elsewhere when bingo, we hit lucky.

'Have you any rooms?', I asked hopefully.

'Yes, yes, come', a lady invited us in. She showed us the room.

'Ok for you?', she asked.

It was a large room and to be honest quite dreary.

'Yeah, it will do', I told the landlady.

Richie nodded, as much to say it would do. To be honest we couldn't be arsed to look anymore. Two nights were booked at only eight quid each. We dropped the bags and looked more closely at the room.

'One bed Rich', I said.

'I did notice', Rich said.

Did the landlady think we were gay, she didn't ask if we wanted separate beds.

'I think we will get into it ok', Rich said.

He wasn't wrong, the bed was enormous, about seven feet long and nine feet wide. Like two doubles pushed together, but only one massive mattress and one headboard.

We left the hotel and went for a meal and a few beers but stayed near the hotel and kept a low profile, as more Spurs fans arrived by the hour. Sirens were constantly ringing out as the Tottenham invasion played its part in this.

Next morning we headed out the hotel as it was room only, getting breakfast at a café.

Before setting off from home we had arranged to meet Percy at the station that morning. It was a case of keeping an eye out in the hope of seeing Percy's distinct fuzzy hair coming out the station. We were confident of not missing him as long as we didn't drink too much while waiting, which was unlikely when in Richie's company.

Percy arrived at around 1p.m., a couple of hours later than scheduled.

'Have you got digs?' Percy asked.

'Yeah, we will get you in where we are staying', I said.

We set off, it was only five minutes' walk from the station. The landlady was in the foyer.

'Have you got another room?' I asked her.

'No, no, fully booked, no rooms,' she said in a stern voice.

'He can come in our room', I told her.

She looked surprised at what I was asking, another person to stay into our room. She must be thinking one bed, three lads, a gay orgy.

'Ok', she said.

It cost the equivalent of five quid to get Percy in.

'Percy you're in for a fiver', I shouted to him.

'That's not bad, only a fiver' Percy smiled.

We take Percy to the room.

'What do you think', I asked Percy.

'Where's me fucking bed then?', Percy perusing his gaze around the bedroom.

'That's it Percy', I said almost laughing.

'One fucking bed between us?', Percy said.

'Yeah, but it's big', I said.

'Aye, who cares, I'll be fucking pissed by the time I get in it', Percy declared.

Its early but we head towards the ground. It's swarming with Spurs supporters, every bar you passed there were songs and chants reverberating from the revelling Spurs fans. Hardly an Anderlecht supporter could be seen.

 The evening was damp after a mid-afternoon downpour which saw less fans on the streets, but as the rain relented more are hitting the streets. I hadn't seen any trouble but there was still the din of police sirens all around.

I asked Percy and Richie if they wanted to walk up the road to see if we could find a quieter bar, they were both happy to move on. We set off and have only walked a couple of hundred yards when I spot this bloke heading in our direction. He's an oldish man in his late sixties or early seventies, he's also got a cowboy hat on, as he got closer, I said to Percy.

'God, he looks like you Percy, only thirty years older'.

The old man had fuzzy blonde hair and a beard, another general cluster lookalike, and definitely a Percy lookalike.

'Any boozers up there?' Percy shouted.

I'm still smiling at the resemblance.

'Are you Tottenham?', the old man said.

'Yeah', we say in unison.

'Come, come with me'.

He leads us up a street to the Anderlecht Supporters Club. We go in, its small and homely not unlike the Spurs Supporters Club at Warmington House outside White Hart Lane. The old Belgian walked in nodding to everyone, they all nod back and greet him like he's one of their old boys, showing him respect, it was nice to see. He went to the bar.

'Three beers for my Tottenham friends'.

He's served straight away, we sit with him, Percy alongside like a long-lost son. Richie finished his beer and said he's off to do some filming and lugs his large holdall over his shoulder containing the massive cam-corder.

Percy is hammering down the Stella Artois and getting steadily pissed, though to be fair the beer was good in Belgium. After an hour we said our farewells and asked the old man to meet us at Tottenham for the return match. He said he couldn't make the second leg. We wished him well and set off to meet Richie who was still filming when we got there. The rain had now started again but the bars had spilt onto the streets. The atmosphere was more carnival than menacing, but a few Belgian women pass with fear on their faces, you don't notice it yourself when you are part of the party.

We left and entered the away turnstiles and headed to the top of the terrace so we were under the partial cover, mainly to keep Richie's camera dry. The end now looked bigger than when we were looking at it the previous day from the main stand. It was filling up nicely, but as we stood more towards the top corner it never got too full, meaning Richie could film more footage.

'Come on you Spurs, Come on you Spurs', the roar went up from the near 7,000 Spurs fans as the teams entered the pitch. Inside the ground everything was peaceful on the terraces, which was pleasing after our name was tarnished in Rotterdam.

The match kicked off and was fairly even, the atmosphere passionate. A corner to Spurs in front of our massed ranks, Paul Miller our centre half gets his head to it and the ball hits the back of the net, we erupt as one, unfortunately Richie's camera is in the holdall.

The second half and we were holding out under the expected pressure on our goal. Steve Perryman our skipper makes a rash tackle and is booked, meaning he misses the second leg. We are all gutted for our leader he's Tottenham through and through, we knew he would be sorely missed in the next meeting, his leadership qualities shine through every time he puts on the Lilywhite shirt.

Graham Roberts our defensive/midfield hard man would come to the fore. Roberts was a player who would give as much back as he took, his tackling would of suited the 60's/70's against the likes of Tommy Smith, Norman Hunter and all. Some of his challenges would make you wince, so God knows what the opposing players must of thought when they saw him steaming in, but as fans we loved him.

Five minutes to go and Anderlecht get the equaliser, which to be fair they deserved. A draw would be the final result, a score which we would have happily taken before kick-off, especially with an away goal. The whole squad come down to our end and receive our adulation.

We left the ground with no sign of trouble, to be honest a draw is always a crowd calmer. We headed back to the bar near the hotel, Richie said he was going back to the hotel to drop his camera off.

'I'll get you a drink in', I said to Rich as he went to the hotel.

After twenty-minutes I said to Percy.

'Where's Richie at?, he should have only taken five minutes'.

Five minutes later Richie strolled in.

'Where you've been?' I asked.

'Chasing a cockroach around the room, it was massive', Richie said.

'What did you do to it', I asked inquisitively.

'I jumped on it', Richie said.

I'm thinking how big was this cockroach. You would normally just stand on it, but Richie had to jump on it, like it was a wild pig.

'It must have been big' I said, still grinning, picturing Richie on the back of a giant cockroach.

A couple of beers later it was back to the hotel.

'I hope its mates aren't waiting for us', I said to Rich.

Rich opened the bedroom door and flicked on the light, no cockroaches, only a patch on the rug where it had succumbed.

All of us climbed into our giant bed, the light was switched off. Night Percy, night Richie, it was just like The Waltons.

We woke early and were soon off for the early train back to Ostend. Percy was heading back to England while Richie and I booked another night in the hotel we had stayed in on the Monday. We planned it this way so we could get to London for the final home game against Man Utd. It was pointless going back North to come back South one day later. The day in Ostend was spent down at the beach, it was a lovely day so we just chilled before setting off back to London on the Friday afternoon for the overnight ferry.

West End – White Hot Lane

Richie and I went over to Kings Cross to meet the rest of the Northern Spurs off the train. Karen had made the trip, joined by Phil, Pete, John, also Alan the Man Utd fan and Keith the Arsenal fan. Arsenal were playing in or around London so Keith said he would meet us after the game and have a look around the West End. The match was really secondary, our thoughts were more on the second leg with Anderlecht. The match with Man Utd ended 1-1 and signalled the end of another league campaign.

Back to Kings Cross where we met up with Alan and Keith who were both well oiled, especially Keith, who would regularly get so pissed at Arsenal home games he would sleep on the Clock End terraces. Of course it was still the days of 'Boring Boring Arsenal' so they could send many a fan to sleep!

A couple of drinks and we were off onto the tube to Leicester Square where our usual pub crawl would begin. By 8p.m. Alan had got into an argument with someone which needed the police to intervene. Alan got a ticking off and told he would be nicked if he caused any more trouble. Alan said he needed time off the beer and was going off to find a lady of the night. Alan never hid the truth he used prostitutes, and in the coming years would be a regular to what Thailand offered.

Going into another pub we are soon getting grief off a few West Ham fans who were calling us dirty yid bastards. We let them leave, we couldn't be bothered with them. Some people just can't have a good night out without aggravation, forget your football loyalties.

The last pub we were in had a little dance floor with the DJ setting up his equipment so we decided to stay, although dancing didn't come naturally to any of us, but hey it was the last Saturday game of the season, we were first on the floor strutting our stuff. I think 'Tiger Feet' by Mud got us up there first. Richie had his camera in hand when he was not up dancing with us. Keith on the other hand was so pissed he couldn't move, never mind dance, and was laid out. We soon had his trainer laces knotted together. I've watched the video of the event on numerous occasions, and what fools you make of yourselves, including John dropping his trousers to show his unbelievably hairy arse to 'Joe Public'. As the night drew to a close we set off from the pub, nudging Keith from his slumber, He stood up wondering why his legs were almost stuck together as he tried to walk, his laces so tightly knotted, eventually having to burn them off to set himself free, then it was off for a kebab and the midnight train home.

We were all back down to London thirteen days later for what would be the biggest match at The Lane since we beat Leeds in 1975 to stave off relegation.

After a few drinks, Karen, Richie and I headed to the ground early. The game wasn't all-ticket but admission prices had been hiked up, as they had for the semi-final against Hajduk Split. League prices at the time were two quid for the terraces, for the Semi-Final they had risen to three quid, and now four quid for the Final, It was expected I suppose.

Being first come first served we thought it would probably be a lock out, so a good reason to get in early. We met Brent before the game who still had his season ticket in the centre section of The Shelf, he asked if we wanted to stand with him instead of on the left side of The Shelf where we normally stood with the more vocal section.

'I can get you in, I know one of the lads where I show my season ticket', Brent said.

It would be undoubtedly the best view, and where we had stood when we first watched Spurs. The only thing with the season tickets section was that they were more your forty years plus age group, more reserved and definitely less boisterous to the section we normally stood, but we accepted Brent's offer, more for it being the best view and not being quite as packed, not a problem for Rich or me, but for Karen who would have felt crushed on the left side of The Shelf.

We entered our usual turnstiles and then into the underbelly of The Shelf. To be honest you could go through any turnstile on three sides of the ground and get to where you wanted, so accessible was White Hart Lane. The new West Stand was the only area where you were limited in moving around the stadium. The only changes underneath The Shelf to how it had always looked was a sectioned off area that had been put in for the season ticket section. Brent had a word with the gateman on the sectioned off area, his name was Graham Roberts the same as our skipper for the night deputising for the banned Steve Perryman. He let the three of us in and we made our way to our viewpoint on the halfway line under the TV gantry where Brian Moore was sat ready to commentate for the live coverage for ITV. The ground was already two-thirds full and the atmosphere building. By 7.30p.m. the gates were ready to be locked. The attendance of over 46,000 just short of its 48,000 capacity due to Anderlecht not selling all their tickets, they only brought over 1,500 supporters.

The noise level grew. As I've said The Lane had a very special atmosphere on nights like these. By the time the teams came out the floodlights were now fully glowing, the playing surface pristine and bright, 'Come on you Spurs' starts ringing around The Shelf, Park Lane and Paxton Road, the noise was better than I had ever heard.

It's off, the whistle blew, the game is edgy, the crowd incessant. Then what we didn't want, Anderlecht scored, they got the important first goal and an away goal at that, for a brief moment we heard the Belgian support. Then we let our team know we were still with them, the noise level goes up, but as the game goes on we were getting more nervous as we pushed to get the equaliser, but we also had to watch Anderlecht's counter attacks. After eighty-two minutes the ball was put into the box, Park Lane End, the end we were attacking. Ossie Ardiles connected his shot cannoned off the underside of the bar, we swayed as one on The Shelf, It's in, it's out, but we had Graham Roberts, his physique like another great Spurs captain Dave Mackay, he wasn't going to let the ball go dead. Robbo drove forward and bundled it into the net. The Shelf erupted, White Hart Lane erupted like it's never erupted, well not like I had ever seen. The old boys I was stood alongside, some in their sixties, normally placid, leaped around like the schoolboys they had been fifty years earlier. Rich took off, I leapt around with any stranger, hugging, it didn't matter if you knew them, they are Spurs, you are Spurs, you are as one.

I would love to have a photo of that scene, three seconds after the ball had hit the net, the scene of bodies going in all directions in delight. I will never forget that moment, ever.

For the first time I had forgotten about Karen. Normally I would protect her from any surges, but here I was some ten yards away from her from where I had been. I found her, she smiled, she knew what it meant to me.

The ground was buzzing, the noise unbelievable. I later watched the match on my VHS recording, Brian Moore on ITV said,

'I can't make myself think, never mind make myself heard'.

It was fever pitch. The final whistle blew, we were happy to take it to extra time. We felt now we could finish them off, the crowd was lifted.

Extra time was nervous, cat and mouse, no-one wanted to make a mistake, and no-one did. Penalties would decide the Final, not my favourite way, it's the luck of the draw.

Our skipper blasted home the first and Anderlecht missed their first. The next three from each team went in, it's up to our young right back Danny Thomas to win the cup. It was his first season at Spurs and he'd been brilliant for us, but his luck ran out and his penalty was saved. It was a blow to us, but in an instant the cry went up, 'One Danny Thomas, there's only one Danny Thomas', it rang around all four sides of the stadium. The fans knew it was one mistake in a fantastic season from him, we needed to let him know what we thought.

Anderlecht needed to score, Gudjohnsen stepped up, the father of Eider who would play for Bolton, Chelsea and ironically Spurs in the 2000's. His penalty was placed to Tony Parks right, Parks at full stretch saved, we jumped in ecstasy.

It had been draining, but the win a fitting tribute to our manager Keith Burkinshaw who had decided this would be his final game. He stated that it was down to commercialism that was eroding the game, what would he think of today's football?

The trophy was lifted and paraded around the pitch. Danny Thomas looked up at us and waved, which started another cry of his name, he appreciated the support. We left the stadium and enjoyed the walk down the High Road with car horns blaring out in joy. The midnight train would see us again savouring a few bottles of Pomagne.

The Scouse Low Life

Waiting for the fixtures to come out was one of the days I looked forward to during the summer. The anticipation of the matches that you were keen to see, Arsenal, Man Utd, Liverpool and now Newcastle, who after eight years were back in the big time.

The opening day fixture would be away at Everton, a tough start, Everton were being talked about as one of the challengers to Liverpool's title crown. It would be the start of five years of Mersey dominance.

Tottenham had lost 'fans favourite' Steve Archibald to Barcelona and replaced him with Clive Allen, a forward who would take a couple of seasons to fully blossom, but none the less a dependable striker.

Richie, Karen and I set off on a hot August morning., Percy was getting the later train, some of the other lads were still on holiday.

Arriving at Lime Street, not much after 11a.m., a gang of scousers were hanging around, but never gave us a second look when I was with Karen.

We walked up to the Stags Head for a few pints and then over to Goodison Park. Everton were expecting a good crowd after poor attendances the previous season, many of their crowds were under 20,000 including our visit, but in general attendances were still falling, due primarily to the country still not being out of a recession. Clubs also started to hike up prices for tickets that were out-stripping inflation and of course that ugly word 'hooliganism' was still rife.

'Where do you fancy sitting?', I asked Richie.

We had already decided against the Park End terrace, a pretty shit view being so low down and dodgy coming out. Park End seats, like the terrace meant you had to come out the one exit to face their mob,

'How about the Bullens Road?', Richie said.

This the stand that presently houses away fans, but then it was only Everton fans. We had been going in the Main Stand opposite for the last three years, but each year it was becoming more hostile as more Spurs fans were going in it. The Scouse scallies had got wind of it and more of them would come in to confront the Spurs fans, who were the type who were only there for the match, not a ruck.

'Yeah, good idea Rich', I said.

The Bullens Road was chosen.

Tickets purchased, we entered and took our seats which were over the eighteen-yard box towards the Gladys Street End which was filling up with Evertonians. Opposite at the Park End where around 2,000 Spurs fans were making themselves heard.

The game kicked off. Everton came at us in waves of attacks and were soon a goal up. But we go back at them and scored four times without reply. Clive Allen scoring twice to take the adulation of his new supporters, those same supporters, or maybe their fathers who had worshipped his dad Les who was an integral part of our 'Double winning team' almost a quarter of a century before. As each of our four goals go in Richie and I jumped up, as well as the other Spurs fans around us. A bloke behind me was getting more upset as each Spurs goal went in until he couldn't hold back any longer.

283

'Fuck off into your end', he said.

I turned round to face the irate scouser.

'We're only celebrating a goal', I said.

It wasn't like we were gloating. As for fucking off into our own end I would have loved to have been celebrating with the Spurs contingent, but I didn't think it was possible, so he would have to put up with it.

'Yeah, you should fuck off into your end' another Scouser said.

Ten minutes from the end and the three points in the bag, some of the Spurs fans around us, mainly family types got up and left. I continued arguing with the Scousers. I hate trouble but sometimes I get a bee in my bonnet, and these Scousers were really pissing me off. All we did was jump up when we scored, sat down, no singing, no winding the Scousers up. They were both around forty so should have known better. I've been in the seats at Spurs when away fans around me jump up, I don't care, to me that's what the game is about, as long as they aren't winding you up.

Karen told me to calm down. The whistle blew. I watched as the team run down to the rejoicing Park End, I also applauded, the Everton fans left.

We got out the ground a couple of minutes later into the still hot sunshine. I was calm now, delighted we'd got the season off to a winning start. The smell of burgers and horse shit from the mounted constabulary lingered in the humid air. We passed the back of the Park End, the Spurs fans still inside, held back, we could hear them singing our songs, it always makes the wait inside much better after a win.

At the top of the Park End we saw Everton's mob waiting for the Spurs boys, it was a a big mob, we passed them and headed to the bus stand where John had his hat taken in the cup match. I suddenly had that feeling of being followed. I turned my head and looked, I saw the guy who was sitting behind me giving me grief in the ground. I saw him pointing as though to say, 'these two'. Before I could say anything to Richie, two scousers laid into him, then a burning thud connected with my mouth. As I reeled from the punch, or whatever it was, another scally kicked me in the balls. This had me almost on the floor. The instigators left the scene not wanting the 'Local Plod' to see anything. We were left shaken, yet again my lip was bust and swelling, blood around my face. My main concern was Karen, she was upset. The gutless Scouse who had sat behind me hadn't the bottle to have a go himself, he had to use a gang of scallies to do his dirty work. But what really pissed me off was that he knew there was a girl with us, he was the one I thought was scum, not the ones who had jumped us. They probably didn't even know there was a girl with us. I felt disorientated, on high alert. My lip was getting bigger, and the blood made me feel like I had Spurs stamped on my forehead, I was almost waiting for the next punch.

I got my bearings and got on a bus back to Lime Street, meeting up with Percy on the train who was with Billingham Bob, another Spurs fan from the Northeast.

'What the fuck happened to you?', Percy said.

'We got jumped', I said in a muffled way.

'Did you have any bother getting out the Park End?' I asked Bob.

'No probs, sneaked past their mob no bother', Bob replied.

'Typical you get jumped when you're trying to avoid it'.

'Rich, Park End next season?' I said.

'Aye', Rich said.

As for Karen, she never went to Liverpool again. She was traumatised by the episode. In fact she went to very few away games again, preferring to stand in safety on The Shelf at home matches. As they say, home is where the heart is.

Titanic No More, The Mags away

As the season progressed Spurs stayed in and around the top three along with Everton, Liverpool and Man Utd. I didn't follow Spurs in Europe as I was saving to buy a house, but still got to many of the league matches. In January we unluckily lost to Liverpool at Anfield in the FA Cup on a wintry afternoon where many of the Spurs fans missed the first twenty-five minutes due to travel chaos.

Our main aim now was the league title. On March 16th we set off again to Anfield for the top of the table clash against Liverpool. We lay second in the table, Liverpool below us. We actually thought we could get a result, but our dreadful record at Anfield always dampened our encouragement, but we travelled in hope.

Certain games stay with you for life, like your first match or a Cup Final, many are forgotten, but not this one, and I can safely say that for many of the 4,000 travelling Spurs fans this game will live long in their memories, just as it does mine.

The morning train journey was the usual card school and looking at the daily tabloids, broadsheets never entered our minds. The usual clichéd newspaper headlines were there year on year, 'Spurs have not won at Anfield since 1912 the year the Titanic was built and sank'. Here we were seventy-three years on from that fateful day in the North Atlantic, our section packed, Anfield packed. Richie standing with me, we belted out our songs, we were in good voice. We knew a win would put pressure on leaders Everton.

It was a tight game with no goals at half-time, but we were playing well. The news came through that Everton were winning 1-0 away at Villa. We kicked-off the second half, attacking the Kop end, pushing for a goal. Then it happened, Mickey Hazard hit a cracking shot, Grobbelaar makes a brilliant save but only puts the ball into Garth Crooks path and he fires home. Our corner erupts as one, its pandemonium, bodies rolling around in the seats and terraces, Richie and mine included. I had seen us score at Anfield before but it either meant little to the result or was a nothing game for us, but this had meaning, it was a feeling of euphoria. The noise from our fans cranked up as we had to hold on for twenty-minutes. 'We going to win the league, we going to win the league', a song not often heard from Spurs fans, then we heard Villa had equalised against Everton.

The final whistle blew, we had done it. That quip of not winning since the Titanic went down could be thrown into the gutter, along with the press. What a feeling we had. I was so happy and especially for Steve Perryman who had played at Anfield around fifteen times without any joy. This was special, his face beaming as he led his victorious team to our corner.

We were kept in a for a while, which was no hardship as we continued to celebrate. Eventually the gates were opened, there were gangs of scousers hanging around street corners, but not to the extent of the Everton gangs.

We got to Lime Street Station, I entered the Buffet to get a bite to eat, as I queued a young scouser, about twelve, said.

'Hey mate can you get something for me?',

'No', I said, 'Queue up like the rest of us'.

'No, I don't want to pay for it, I want you to nick me a sarnie', he said as bold as brass.

Like I was stupid enough to steal something for myself never mind a little scally.

He walked away shaking his head like I had done something wrong.

I met up with Richie and discussed us winning the league, there was every chance now.

Richie had the fantastic trip to Real Madrid four days later, which ended with an aggregate 1-0 loss, a home defeat in the first leg killed our hopes. Back to the league we beat Southampton 5-0 but then lost at home to Villa.

In the first week of April we had White Hart Lane's biggest game of the season, a packed house for the visit of Everton, anything other than a win wouldn't be good enough. Everton had improved dramatically from the team we beat on the opening day of the season and it would be them who took a tenth minute lead to send the thousands of Evertonians wild. Their second goal followed in the second-half, but a Graham Roberts thirty yarder cut the arrears, but Everton hung on. That was it, our title hopes had gone. Our form dropped off and we ended a long way behind the eventual Champions Everton, Spurs finishing third.

Our last away game of the season was for me, the much-anticipated game at Newcastle. It was our first visit there since Newcastle's relegation season, eight years previously.

I got a call from Keith the Arsenal fan to ask if I was going.

'Of course, I am', I replied,

'Do you want a lift?', Keith asked.

Keith had got disillusioned watching Arsenal, something I wasn't surprised about!

'Yeah, I'll have a lift, can you pick Phil and Pete up at Darlington?'.

'Yeah, no bother' Keith said.

I was pleased to be going by car. I'd heard the Geordies had a big welcome mob for any club with a decent following and made even more special for Londoners. They would wait in their droves outside the railway station next to what was Yates Wine Lodge hoping to pick off any stray away fans.

Keith picked Karen and me up and then drove to Darlington to collect Phil and Pete.

Keith said he was going to the odd Newcastle game and this match was the one he was looking forward to the most. He would be standing in the home paddock to give us grief, his Spurs, Arsenal rivalry still shining through.

We arrived in Newcastle early and parked up near the railway station, about three hundred yards from Yate's Wine Lodge. It was just past 11a.m. and already there were hundreds of Newcastle fans loitering, waiting for Spurs fans. We left and entered a quiet bar.

'We having a round?', Keith asked.

'Yeah we all agreed'.

Five drinks were bought, Keith drank his first pint before I'd had a mouthful.

'I like a quick first pint', he declared.

He went for another and another. We were slowly getting pissed.

I was never a big drinker, but I was getting through my fair share, but also keeping an eye on Keith who kept slipping in extra pints between rounds. At 2.30p.m. we staggered to our feet, even Karen had drunk a good few. I had knocked back eight or nine pints, far more than I normally would. Phil and Pete were okay, Keith had drunk twelve and he was our driver!

We left the pub and hit the warm May air, my feet and legs were in a world of their own. We weaved our way through the Geordie faithful. Keith went his own way, he didn't wish us well.

We entered the uncovered Leazes End corner towards the Main Stand paddock where the Geordies were stood and no doubt Keith. They were giving us loads of abuse. Our section of a 1,000 supporters had a huge perimeter mesh fence obscuring the view of the ground, which was in decline to the one I had first visited ten years earlier, and was now a very open stadium. The Gallowgate End opposite was packed, a constant din being created, only stopping when we scored. The commotion from our fans as that goal went in left me laid on the terrace as my drunken jelly legs couldn't hold me up.

As the game went on I got my cohesion back. A coffee at half-time helped.

With the score 2-2 and twelve-minutes left, our young midfielder Ian Crook scored what would be the winner, celebrations ensued. I was delighted to have beaten them for a second time that season. The game at The Lane earlier in the season Spurs won 3-1, but what really shone was the performance of the mullet-haired Chrissy Waddle who was outstanding for the Geordies. I think White Hart Lane took a shine to Waddle that day, with Waddle saying the same, that he would love to team up with Glenn Hoddle. Of course his dream was realised in the summer of '85, much to the disdain of the Geordie faithful, them saying, 'Why does a Geordie want to play for a London club', but Waddle had made his mind up. The Lane would see some stunning performances from Waddle, though it would take time for his brilliance to shine through.

We left St James' Park, out onto the street in a procession, a long line ten deep. Northumberland police were trying to keep us in line. I was now feeling reasonably sober so was aware of the Geordies over the road building up in numbers.

The police wanted us back to the railway station as quick as possible, but the start of verbal's going back and forth had the police losing control, a possible stand-off looked likely.

A couple of bottles headed in our direction, 'Brown Ale of course', they smashed around our 1,000, just missing some.

'We hate the Cockneys'. The usual chant from Northern Fans towards Londoners.

'Where were you at White Hart Lane?', The Spurs fans responded.

Of course, the Geordies were there, 3 or 4,000 of them. One I distinctly remember was trying to climb over one of the fences that split the Park Lane End into pens. As he got on the top of the fence he slipped and fell headfirst, only being stopped when the spike on the top of the fence pierced the bottom of his jeans and stopped his fall, which left him dangling on the fence, much to the delight of The Shelf Side.

A few Geordies crossed the cordon to try and get at us, some Spurs fans met them in no man's land. Before they clashed the police got in between, the dogs barking, their muzzles were off, order was restored.

'We need to get out of this escort', I said to the others.

We slipped out, trying to get down a side road.

'Hey where ye fuckan goin?'. A burley cop stopped us in our tracks,

'To the car' I said.

'Get back here', he said, truncheon in hand. Another bottle headed in our direction.

'Watch it', a group of us shouted, the bottle missed us, the burley copper looked amongst the Geordie throng searching for the instigator, his gaze not on us now. We nipped out of the escort and headed back to the car to wait for Keith.

We could see the railway station, a mass of Geordies were outside Yate's Wine Lodge, as though they hadn't moved

291

since this morning, missiles rained down on the incoming Spurs fans.

Keith turned up after twenty minutes.

'Where you've been?', I asked Keith.

'Thought I'd go for a couple of pints', Keith smiled.

We got in the car, not even thinking our driver has had around fifteen pints, we were just pleased to be getting out of this city.

Keith got us back safely.

I got home, went in the bath and almost fell asleep, eight or nine pints is more than enough for me in one day.

I rang Keith the following morning.

'How you feeling?', I asked.

'What you mean?', Keith asked.

'Thought you might have had a hangover', I said.

'No, I'm fine, got back home and had another six pints in Bishop Auckland after dropping you off", he said. I shook my head in amazement.

Musicals, Heysel, Bradford, Dad

Musicals! I just didn't understand them, I often thought they spoilt a film. A good story would be ruined when someone would burst into song or start dancing. It wasn't real, no one having a conversation would suddenly begin to sing and dance, life wasn't like that and it would annoy me. My mam loved them, watching the Sunday matinee on TV, I would also watch them aged between ten and twelve years old. My dad would come home from the Workingmen's Club, have his Sunday lunch and go to bed to leave mam and me to watch in peace, that is until the singing and dancing started then I would get up and say, 'It's not real life' She, not even hearing me, so engrossed in Howard Keele and Doris Day and the like.

Oklahoma, South Pacific, Calamity Jane, I've seen the start to all those films and got up and left, probably to play Subbuteo.

Last game of the season was home to mid-table Watford. I was looking forward to our annual pilgrimage around the West End, possibly more than the match.

The game was a disaster. When they say players are thinking about their holidays, well our players had already got a suntan and were into their second week. A 5-1 defeat is bad at any time, but when it's on your home patch and you're playing a team well below you in the league it's a bitter pill to swallow, it was a case of drowning our sorrows.

To be fair the game was soon forgotten as we went from pub to pub around the West End, breaking into groups of two so we could by-pass the bouncers. The last thing they wanted was seven or eight football fans coming into their pub in a group, but once inside our groups of two would all regroup again.

Once inside the pub I caught site of a newspaper seller selling the London Evening Standard which contained the football scores, none I'd seen that day, so went over to buy one. I would normally just look at the back page, but the front-page headline hit me hard. 'Dozens of people die in football tragedy'.

Fifty-six people died and two hundred and sixty-five people were injured in the fire inferno at Bradford City when a wooden grandstand caught fire. Things like that really hit home to me, I put myself in their position, devastated families, people saying goodbye at lunchtime to their loved ones never to see them again, I don't ever want to know what that feeling would be like

Finally at the bottom of the article, almost like an afterthought, a young Birmingham City fan had died at the match versus Leeds when he was crushed by a falling wall as chaos ensued all around St Andrews. That life was every bit as important as the fifty-six at Bradford, but because it was due to hooliganism it appeared less relevant, but that young life was trying to escape the madness.

It didn't surprise me, Leeds yobs had caused mayhem all over the country and Birmingham were no angels, but again it brought the game into the gutter.

We chatted about the incidents in the pub and bought John another pint, he was skint having been part of the Miners' strike. John having a weekend at the football instead of being one of Arthur Scargill's foot soldiers, creating picket lines and having running battles with the over-zealous plod who seemed hell bent on coshing anyone who didn't have a police uniform adorning their bodies.

The pub called for last orders. It's strange to think it was barely 11p.m. in one of the most famous cities in the world and its closing its doors to the masses, but that was of the time, so we were used to it. Anyway we had to get to King's Cross for the Midnight train.

We left the bright neon lights off Oxford Circus and headed down the steps towards the Tube Station. Approaching the escalators we soon noticed they weren't running so had to walk down the stationary stairs towards the trains. As we got to the bottom, a couple of buskers with saxophones stood in-between tunes.

'What can you play?', I asked.

'We can do a Glenn Miller medley', one said.

Perfect music for a couple of saxophones. They started playing, the acoustics of the subway created a slight echo which not only amplified the sound but made the sax's sound like there were ten, a proper Glenn Miller orchestra. The upbeat 1940s music got us all dancing at the base of the escalator. Within minutes it was like an old dance hall as tens of people were jigging around. I turned around looking at the stationary escalator, its full of dancing people, clapping along, no one was moving. People who were going wherever had suddenly stopped and burst into song and dance. Musicals! They are realistic, as of 1985 anyway. I can't watch a musical now without thinking of that night. I wonder if Rodgers and Hammerstein had been influenced in a similar way.

With the season over I could look forward to the European Cup Final featuring Liverpool against Juventus. I enjoyed watching other teams play and still do, you don't have the pressure of watching your own team trying to win, a neutral game is much more relaxing. The Final was held in Belgium, in an old stadium known as 'Heysel' and would be remembered for all the wrong reasons.

It was soon obvious that the stadium was inadequate, one end housed Italians in one half, the other half Liverpool fans, with little segregation between them, it was a disaster waiting to happen. Reports said the Italians were constantly sending missiles into the Liverpool fans section until they'd had enough, sending the Italians fleeing as they surged towards them. Fights broke out with many Italians trying to escape not wanting to get involved, until they were trapped at the front wall, which finally collapsed through the pressure of bodies.

I'm not just blaming the two sets of fans for what happened, we know Italians are renowned for throwing bottles, coins, etc. and when English fans retaliate its usually the English who are blamed. Unfortunately it's the innocents who are the victims.

Watching the horror unfold in front of my eyes, people piled on top of one another as the wall collapsed, the life sucked out of them. I remember one Italian, bodies four deep on top of him, his arms outstretched pleading for help, only his head and shoulders clear of the bodies on top. Suddenly the pile above him fell forward and he was gone, crushed, suffocated.

I looked across at my Dad in his favourite chair looking at the TV but not taking it in, well that's how it looked, my Dad had recently been diagnosed with throat cancer and had weeks to live. It wasn't only the poor souls on TV dying. I could feel a tear well up in my eye. Another glance at Dad and that tear rolled down my cheek. My Dad was a tough bloke when he was young, well before I was born, Some would say a hardcase nowadays. I had spoken to a few of my Dad's mates' years later and they were all in agreement. 'George would flatten anyone in the town whatever the size of them' they said. My Dad wasn't big, 5ft 9in and weighing twelve stone, but his friends said what he did have was incredible speed with his fists. They all said it was a missed vocation in his life, he should have been a boxer, but now his fight was leaving him.

Six weeks after that European Cup Final I sat with Dad, him in bed sedated with morphine, he weighed five stone, his body little more than a bag of bones. It was my turn to sit with him, Mam downstairs having a break. I talked to him about everyday things, something I had rarely done with my Dad. The forty-year age difference made it seem like we had little in common, in fact I knew so little about his life from when he was young, this the reason why I wrote this book, so my children can read it and at least have an idea what my life was like before they came along.

My dad took a large breath, then nothing for around five seconds, like he was holding his breath, then an outward breath and no more, he had gone. I sat a minute, tears streaming down my face hoping he would breathe again, but it wasn't going to happen. I shouted to Mam 'he's gone'. I was sad but pleased it was over and his pain was no more. I felt cheated in a way. I was twenty-four, him sixty-five, we should have had longer together. I think of my Dad especially on July 4th, the day he died. I never think of America.

Down and Dirty – Take It or Leave It

Two weeks before my dad died I had booked up on a coach trip from York to see U2 at the Milton Keynes Bowl. Phil had sorted tickets. It was a break from the gloom at home. I stayed at Phil's the night before so had the inevitable hangover on the Saturday morning when I met Phil's mates, lads I hadn't met before. Tommy a Southerner and a big Chelsea fan, Pete a York lad but a West Ham supporter, Chris, John and a couple girls who they knew.

Sometimes you meet people, and it just clicks, you feel like you have known them years, they made me feel so welcome. As a result in later years I would go to York Races every year and meet up for the racing and the pub crawl afterwards. A special mention to Pete who died in 2010 from the demon drink, a lovely lad, I didn't make his funeral, but I was so pleased his mates had got the church to play the West Ham anthem 'I'm forever blowing bubbles'.

We hadn't been in Milton Keynes long when the heavens opened. It wasn't even a warm June day, we got soaked and the ground became sodden, like you see at Glastonbury when it's been one of them wet festivals. Once you're soaked you can't get any wetter. It started with Billy Bragg, Spear of Destiny, the Ramones and a young American band I hadn't heard of at the time, who would go on to headline some of the biggest shows in the world, they were 'REM'. In fact, they had to wait two more years after this show to get their first UK hit, 'The one I love'.

U2 came on and the crowd were a throbbing, steaming mass, sliding in the thick mud. U2's fan base were late teenage and early twenty somethings, many of whom had followed them from their beginnings five years earlier, they were boisterous with attitude.

Many of them same fans have carried on following the band, now middle aged, they now listen to the music instead of po-going. But in '85 we bobbed around only twenty metres from the stage with the vast 60,000 crowd mainly behind us. Once the first chords of '11 o'clock tick tock' came through the massive speakers there was a surge forward of writhing bodies. One of the girls, Chris's cousin who was in front of me suddenly went down amongst the mass of legs. People were totally unaware, so engrossed in the driving music. Cold, rain, alcohol, hunger, may well have had an effect on her. I dived down into the thick mud to find her, you don't worry about your own safety. I managed to get to her, people around me still unaware, still bouncing around, then the rest of the lads noticed and helped. She had fainted. I was just pleased to have seen her fall, it could have been tragic. The show was a huge success, we were all buzzing from it, and rather dirty as we boarded the coach to York.

My dad died less than two weeks later.

The following week the greatest ever live concert took place. 'Live Aid' a show no one will ever see the likes of again. I watched it from start to finish, it was an emotional ride, seeing the emaciated bodies of dying people from the video's shown in-between the music. It hit home after seeing my dad waste away, I had more than once tears in my eyes once again.

I should have been looking forward to the fixtures coming out, after all we'd had a decent campaign the previous season finishing third, admittedly a long way behind Everton who were worthy champions and also trailing Liverpool who were runners up.

It should have been another European season for us but was halted by the shenanigans of the Liverpool and Juventus fans in Belgium. Not only were Liverpool banned from Europe, but all the other English teams were banned for five years. It gave U.E.F.A. the opportunity to rid the scum of the English that had blighted trips on foreign soil. Yes, we had a reputation, I had seen it first-hand, but I had also seen the provocation of foreign supporters attacking English fans in bars for no other reason than they were carrying the colours of their clubs. It was an over-zealous reaction by U.E.F.A. and in particular to Everton. How that must have hurt to know it was their fellow Liverpudlians' who had prevented one of the best teams to have won the league in years from competing in the European Cup, especially seeing the Italians allowed to compete with a slap on the wrists.

The fixtures had arrived for 85-86, of course I checked them out, but I wasn't bothered, in fact I had lost interest. Looking back I think the loss of my Dad had a bigger impact on me than I thought, I was also saving up to get married to Karen the following year and that was taking time and cash. But I think the biggest factor had been the loss of lives caused by the hooliganism. The lives lost at Bradford in the inferno was a tragedy, but that was an accident. It was the thirty-six Juventus fans, the youngster at Birmingham and the hundreds injured and mentally traumatised that had hit home. I had seen enough!

1985, for me was the year where you either said 'I Can't wait for the season to start or that's it, I've had enough'. Going to games was getting pricey compared to the 70's. Fifty pence to stand or a quid for a seat had long gone, we know everything goes up in price, but sheer greed had come into the game. Agents began representing players, who also wanted their little piece of silver.

Commercialism had now been around for a few years, corporate hangers on in their three-piece suits who in all honestly couldn't give a shit about the match, they were more interested in 'boiled potatoes or roast sir'. I hated it, the beautiful game was going down the pan, and none more so than my beloved Tottenham.

One year earlier we had an average gate of 30,000, in 1985-86 it would drop dramatically to a little over 20,000. Many fans had thought like me and given football the elbow. White Hart Lane looked spartan, with one Saturday gate having less than 11,000 and a midweek league match little over 9,000. It's a wonder we didn't get that well know chant 'where were you when you were shit' in the following seasons. But it wasn't just Spurs, many clubs around the country were having a hard time.

Come August 1985 first game of the season, home to Watford, was I there? Of course I was. Richie, Phil, Karen and I were down as usual. We went to our usual boozer pre match, the pub we had now used for three or four years, The Railway Tavern, just outside White Hart Lane Railway Station. It was a good little pub, usually the same lads in every other week and on occasions Len (the Duke) Duquemin would sit at the bar. Many didn't recognise him, but he was our centre forward in the forties to the early fifties, a league winner and England striker. He was revered in his day, now an old man having a few pints amongst the fans.

We got talking to a few Spurs lads we knew, lads who were regular home and away supporters, but like one said, it's part of your life and he was right. It doesn't matter who you support if you've followed a club it lives with you forever. Even if you stop going there will be a part of you that looks out for the result, it may not mean as much, win or lose, but you look all the same.

We left the pub, Phil decided to come on The Shelf as none of the others Northern lads were down. Phil was a Park Lane Ender, so it was quite rare to get him on The Shelf.

We chatted about our three new signings, Paul Allen from West Ham a busy midfielder, but the chat was more for the Geordie we had bought, Chrissy Waddle, the flair player that Tottenham fans craved. A lot was expected of him after many had seen his exhilarating performance against Spurs the previous season for Newcastle. John Chiedozie our other signing wasn't really mentioned.

30,000 turned up to see Waddle's debut which was one of our best gates of the season, and he didn't disappoint scoring two in a 4-0 win. His season however became sporadic, some games he didn't look interested, but after that initial season he became world class at times.

The game kicked off when Phil said.

'I feel ill'.

Phil hadn't drunk much in the pub but within a minute he had sat down on the Shelf terrace.

'Do you want to see someone?', I asked.

'No I will just sit here, Phil said.

And sit there he did until the final whistle, missing all four goals.

We managed to get him back to York where Phil spent the next day in bed. We never found out what was wrong with him that day.

It was a poor season, win, draw, lose, you didn't know which Spurs would turn up, another reason why attendances suffered.

When we were drawn away to Oxford United in the FA Cup it was like, right all our eggs are now in one basket, let's have a good go at winning the cup.

Harry and Colin were our two drivers, no one else had bothered to learn to drive. Harry was up for driving to Oxford in his Mini Metro, it would be a long drive on a cold wet January day.

We had a few beers near the ground and then walked to the quaint Manor Ground, home of Oxford United, and oh dear what a ground.

Oxford's rise through the divisions had been meteoric but the ground hadn't kept up with that rise, it was strictly fourth division, and the away end was a disgrace. An open end was fine for our 3,000 fans, but it was split down the middle by a thick girded fence with a tight mesh so you couldn't really see through it when the ball was in the corner. But the front perimeter fence was in a league of its own.

At the time the first few football fanzines were coming out, it would be a way of uniting fans from different clubs with banter, humour and some good-natured piss taking. I loved them and decided to subscribe to 'When Saturday Comes' which is still going today. An article in one of the editions was 'Name the worst away end you have had the misfortune to have visited', I had to write. 'The worst end is undoubtedly Oxford United with its twenty feet high thick girded and small meshed perimeter fence, which means unless you are at the back you don't see anything of the near goal. If the Germans had used this fence in the film 'The Great Escape' Steve McQueen would not have jumped over it on his motorbike.

My letter was published. I didn't receive anything, but it was nice to be recognised.

We were 1-0 down with a quarter of an hour remaining, the rain was constant, driving down on us unfortunates. We were soaked to the skin and very cold. A cross came in and John Chiedozie equalised.

What I do remember as the end erupted with the usual melee, hugging anyone, we were all brothers after all. Just as we all settled down I looked around and saw a very strange sight. We had all been so wet and cold the sudden exertion had made our end look like hundreds of kettles had just boiled, all you could see were clouds of steam, it looked quite surreal. 1-1 final result.

The replay was an easy win.

Next up were Notts County in the 4th Round, easy win. Then a 5th Round tie at home to the Champions Everton, who were going well again in the league.

Richie and I travelled down to London, only finding out when we got to Kings Cross the match had been postponed. A sickener, a quick pint and we set off back. What made it worse was the game was going to be live on TV, so the five-hundred-mile round trip seemed even more pointless.

Everton beat us in the re-arranged mid-week fixture, 2-1.

The season was over, but I still had the away game at Newcastle to look forward to.

Newcastle away is the game I like to win more than any other, or as Kevin Keegan once famously said 'I'd love it if we beat them, I'd love it'. That sums it up for me, to beat the

Mags in their own backyard it's the same feeling Spurs fans have beating Arsenal. It must be like that for thousands of fans all over the country who follow their team from afar. You want to beat your nearest rival team, if that makes sense.

Phil and I travelled up to Newcastle by train. After the antagonism the season before, especially by the Central Railway Station it seemed a bit silly to travel by train knowing the expectant Geordies would be waiting in numbers, but hey anything for an adrenalin rush.

'Think they'll be waiting for us outside the station?', I asked Phil.

'Don't know', said Phil, his interest more in finding a decent pub.

Phil didn't have much time for Newcastle fans. He'd lost too many badges and jumpers to the marauding Magpies to have any love for them, but like myself he enjoyed going to the city.

Richie and Harry met us inside the railway station, they had been there long enough to check out the situation outside the station.

'There's a big mob outside Yates Wine Lodge', Harry said.

'What do you want to do?', I asked.

'I've found a side entrance down there', Richie pointed in the direction.

We made our way out the station leaving the Geordie masses a hundred yards away and kept going in the same direction coming to a pub called 'The Dog and Parrot' which would become our regular first-stop pub for the next twenty years. We found out many years later that it was a gay pub, maybe that's why the macho Geordies didn't bother with it, their loss, it was a decent boozer.

We stayed in the pub until around 2.30p.m. Walking out into the air, I knew I'd had a good drink, as did Phil and Harry. Our walking had a distinct sideways crab movement. On the other hand, Richie had drawn out a pint of cider for three hours. He had possibly only drunk half of it, the other half had probably evaporated.

Once in the away section with our supporters, similar numbers to the year before, we could now let off a bit of steam. You always felt on alert in the Geordie pubs with their dislike of anything London.

Although our home gates were suffering, it was the usual faces on our travels, they couldn't give up on the awaydays.

The Geordies were soon slating Chrissie Waddle unmercifully for his move South, but he revelled in it. The match was good and a fair result ensued, ending 2-2.

We got out the ground without the aggro of the previous year, as I said, a draw is always a pacifier, everyone leaves in a decent mood.

Nipping down a back street after sneaking out of the police escort we found a pub and had a couple of pints, then headed down to the station, it was just after 7p.m. The next train was 7.45p.m.

'Time for a beer', Phil said.

Richie and Harry had already gone. Phil squeezed in two pints.

We headed back to the station, onto the platform to see the train pulling out as we entered. The next train South was 11.30 p.m. The next three and half hours were spent in several pubs, by which time I was palatic, with Phil well on the way. We staggered once again to the station and boarded the train which had a group of Geordies on board. They soon clicked we were Spurs and started giving us, 'Spurs are on their way to Auschwitz, Hitler's goin to gas them again'.

With all our inhibitions gone through alcohol we joined in with the proper words.

We didn't give a shit if they laid into us, we weren't going to feel much in our state.

'What ya think of Chrissy Waddle?', one asked me.

'He hasn't had a great season, inconsistent, but once he settles, he will be ok', I slurred.

'What tha fuck you on aboot, he's fuckan magic' another says.

I was thinking, he's so magic that's why you've been slagging him off all match.

'Divn't na why he's gone to some fuckan Cockney shite team anyway', another Geordie putting his tenpenneth in.

The train soon pulled into Durham, they got up and had to get their last say in.

'Aye fuck off back to London'.

The thick Geordies couldn't even recognise our Northern accents.

The Geordies looked at us as the train set off and gave us the hand gesture of being wankers. We smiled.

'Geordie scum', I said to Phil.

The train terminated in Darlington. We staggered to our feet and almost fell onto the platform. It had been a good day.

Phil had been in touch with his sister who lived in Darlington, she would let us stay for the night.

I entered the house and banged off each wall like a ball on a pin ball machine, my state obvious to Phil's sister. We exchanged pleasantries, and I'm shown the settee, my bed for the night. It was now 1a.m. in the morning, I was in a good mood as I fell asleep.

I awoke at 7a.m. From being in a joyous mood six hours earlier, I was now dying. How could this happen?

The aroma of bacon and eggs was wafting through the house, the last thing I wanted to smell. I had to get out, my head was about to explode. I thanked Phil's sister saying I had to get home, this wasn't true, but I didn't want the embarrassment of throwing up in her house. My exit made, I was sick twice on my mile walk across town to my brother's house. I talked to myself on the walk, 'never again' I said, but of course it would happen again, on numerous occasions.

The season petered out, a term often used by Spurs supporters. A few high scoring wins in front of paltry attendances reflected the mood of the fans. Anyway, I had more important things at hand, my wedding to Karen and decorating the cottage we had bought.

My Wedding was great, Gary the Liverpool supporter was my best man, an honour I had done for him a couple of years previous. Its so nice to have your family and friends on such a joyous occasion, unfortunately my Dad had passed away the year before, maybe he was watching from the upper tier. All the Spurs lads turned up, most of them staying in Bishop Auckland about fifteen miles from the reception. The hotel being abused later that evening by drunkard Spurs fans.

I also had my engagement party in Bishop Auckland the previous year at the same hotel, Harry almost thrown out for throwing a bottle at Keith the Arsenal fan. You can't beat a bit of North London rivalry!

The Treble (well almost) and Standing with the Enemy

People talk about the Spurs team of 1986-87 as the best team the club have had since the '61 double team. I disagree, I believe the team five years earlier, the team of 81-82 was better. I don't say that because I was watching Spurs more often in 81-82   than 86-87,   even in the late 80s I was watching over twenty games a season, so I was still well in touch with what was happening in London N17, but with a mortgage and utilities to pay for, you did start to distance yourself to a degree from football. It isn't the 'be all and end all' anymore.

The '86 team was good under the leadership of David Pleat who had become manager, taking over from Peter Shreeves. To be honest Shreeves was more a coach, serving in that capacity for many years at Spurs, he was too much of a friend to the players, you need to distance yourself when you're a manager and Shreeves was never going to achieve that.

Spurs still had players covering those two teams of '81 and '86, but only Ray Clemence and Glenn Hoddle played regularly in both sides, with Roberts, Ardilies and Tony Galvin playing to a lesser extent.

What the '86 team did have that season was a striker who would go on to break records, that was Clive Allen. Thirty-three league goals, forty-nine goals in total, a club record he had taken from the great Jimmy Greaves.

We had also signed a centre half which many said could have been one of our greatest. In Richard Gough we had found a colossus of a player, he fitted in perfectly, but we only had him for one season. When Glasgow Rangers came in for him he wanted to move back North of the Border. His loss would leave a massive hole in our defence the following year.

The season had some highs but the lows out-weighed them, and the worst was the epic trilogy with Arsenal in the Littlewoods League Cup Semi-Final. Having won at Highbury 1-0 with another Clive Allen goal we left the ground on a high. In the second leg at The Lane we really fancied our chances, but our home form wasn't brilliant, and it shouldn't have come as a surprise to lose 2-1. The replay venue was decided with the toss of a coin to see which ground would be used for the third game. Spurs won the toss, we cheered a home advantage, but the 8,000 Arsenal fans also cheered, they were as pleased as we were.

I got the time off work and headed back to London three days later to endure the worst day at White Hart Lane I could remember. Clive Allen putting us one up, we could feel Wembley, but two Arsenal goals late on was gut wrenching. To hear your enemy celebrating, the sound of 'Wembley, Wembley' ringing around your ground from the away end was a hard pill to swallow, but that's football.

Our FA Cup run was going along nicely, beating Scunthorpe and Crystal Palace in the third and fourth rounds respectively, we then drew Newcastle at The Lane. All I could think of was the train down would be full of Geordies. This would be a game I definitely wanted to win.

The thing with Geordies is they get everywhere, I knew they would be down in their droves, 15,000 had been banded around, a figure I hoped wasn't true, 1,000 is too many for me. Arriving at Kings Cross they were everywhere, like Zebras on the Serengeti. It was no better on the tube with chants of 'The Blaydon Races' and 'Geordie Boys we are here, shag your woman and drink your beer'. It was like having flashbacks of past meetings.

Coming out of Seven Sisters we headed up to the Beehive pub, normally quiet a little after 11a.m. but not today. The hordes were already in, one pint and then we were off. The long walk-up Tottenham High Road passing each pub to the sound of the Geordie voices, even The Black Swan, a pub we never went in and traditionally an African/Caribbean pub, had Geordies in.

'We'll go to The Antwerp' I said to Richie.

The Antwerp was a nice little boozer only ten minutes from the ground but was out of the way, a pub we frequented quite often in the mid-80s. We went in the pub and at last it was the voices of Londoners. A lot of the older blokes would go in the Antwerp, faces I had seen on many occasions in my ten years of coming to White Hart Lane. I heard a few Northern voices, but not Geordies, more like a South-West Durham accent like my own, I looked around and to my amazement my brother Dave was five yards away. I went over for a chat, he just as amazed to see me.

'What you doing down here?', I asked, silly question really.

'Some of the lads from work had put a bus on so I thought I would have a day out', Dave said.

'I can't believe you found this pub'.

Dave wasn't a Newcastle fan, he didn't follow anyone really but did watch Middlesbrough quite a lot in the early 70's. I remember him telling me about a really good midfielder at Boro, a young lad called Graham Souness, 'He will make a good footballer'. I did say 'Yes he learned his trade at Tottenham', what a mistake that was by Bill Nicholson. He didn't make many but that was one big mistake to let Souness leave.

I wished Dave well. I knew Dave would want us to win, he had been to a few Spurs games with me over the years. We soon left The Antwerp and passed the masses of black and whites as we made our way down the Park Lane End and round to The Shelf Side. Once inside I looked to my left to the approximate 10,000 Geordies filling the end and the corner of The Shelf. I wasn't bothered how we did it, I just wanted to beat them. I didn't care if they were their usual aggressive selves on the train back home, I wanted them out of the cup.

It wasn't a classic by any means, but we won 1-0 and at the end of the match it was us singing 'Spurs are on their way to Wembley'.

To be honest it was a quiet journey home. Were the Mags mellowing?

The 6th Round gave us another trip to London, but this time it was away at Wimbledon. It was strange to go to an away game and have more fans than the home team. The 9,000 who had got tickets, including myself and Richie in the 15,000 crowd saw us win 2-0 and set up a Semi-Final at Villa Park against Watford, but first there was mid-week trip to Newcastle in the league.

I had managed to get a lift with a Newcastle supporter who worked with Karen. I didn't know him at all, but as I still hadn't yet passed my driving test I was pleased to get a lift.

He seemed a decent lad, and said that he would be standing in the Gallowgate End. He asked how many Spurs fans were coming and if I would be standing with them. I said I would stand with him in case our supporters got locked in after the final whistle, I didn't want him waiting for me after the match.

We entered the centre of the Gallowgate End and moved to our right until we were in the right-hand corner towards the East Stand where the real hardcore Geordies would congregate. I looked down to the open Leazes End to see around 500 Spurs fans. I would have liked to of been one of them, but tonight I would see it from a different perspective, and what an eye opener.

I thought some of our fans were hard to please, but this was another level. I didn't expect the torrent of abuse that the Geordics would give out. I knew they would slag us off, but they gave just as much to their own team and even their own fans.

311

This bloke came past us just before kick-off, he was wearing a suit so I presumed he'd just finished working in an office. This Geordie shouted out to him, which stopped the man in his tracks.

'Ow! Where ye gannan, to a fuckan weddan? What tha fuck ya dee'an in that clobber, it's a fuckan football match man'.

The look on the face of the suited man was a picture of contempt.

The game started and it wasn't what Spurs were doing that riled the Geordies, it's what their own team aren't doing. All they wanted was the ball up to our area.

'Howay man, kick the fuckan ball forward', they yelled.

Kenny Wharton, the Newcastle fullback/midfield player who just happened to have a bit of acne on his face was the target of the boo boys. It was a shame really, he's a local lad, and that should be enough for your own fans to give you a lift. Wharton got the ball in the right back position, near the corner where I'm stood and played an easy pass out of play.

'Wharton, ya fuckan spotty faced cunt, what tha fuck ya dee'an, fuck off'. It was constant, made worse when we scored. There was a distant roar from our pocket of fans, oh I wished I was there, I bent down as though to fasten a lace, 'get in' I yell to myself. But fair play to Newcastle, they came back at us and equalised. The Gallowgate erupted, I didn't move, but I was jostled so no one noticed. The game ended in a draw. It had been a good game and an experience, but one I wouldn't repeat, especially not in that ground.

Wembley, Wembley

'We the famous Tottenham Hotspur and we're goin to Wembley, Wembley, Wembley' we sang in our masses on

Villa Parks' huge Holte End.   But our 4-1 win against Watford felt a little hollow.

Colin drove down and parked up within half a mile of Villa Park just before 11a.m., but we found not one pub open near the ground. 'Police Advice' it said. 'Why?'. There had never been any issues between Spurs and Watford fans. There was no animosity around the ground and I'm sure if pubs had been open the two sets of fans would have happily drank together with not a hint of trouble. To be frank it killed the day for me and the rest of the lads, a couple of beers gets you in the mood. It hit Colin the most, no drink for the driver, what a disgrace!.

The atmosphere inside Villa Park was muted, like an early kick-off feel, especially for it being a Semi-Final. It was an easy win for us, with Watford's third choice keeper having to take unrelenting stick for his numerous mistakes from the Spurs contingent, 'You should have stayed in your wine bar, you should have stayed in your wine bar', we sang, a play on his recent previous job as a waiter.

It was off to Wembley against Coventry City, who had never played in a major final and had won nothing at all in their history. Let's get Spurs to end the sequence, I can here you say.

I met up with the lads on the train, we had all got tickets. Phil had stopped going to Spurs this season, I'm not sure why. Into London and onto the tube to Baker Street to take in a couple of pubs, but I didn't have a good vibe. Coventry were the underdogs, finishing mid-table, whereas we finished third.

The teams came out, Spurs having made a total cockup with their kit, half of the team had Holsten emblazed on their shirts the others half had no sponsorship, apparently the club were supposed to have taken two full kits to the match with Holsten on the front, but they managed to put some of the reserve kit in the skip as well which didn't have any advertising, it all got mixed up when the players put their kits on, once the tracksuit tops were put on no one had noticed. Holsten were livid with the blunder, Spurs had to give them free advertising around White Hart Lane the following season.

Richie yet again not happy we had been allocated the tunnel end of Wembley, saying, 'We will struggle today', but we got off to a flier, one up through the goal machine Clive Allen, but after that it all went wrong.

With the score two all, our captain Gary Mabbutt sliced a cross which looped agonisingly over Ray Clemence. The day wasn't to be ours, and to be fair Coventry deserved their 3-2 victory. Their support was more up for it, and you sensed the joy of their fans and what it would meant to them. It would have felt like it had for me in '81.

Coventry have never emulated it again, in fact only 19 months later they lost to non-league Sutton United in the 3rd round, but that's cup football, joy to despair.

I left Wembley and wasn't that disappointed, not like how I felt after Arsenal had knocked us out of the League Cup Semi-Final a couple of months earlier. Maybe I was getting older and the results meant less. My main disappointment that day was it hadn't been the final swan song for the great Glenn Hoddle, his last match in a Lilywhite shirt.

The one thing that pulled me to matches was the camaraderie of my football friends. We were now choosing our games more, and at times just a few of us would make it to games together. Going to football meant more than just the match, it was the bond you had from that close-knit friendship of having travelled around over the last ten years, we had been through a lot of wins and losses in that time, the losses brought you together more, you had a shoulder to cry on, but most of all the laughs, you can't put a price on those.

I remember my dad saying, in 1980, after I had been to forty-one games that season,

'How much have you spent this season going to games?'.

Travel, admission, programme, I didn't really drink much apart from the Idris Ginger Beer, after working it out it was approximately a thousand pounds.

It doesn't seem much nowadays but at that time I was earning less than two thousand pounds a year at work.

My dad's reply, was, 'You bloody idiot'.

I replied, 'From a man who wastes all his, on beer, fags and betting'. He said nothing, but I did.

'And it's been worth every penny'.

I wouldn't have changed a thing, Tottenham have given me so many highs and lows, and a group of friends who will be there for life, you can't put a price on that.

In the summer of 1987 I got to Wembley again, this time for U2s Joshua Tree tour. This was the mega selling album which finally propelled the band to the top of the pile. The biggest band in the world, some would argue the best, but they were definitely the biggest at that time. When tickets became available it was a no-brainer.

Phil again sorted tickets from York. On the coach down I had another hangover from the night before, but by the time The Pogue's came on to do their set I felt great.

We made our way towards the stage, 80,000 packed in. I had always dreamed of playing at Wembley as a kid, this would be as close as I would get. As I looked at the filling stands, the pitch packed, it came to me I was stood where Ricky Villa started his mazy dribble six years previously in the Cup Final, what a memory.

The band came on with a huge sway, the customary U2 flags held aloft. The band went through their repertoire, then 'The Edge' played the riff we all knew, within a second Wembley was a sea of bouncing bodies as 'I will follow' reverberates through the giant speakers. I was totally immersed, song after song in the whole event. I will never go to another gig as good as that one. I love the Joshua tree, it should be in everyone's collection. For me it was the final album, the curtain call of U2 being the rock band they wanted to be. Their direction began to change, infusing dance into their next albums, even Larry Mullen (drummer) questioned the direction of the band, saying we are losing our rock roots. But do you knock it? They have been brave, trying new ideas, and rather than losing fans they gain another audience. When once on par, Simple Minds stayed true to their stadium rock, they were left behind. I've been to see U2 a couple of times since, they are still a brilliant live band, but I hanker to the first five albums, and I would think a lot of the older fans who have grown with them would say the same.

Cup Debacles and Flat Caps

By the start of the next season John had moved to Wakefield, the mining industry now all but dead. John was an electrician, so his skills were transferable. We of course would meet up with John on away trips, but he had now met some of the Yorkshire Spurs around Leeds and Bradford so would travel with them, one of the original Northern Spurs had left us, but Phil was back on board, back to watching his beloved Spurs.

We met up with John at Derby, us standing on the terrace behind the goal and John in the seats above us. You were so

316

close to each other that John could have shook our hands, so compact was the old Baseball Ground. As we chatted to John it was obvious that he was totally pissed and had a joint in his hand. His Yorkshire mates were further back in the seats.

Suddenly a scuffle broke out in the seats, stewards piled in and were pulling John's mates out. John dropped the joint, the steward grabbed John, by now the boys in blue were involved, This was all happening a few yards above us, pandemonium as people were being led out. John in his rat-arsed state was pleading his innocence, if anything he was going out for being pissed.

'You're nicked', the long arm of the law said.

'What for?', John asked.

'For possession of contraband', plod said.

John was hauled out, we cheered, Harry couldn't contain himself, he laughed with glee.

'Gan on ye moth', Harry folded up with laughter.

We saw John at the next match, he was released and warned.

'It was me fuckin mate, he just gave it to me and I get chucked out', John pleaded his case.

The rest of us found it funny.

Our manager at the time, David Pleat was booted out the club for alleged curb crawling. True or not it was sweet music for the Arsenal fans, within days new anti-Pleat songs were spreading across the Highbury terraces like the plague. For us Spurs fans the thought was, the board of directors had their excuse to get rid of Pleat from the hot seat after an indifferent start to the season. They favoured Terry Venables, an ex-Spur from the 60s, but not a crowd favourite from his time in a Spurs shirt. His success at Barcelona couldn't be overlooked though, the chairman must have thought he had to make a statement of intent to the fans who were split on the sacking of Pleat. The news was all over the press, yes it was a big appointment for Tottenham, who had to also appease the fans after losing Richard Gough to Rangers and Pleat's decision to off load fans favourite Graham Roberts, who was said to of been heartbroken to be bombed out the club.

Venables first home game against Liverpool had the turnstiles clicking to the tune of 48,000, double our average, but still a defeat, as our mediocre team struggled to stay in mid- table, the Venables touch was not working yet.

With our hum drum league form it was a nice distraction to get a good F.A. Cup draw, an away match at Oldham Athletic. It was good to go to somewhere new you hadn't been to. The one disappointment was that Oldham had an artificial pitch, it was something I dreaded coming into the game. We had seen Q.P.R.s green carpet and the ridiculous bounce the ball had on its surface like a power ball, but I had some sympathy with Oldham, their ground was so high up in the Pennines with harsh winters of snow and ice they didn't want postponements every other week.

Col drove down with Harry, Richie and me, Phil, John and Pete were coming on the train. We all met up and found a good pub about half a mile from the ground. We got settled in front of the coal fire, the beer was beautiful, one of the best pints I had ever had, 'Samuel Smiths' if my memory serves me right. It was going down too easy. I looked out of the window, the rain was incessant bouncing off the road.

You get that dilemma, you're warm, you're enjoying the company, the ale is going down a treat, do you actually go to the match. Stupid as it may sound you think about it, especially knowing we were going into a large open end, no roof, its pissing down, with no sign of it relenting. The only plus point is you know it's not going to be waterlogged due to the artificial pitch. Of course you drag yourself out, but at the last possible minute.

Phil must have known the forecast was going to be bad as he had brought an umbrella, not a sight you often saw on the football terraces in the late 80s, but a popular sight in grounds right up to the mid-70's.

We entered the large curved open bank, and even though we had almost 5,000 fans present it still looked quite spartan, with groups huddling together to keep warm on this wet January day.

The team played well considering the conditions on the artificial surface. Ossie Ardiles in his last season with us really shone, his small frame, balance and delicate touch seemed to like the new surroundings, even if the rain was persistent.

Phil with brolly in hand pulled out a flat cap from his pocket, John in his boisterous drunken state shouted.

'Wah, it's fucking Jack Sugden (Emmerdale), Phil give as yer brolly seen as you've got your farmers hat?'.

Phil handed John the brolly, but instead of putting the brolly over his head John put it down into the closed position. John was stood behind Phil so Phil hadn't noticed John closing his brolly. John lifted the brolly and carefully plucked Phil's cap off his head using the end of it. John now had Phil's cap high in the air holding the brolly above his head.

'Give us me cap back?', Phil demanded.

As if John had any intention. John began to spin the cap on the point of the brolly, Phil couldn't reach it, the cap gained momentum, spinning like one of those plates on a pole that you used to see in old cabaret acts at the London Palladium. The hat was now going so fast with John's wrist action that the brolly couldn't hold it anymore. The cap left the brolly end and went high into the air, caught on the winter breeze, the glint of the floodlights catching its flight. Our supporters took their gaze from the match and like us wondered where it was going to land. We were halfway up the terrace, but with wind assistance it sailed over the high security fence at the front of the terrace and landed near the goal. The look of anxiety on Phil's face turned to thunder. John screamed with laughter, we all found it funny apart from Phil. He looked in Johns direction, I'm not sure if John could see Phil through his tears of laughter. Now Phil was not one for swearing much but today was different.

'You fucking bastard, you're a cunt John'.

John knew it, but it was worth it to get this reaction.

'Phil you're going to have to get it' John told Phil, hardly managing to get the words out, the tears of joy rolling down his cheeks.

Phil knew he was right, or was it better to cut his losses and leave it. Phil looked at John.

'You can go and fucking get it',

'Am I fuck', John still laughing.

Phil reluctantly made his way down the front, where he stood with the large steel fence in front of him.

'Hey, hey'.

Phil made himself known to the small soaked ball-boy sat on his little stool by the goal. The boy turned around.

'Yes mister'.

'Can I have my cap back?', Phil asked.

Its role reversal, I had asked many times as a kid to my next-door neighbour 'Can I have my ball back' when it had gone over their fence, now here we were, Phil a twenty-nine-year-old asking a ten-year-old. The boy passed the hat back to Phil. I could imagine him saying to Phil.

'If it comes over again, I will put a knife through it and tear it up'.

Phil sheepishly puts the cap back on and makes his way up to us.

'Howay Phil, it's only a laugh', John still happy with himself.

'Fuck you', Phil's instant reply,

'And give us that fucking umbrella'. Phil had seen enough of spinning caps for one day.

A good 4-2 win, all was forgotten, and another story to be told in later years in some other far-flung town. Port Vale away, our prize in the 4th round.

There are days in any football fan's life they'd sooner forget, Port Vale was one of mine. It doesn't happen often losing to a lower league club, but when that humiliation is against a club a couple of divisions lower it's a hard pill to swallow, and for a team the size of Spurs it's happened too often.

The day started well, most of us travelled, the attraction of another new ground too hard to resist. The travel down involved our usual card school, making the journey go quickly.

We soon arrived in Stoke, and this was where the day started going downhill. We should have stayed there and gone for a drink, but instead boarded another train to Burslem, about five miles down the track from Stoke. Coming out of the station there appeared to be nothing. We couldn't find a pub, and neither could many of the Spurs fans milling around, with the usual comments as we passed.

'What a fucking shit hole'.

Mind you if you were wanting to buy a bit of pottery you were well covered, with numerous shops selling their wares.

We walked to the ground where we eventually found what looked like a Supporters' Club which was small and already packed. Everyone had descended on what seemed the only watering hole open.

'We should have stayed in Stoke', was the thought we all had. We manged to get one drink, then set off to the ground to another open end, fortunately it was only a cloudy day with no rain forecast.

The lads would usually ask me what the away ends were like if we had never visited a ground before, I had a fascination for football stadiums and knew what every ground capacity was and even how many could sit in every stand, a bit sad really. The lads often taking the piss out of me for knowing useless information on capacities and attendances.

I had gone to Port Vale, taking time out from going to the Darlington match yet again.

At the start of the season I had approached Darlington about running a programme shop, the club happy for me to do it as long as I would purchase at least fifty unsold programmes from each match at half price. I was happy to do it, I had amassed a large programme collection which I could sell in the shop, and the fifty Darlington programmes I would swap for Premier club programmes with other dealers. I enjoyed it, I would make around forty quid a game which wasn't bad for a couple of hours in 1987, and of course I could watch the Darlington match. However Spurs would always come first, and I would often say to my loyal customers, 'I won't be in next match, I'm off to see Spurs'. I would miss at least six or seven Darlington home games to see Spurs, but when Darlington were away I could get to any Spurs match.

I ran the shop for the next five seasons, but not once did I have the desire to make Darlington my number one team. Though Port Vale could have sent me there.

We were in the ground for 2.45p.m. The 6,000 Spurs fans were trying to make themselves heard, but it's never easy in an open end, the acoustics don't work. Port Vale were up for it, the Vale crowd were up for it, it's their Cup Final, you could imagine the Vale's manager saying.

'Hit them hard from the start, these fancy dans will buckle'.

He wasn't wrong. 'Vale scored'. Okay, we now knew we were in a game, but surely it was the kick up the arse we needed. But no, it didn't happen, 2-0 as Vale scored again. You could see no fight, we played like we'd just taken eleven strangers off the street, it was a shocking performance. With ten minutes left our fans were streaming out of the ground, the remaining one's left chanting, 'You're not fit to wear the shirt'. They were right, any of our 6,000-travelling support would have dreamed of wearing that Spurs shirt and ran till they dropped, but not this Spurs eleven. We pulled a goal back, but it was only a token. I stayed to the end along with the other Northern Spurs, we always did. I never booed the players, even if it has been a shit performance, and this had been the biggest pile of shit I had seen in a while, I just don't clap the team, that's it, I don't really get irate, what's the point, Pete does, with cries of.

'Fucking shit, why do we bother'.

Colin on the other hand occasionally says,

'That's it, you'll never see me again'.

Of course he'd be there the following week.

Just before the final whistle the police lined up behind the goal in case of a potential pitch invasion by our fans. The whistle blew. Vale fans streamed onto the pitch to hug their heroes, there was no animosity from them towards us Spurs fans, but some of our fans were going mad with the apathy of the performance, they wanting to get onto the pitch, more to go face to face with our players and read the riot act.

They soon began trying to get on the pitch, there's no fences just a three-foot wall which the first few were starting to scale, the police batons were drawn and they struck anyone who made the attempt to climb. I watched from my vantage point halfway up the terrace.

I focused on one copper in front of me, middle aged, a bit on the tubby side, his days of chasing villains long gone. Spurs fans were still climbing the wall, this copper was lashing out, his face red, helmet now discarded, walloping anyone his truncheon would reach, He was in a frenzy, it reminded me of that kids' game 'Wiggly Worms' where a worm pops up and you had to hammer it down. I watched in amazement, his velocity never ceasing. I looked at Pete and Richie.

'Look at him, he's lost it'.

We stood watching him, laughing at his desperation to hit anyone, at least it cheered us, even though it was our fans on the receiving end, but his desire was becoming obsessive. He even began leaning over to hit innocent people passing as they left the ground, talk about over-zealous.

We left the ground and headed to the station. We were soon on the train, quickly back into the card school. Darlington Station soon arrived.

I got home, switched on Match of the Day, Port Vale v Spurs, first match. Of course it would be, every football fan around the country could see how the mighty Spurs were humiliated by the minnows of Port Vale. I watched it, I always did, like some masochist hoping it might change the outcome, of course it never did. These types of results will happen again, you only hope that next time it's not you. Let the ridicule be for someone else.

Come and Join Us

Having moved to a small village when I got married, I would go out to the local pub and soon got to know the locals. One young lad who came in quite regularly was Paul. I think he was about eighteen, a Liverpool fan and a frequent visitor to Anfield. Once I got to know Paul I found we would often be on the same trains back from matches. He liked to hear my stories of past games and got to know the regular Spurs lads well enough to ask if he could come to a match with us, of course it wasn't a problem. We were soon due to play Sheffield Wednesday so I asked if he fancied going.

'Yeah, Paul said, Who's going?'.

'Me, Phil, Pete, John, Rich and Harry', I said.

'Yeah, great seeya next week'.

The following week we were in Sheffield by 11a.m. and entered a pub, we wandered around several. Anyone who has been to Sheffield Wednesday will know it's around four miles from the city centre, which is where we were drinking. We totally lost track of time as the beers were flowing, it was now 2.45p.m. and a 3p.m. kick off!

'We'll have a quick one' John said.

We all agreed, even Richie wasn't too bothered, his second pint of Sweet Cider dulling his appreciation of the time. Out the pub at 3.05p.m., we staggered to a taxi.

Paul looked really hammered, he had been frequenting the toilet regularly. He had always suffered with kidney issues since he was very young and wore a bag which needed emptying quite often, especially if he'd been drinking. Normally he would only have a couple of pints when going to watch Liverpool, more often going shopping before games buying the latest fashion, usually a pullover. He would pay almost a hundred quid even in 1988, total madness, I could never see the logic.

I never let on to the other lads about Paul's condition, I didn't want to embarrass the lad. The taxis dropped us off outside the Leppings Lane End away section. We went in trying to look remotely sober, onto a sparse terrace with loads of space.

The game was a bit of a blur, and we were soon challenging each other to do somersaults over the crash barrier. All of us were having a go, not easy in our state.

'Paul you're next', Phil said.

'No, it's ok', Paul said.

'Come on yer moth', John shouted.

Paul wasn't getting out of it, we got hold of him, Paul was short not much over 5ft, we put him on the barrier. Paul was pleading, but to no avail and we spun him round several times. I had totally forgotten about his bag, the rest of the lads unsure why he was so keen to avoid the activity, but I did now. I noticed Paul's jeans go a darker shade of blue, the bag could take no more, it had emptied. Fortunately, no one else noticed.

We scored for the second time. Phil ran to the large perimeter fence in front of us and started to climb it in exuberance to acknowledge our goal scorer, as he reached the top he is told in no uncertain terms to get down by the stewards. Like a cat up a tree it's easier going up than down. Phil slid down, I've never seen Phil so out of it.

A third goal for us, Phil headed for the fence but his legs had gone. Paul, by now is hanging onto a barrier just to stop falling over. The whistle blew, our 1,500 fans gave the team a thunderous ovation.

We headed down the infamous Leppings Lane tunnel. Paul pleaded not to let go of him, we let go.

'Get hold, get hold', Paul hit the floor, the bag goes again.

A steward picked Paul up.

'Get yer sel sorted son or thar'l be nicked'.

We managed to get a bus to the station and were soon on a train North- bound, along with another group of Northern Spurs who we didn't know. One of them shouted to his mate,

'Can you smell piss?, fucking stinks of piss on this train'.

I smiled knowing exactly what he was on about, Paul was asleep, oblivious to the conversation.

We changed at Doncaster and boarded a train to York along with the other Spurs fans who came into our carriage, it wasn't long before the same lad shouted.

'I don't fucking believe it but this train fucking stinks of piss as well, can you smell it?, it's the same piss smell as on the last train we were on'.

I couldn't help but have a chuckle to myself.

I got Paul home, he was coming round a bit.

'Had a good day?', I asked,

'You're a fucking mad lot, but yeah it's been good'.

Paul went to Sheffield Wednesday again the following week, following Liverpool, but in a much more sober state, a steward stopped Paul before he went into the ground.

'Weren't you here last week with Spurs?'.

'Yes', Paul replied.

'You were fucking arseholed', the steward said.

'I know, I can hardly remember any of it', Paul said.

Mad Frankie and the end of The Shelf

As the season played out its final few games, in what was a season to forget, we still travelled down as routine. After losing at home to Norwich we made our way to the Kings Cross Buffet as we weren't going home until the 7p.m. train.

As usual the Buffet would have fans from other clubs, West Ham, Chelsea, Q.P.R., Millwall etc. Everyone seemed to get on fairly well as we all had the same common ground of not living in London but followed London clubs. On this day there were a few Arsenal fans in, this was rare as Spurs/Arsenal are always one at home the other away, but today Arsenal had played Nottm Forest in the F.A. Cup at Highbury.

Our defeat to Norwich was made easier when seeing the glum faces of those Arsenal fans after they had lost 2-1. One of those faces was Frankie, the Arsenal fan from Murton where Harry and John were from. Frankie had stood with us on The Shelf the day Arsenal fans had thrown the petrol bomb in 1980.

Frankie was a funny lad, usually drunk and loud. Frankie caught sight of us and gave us a shout, we came over and sat with him, Frankie looked well oiled.

'I didn't see much of the game as I was asleep on The Clock End Terrace', he told us.

Of course, we had to give him the chant of 'Boring, Boring, Arsenal'. This chant would stay for a few more years, until a little-known Frenchman (Wenger), would change the club into a slick attacking team that we would envy, but not admit to.

If Frankie ever travelled back on the train from a match with us, he would invariably fall asleep, and it would be our chance to get to work on his face with a pen, he would be so out of it he wouldn't feel a thing. We would give him the obligatory tache, 'T.H.F.C.' on his forehead, or change that to

'Spurs Rule', 'Arsenal are shit', then tie his laces to the table. John once tied some miniature bottles to his coat so they knocked together when he was staggering home. He had been convinced he was being followed.

As we sat in the Kings Cross Buffet, Frankie in his drunken stupor asked us.

'When is it mother's day?'.

'Tomorrow', I told him.

'I've got fuck all for her', Frankie showing concern. He must have thought a bit about her.

'I'll have that', Frankie was looking at a picture on the Buffet wall of a Hunt scene, 'hounds chasing a fox'. It was at least two feet wide and screwed to the wall.

'What!, you can't have that, its fastened to the wall' I said.

The fact the place was full of people didn't seem to deter Frankie. He staggered to his feet and started to pull at the picture, but it wasn't moving.

'Any of you lot got a screwdriver?', he asked through glazed eyes.

'No', we replied, we didn't expect to be doing any D.I.Y. today.

Frankie was determined, he was now stood on a seat pulling like hell, not a care in the world that people were watching, suddenly a screw eased from the wall.

'I'm getting it'.

He pulled again, the plug and the screw flew out the wall. It was a job half done. Frankie was now spinning the picture round and round to try and loosen the other screw. After much spinning it finally left the wall, people around us were shaking their heads. The picture was put on the table and Frankie went for another beer, not bothered about defacing the décor. He came back with his bottle of cider and sat down.

'Yes, I think she'll like that'.

Frankie slugged down his cider, picked up the picture, tucked it under his arm and casually walked out the buffet.

As we made our way North on the train, Frankie's picture lay on the table. Frankie glanced across to the adjacent table where an elderly but elegant well-dressed lady sat, she looking at the picture. It looked the sort of picture that she would have in her home by her appearance, a hunt scene looked right up her street.

'Nice isn't it?', Frankie said to her, 'Got if for my mam for mother's day'.

'Oh, how thoughtful' she said.

But I thought, 'Is she thinking why has he bought a picture and discarded the wrapping'. If only she knew the story behind it.

May 4th, 1988, doesn't mean much to most, but to me and countless Spurs fans of my generation or older it was the end of The Shelf. At least in its proper glory, the one that Archibald Leitch had designed and engineered fifty years earlier. It was a pity that little over 15,000 saw its demise against Luton in the final game of the season, but at least it was under the lights when The Shelf looked at its best.

Richie and I were the only two who were Shelf Siders, the rest of the lads Park Lane Enders, they only going in The Shelf if visiting supporters got the whole of the Park Lane End. It didn't matter where you stood at White Hart Lane, every Spurs fan knew The Shelf was what made White Hart Lane have that unique look.

For a good part of the season a group of Spurs fans had demonstrated under the banner S.O.S. (Save Our Shelf). A lot of effort was put in by the group but Tottenham officials had said it was not viable to spend millions on a stand that was becoming a crumbling dinosaur. We thought it would be worth it, but it was a war we wouldn't win. The club said as a compromise they would save 3,000 standing places, it would affectionally become known as The Ledge.

The Shelf Side would change in appearance, the original pitched roof was removed and in its place a flat roof which would have two huge supporting pillars that would sit one third up the lower terrace at either end. Not only was it an eyesore but a major blind spot for fans view of the goals, but at least the stand still existed, even if it did lose almost half its capacity.

For people born after 1988 The Shelf Side now looked pretty much like any stand around the country. That age group can only listen to stories and look at old photos to appreciate The Shelf's glorious past, only wishing that they could have stood on the old terrace. There are many fans around the country who will pass on to their sons and relatives what it was like to stand on the old iconic terraces of the past, the Kop, Kippax, The Holte, to name but a few. For me The Shelf will always be synonymous with White Hart Lane. Thanks for the memories.

Heartbreak, Crumbling at Bradford, The Big Chill

The next two seasons, 88-89 and 89-90, probably mean the least to me as a Spurs fan. Not that Spurs were rubbish, well they weren't that good in 1988-89

Spurs would finish third the following season, albeit a long way behind champions Liverpool and seven points behind runners up Aston Villa, having a good finish, winning seven of the last eight games, catapulted us into third place, but it still didn't mean too much.

The problem for my lack of appetite for anything Spurs, was that in the November 88 my mam began to get buzzing sensations in her head and as time went by it became more regular. The doctor sent her for tests which came back showing she had a tumour on her brain. They said they could operate but the specialists weren't promising her a full recovery. My mam's operation was set for January.

We had been drawn to play Bradford City away in the F.A. Cup 3rd round, another new ground to visit. Tickets were obtained courtesy of Brent yet again, a godsend to our Northern Spurs contingent. Col was driving, with Richie, Harry and me, Phil coming on the train. Pete had emigrated to America around this period.

We got to Bradford early and parked down a side street near the ground and called in a pub directly up the hill from the ground, by noon it was packed, half Spurs, half Bradford, all getting on great. A roar went up, from behind a curtain the compere said.

'Our first girl for the afternoon', a cheer goes up. She's soon down to her bra and knickers. Harry, with his short stature was now stood on a chair, he wasn't going to miss this action. With roars of approval the clothes were discarded. The afternoon was going well, one after another the girls peeled off their inhibitions as they took the adulation, the cries became louder. 'Time to go', Richie declared.

We left the pub and walked down the hill towards 'Valley Parade', the home of Bradford City. I was all over the place, as drunk as I can ever remember, how I wasn't arrested or turned away once at the turnstiles I don't know. I followed behind the rest through the turnstile into a small covered end. I soon lost sight of the other lads and I was now stood with no one I knew. The game was a bit of a blur, my gaze always seemed to be one move behind play. I do know we played shit by the constant groans, which go up a level when we concede. Its Port Vale again, I'm now saying 'please score'. It didn't happen. We were the laughingstock again. For the second season running we would be the main match on 'Match of the Day' for everyone to laugh at us.

Our end emptied quickly at the final whistle, they weren't getting our applause today. I fell over, where were my fellow Spurs supporters who were tight against me like scaffolding? Of course they'd gone, back South, they weren't interested in a drunk, and especially one now laid on the terrace like a man in the gutter like I was. I staggered to my feet, someone gave me a helping hand, I couldn't even thank them, my speech was so incoherent. I got out the ground and amazingly found the car, I was back before any of the lads. I sat on the pavement and leaned against the wall.

'Stoker, Stoker', Col shouted, I heard the distant voice.

'Are you alright?', Richie asked.

'Yeah', I replied.

By the time the lads had returned I had rolled over and laid face down on the pavement, they thought I had been turned over by Bradford fans. I was bundled into the car and driven back to Darlington.

Once home I had recovered enough to watch the game on 'Match of the Day' to see how badly we had played, and yes, we were bad.

My mam had her operation the following week, at hospital in Middlesbrough, but it didn't go as well as we had hoped. The surgeon told the family that the tumour couldn't be reached without causing brain damage. That was it, Chemo and Radiotherapy, which was only to slow down the inevitable, that my mam was dying.

I don't care how good a Dad you are, most children are drawn more to their mam. I was no different. That strong bond brought about from those early years where the mother is nurturing her young, feeding, talking, while the dad is usually at work, playing their part but not in a physical presence.

A week after the operation, with mam still in hospital Spurs were due to play at Ayresome Park, which was only a few hundred metres from the hospital. Phil asked if he could call in to see mam before the game, which was touching. He had stayed at my old family home on occasions, Phil felt it was the least he could do to show how he had appreciated those visits. The pre match drink could take a miss for this match, which after the state I got in at Bradford was a blessing.

My mam was in good spirits during our visit, and was pleased to see Phil. She never talked about the inevitable, even though her hair was falling out, her hair something she had always cherished.

We left for the match, Phil wished her well, what else can you say.

The following week mam came home to be looked after by my sister, who fortunately lived next door.

The game ended in an entertaining 2-2 draw, but what was happening to mam never left me, but for ninety minutes of a match it did take your mind off what was to come.

A lot has been written about the decline of football hooliganism towards the late 80s. Don't get me wrong it was still going on, but you did feel less intimidated around certain grounds. Much of this quell in disorder was put down to the music of the time and primarily the Rave Scene, which the young enjoyed, dancing and popping pills which chilled them.

Many of these would have been young football fans. Ecstasy being the pill of choice calming everyone down, it was now love not war. Maybe the popping of pills had an underlying hand in changing the views of the football youth that violence didn't need to be part of football.

But for me the game changer was on the 15th April 1989, the Hillsborough disaster. I wasn't at a game that day but had the radio on listening to the latest scores. I heard within minutes of the kick-off things were going horribly wrong on the Leppings Lane Terrace where Liverpool fans were housed.

I knew it wouldn't be trouble, my mind raced back eight years previously when I was in a similar crush in the Semi-Final against Wolves. By the time the game was halted people had already died. 'Gods way of punishing Liverpool fans for what happened at Heysel four years earlier' that's what some sick people said. But the real culprits were the Football Association for allowing the death trap that the Leppings Lane terrace had become, with its iron cages killing the innocent, and the local constabulary for their incompetence in allowing fans to be ushered down the centre tunnel already bursting with supporters. Why hadn't the police guided the fans to the fairly empty pens on either corner. The crush didn't surprise me, the police didn't care.

I had been at Old Trafford in 1987 on a hot September afternoon. Man United had allocated us the corner of the Scoreboard End Terrace, which then stretched towards the first goalpost. As kick off approached Richie and me who were stood nearer the corner flag were getting more and more crushed, people around us were screaming at the stewards to open the gates either side of us to access the empty pens, but they would have none of it. I managed to ask a copper what was going on, even he looked concerned.

'Why is it so full?', I asked.

He was honest and said, 'We gave you space for 3,000, but you've got over 4,000 here'.

'Open the pen next to us?', I said.

'We're not allowed' he answered.

Safety didn't matter in those times, and you have to remember when this game was played capacities in these pens were far greater than now.

We watched that Man Utd game in discomfort. You always knew when terraces were full because all you could see were people's heads, not even the shoulders because there were two people on each step of the terrace. We left Old Trafford that day with red faces, was that the sun or the crush, probably a bit of both.

Ninety-six died on that fateful day at Hillsborough and another has tragically died of his injuries (Aug. 2021) to bring it up to ninety-seven Justice for them is partly done, in as much as certain establishments have been named as a reason for the tragedy, but there are individual people who still haven't been brought to justice.

It's now taken over thirty years of torment for families to have the names of their loved ones cleared and proved that they weren't the cause of the horrors of Hillsborough. It was a disgrace to say drunkenness was the cause of so many fatalities. Some family members would never see a conclusion, they having died never seeing their family members having their names cleared. R.I.P.

Within days fences were being torn down at most grounds around the country, which was great to see, taking the ugly part of our stadiums away.

The F.A. then panicked, stating all grounds should be all seater, the top division to start with, then the divisions lower would follow. It wasn't the terraces that killed Liverpool supporters it was the fences surrounding them. The vast majority of fans were against all seating.

I could understand if Liverpool fans wanted seats, that was obvious, but the rest of the fans should of been given a vote. I thought England was a free speaking country not a communist state.

Football fans united after Hillsborough, and there was a new feel of friendliness when visiting grounds. More and more fans would wear their replica kits at matches, and not just at home games, but at away matches too. People didn't feel so intimidated. Our trip to Derby around a month earlier was the storm before the calm.

We had gone in a pub near the railway station, which was full of Spurs fans, or at least that's what we thought. It was quite a big pub with a large bar, and another room with a pool table in. There was no sign of trouble, everyone was in good spirits, when an argument could be heard in the pool room. Around six Spurs lads and six Derby fans had got into a slanging match, we later found out that the Spurs lads were all from the Derby area. Then it really kicked off, punches first, then pool cues, pool balls, then any glasses and bottles laid around, and there were plenty. It was like the wild west, most people ran to the exit, one mad rush to avoid the many glasses whizzing around our heads.

'Time to go' I said.

It didn't need a reply. Phil, Rich, Col and Harry ran to the exit, everyone pushed their way out onto the street. I slipped in the rush on the broken glass. I couldn't get up as people climbed over me, but I managed to get under a table, the fight still continued. Police sirens could be heard, the crash of glasses stopped.

I waited in my state of seclusion for another minute then eased my way out from under the table. I looked around, it was like battle zone, glass everywhere, tables and chairs overturned but I was lucky, not one cut.

An elderly lady came out of the back room with a dustpan and brush, a bit inappropriate considering the mess. The landlord walked in, looked at me and said.

'Yes sir, what can I get you?'.

Had he seen the damage.

'What', I was still in shock.

'Beer or lager?', he said.

'Beer please, I'm surprised you're not closing for the day'.

'No, no, we will have this cleaned up in no time, this happens quite regularly, we are used to it'.

People began coming back in, within fifteen minutes you wouldn't have known anything had happened, a full, tidy pub, but now we had two riot vans outside keeping the peace.

Despair

As the summer of '89 passed we had what they say now, a marque signing having bought Gary Lineker. A typical goal poacher striker and undoubtedly one of the best in Europe, the downside was we had sold Chris Waddle who had been brilliant the season before. Lineaker later said he wouldn't have signed if he knew Waddle was leaving. It should have been a team sheet of Waddle, Gascoigne and Lineker, now wouldn't that of been an exciting prospect. I planned my first trip to The Lane for the opener against Luton.

My mam was deteriorating now, the tumour had grown and was taking much of her movement away, she couldn't walk, but what hurt me more were her mood swings. She would be very sharp over minor things and would often shout at me on my visits. I knew it was the condition and the

338

medication, but it was hard to take, she had barely ever shouted at me until this disease had taken over her life. The medication was being upped on a regular basis now, at least it took the pain away, I would have hated her to have been in pain.

The mam I knew and loved, although I seldom said it to her, a weakness on my part, my upbringing was that men are not to show emotion. But now I think it's a weakness not to show emotion, I learned it was okay to have a cry.

I had joined the members club at Spurs for that season. It didn't guarantee you a ticket but it gave you a discount on admission. The ground was still in a mess a year on from the closing of The Shelf in '88, the club even had to cancel the first match of that season, literally a couple of hours before kick-off because the stadium couldn't get a safety certificate. It meant you had thousands of supporters, not only Spurs but our opposition Coventry making their way to White Hart Lane for a non-event. It was a fiasco and you can imagine how it panned out around the ground. The fans felt they were being taken for granted, it did leave a sour taste.

Now here we were twelve months down the line, and still The Shelf Side would remain empty, work still going on for another couple of months before White Hart Lane became four sided again.

Richie and I made the trip. We went and joined the queue early at the Paxton Road End, now known as the Members End. The queue snaked down the Paxton Road, by 2.30p.m. the officials had locked the gates. Thousands were turned away, 'So much for paying for membership'. Richie and I ran down towards the West Stand but saw the notice 'All seats sold', the Park Lane End was now reserved for season ticket holders, so no entry there. We were locked out. I wasn't going to give up, I hadn't travelled two hundred and sixty miles for nothing. It was down to the dreaded touts.

I hated touts but they provided a service, but a service I despised. Rich and I split up and would try and get what we could.

'Tickets, tickets for the match'.

You could hear that well heard drawl, usually from a middle-aged suited type speaking out the corner of his mouth in case some plod might nick him. I found the bloke selling his wares.

'How much?', I asked.

'£30 for two' he said

'I only want one' I said, I had lost Richie in the crowd.

'They sell better as a pair' he added'.

'Come on just one', I pleaded.

He wasn't going to budge, then I heard a lad asking for a ticket, I shouted over to him.

'Here, two tickets me and you'.

'Yeah how much?', he asked.

'He wants thirty'. They were nine-pound tickets.

'We will give you twenty-six quid, you're not going to get rid of them now it's almost three o'clock'.

The streets were getting quieter so he agreed.

I missed the first ten minutes by the time I got to my seat in the Park Lane End, as it happened the only part of the ground I had never sat in. Richie managed to get a seat in the Paxton Road end. We won 2-1 played in front of little over 17,000, how we missed The Shelf.

I was woken, I could hear the phone, it was 1a.m.. Thursday September 13th. I got up, answered the phone, it was Chris my sister.

'It's mam, the doctor has been and said she hasn't long left'.

I put the phone down, dressed quickly, asked Karen if she was coming.

'No, it's best only immediate family are there, she said.

She was immediate to me, but I didn't have time to argue. I jumped in the car and covered the twelve miles in fifteen minutes.

When I arrived my brothers were there, my sister Chris of course, my Aunt from London but not my other brother John, who was still in Leeds.

When I look back, Chris had not only been a daughter to my mam but an unselfish carer, as well as having a teenage daughter to look after.

Mam's breathing was an awful sound, like a gurgle, she was in no pain, morphine now almost unlimited. Suddenly a heavy breath, a last breath, I had heard it before with my dad, a final outward breath. My mam's eyes opened as though to say a final farewell to her loved ones, and she was gone.

I was pleased in a way her pain was over, but it hurt, it really hurt. I went out into the back garden, it was in total darkness and walked its length, I knew it well enough. Once near the top I laid down, looking at the night sky, it wasn't too cold, but wondered whether I would have noticed anyway. The tears began to roll down the side of my face onto the light dew of the grass. I remember thinking back to when I was a child and wondering how this day would feel. I don't know why I thought about things like that when I was young, possibly the thing I didn't want to lose most was my mam. That pain was as bad as I thought it would be. I stayed in the garden for half an hour, no-one bothered me, we all have our ways of grieving. But this was only the start, my pain would escalate to new heights.

I was back at my mam's the next day, it was strange, an empty feeling hit me, I could feel the tears welling up again. I wandered around the house I was born in, going into mam and dad's room, by now the tears rolling down my face clouding my sight. Into my old bedroom once adorned with Tottenham team group photos. I would never see the house again dressed as I had always known it. Strange how bricks and mortar can make you so emotional, but I suppose it was the memories of the house and what had happened in it that had got my emotions going.

I went downstairs, Alan my brother had just come in, the family had to make a start on sorting and clearing the house. It was a council house, so no house to sell, but once the funeral was over it would need emptying fairly quickly.

'Alan, what do you think if I went to the match on Saturday?', I asked.

'Who you playing?', he asked.

'Chelsea at home', I said, almost apologetically.

'What's stopping you?', Alan said.

'The timing, it will be less than three days since mam died',

'What would mam say to you?', Alan almost giving me the answer,

'It will cheer you up', he said.

He was right, mam knew my love for Spurs

.

I went to the match, I had already got a ticket not wanting the hassle like the Luton match. The ground still three sided, I was now in the Paxton Road along with Richie. It was strange to watch what should of been a big London Derby, with less than 17,000 attending and no Chelsea support, except for a hundred sprinkled in the West Stand.

Alan had said, 'It will cheer you up'! Far from it, defeated 4-1, we played like how I felt, I wanted this next week over as quick as possible.

What I dislike most about a funeral is the wait. You are getting over the loss to a certain extent, then it is brought back to the fore on the day of the funeral. I was holding it together until the drive to the church, then the walk down the aisle to the front. Everyone turns to look, you feel like a celebrity, or a stranger going into a rough pub, its uncomfortable which ever. No glee like a wedding, only sorrow. I turned my eyes on the coffin, I was now welling up, an occasional slap on my shoulder didn't help, as though it would at this time. I listened to the vicar, but only half heard his words, my mind skipped back to my childhood, I had the memory I wanted, a strange one, my mam looking in the mirror, me aged about ten, looking at the reflection of her smiling, brushing her hair, pruning herself for the local dance, she loved dancing. This is my memory of her in happier times. I don't have the memory of her last six months of misery. This is what I think of mam to this day, of her smiling.

The coffin was taken to the crematorium, we followed, now for family and close friends. I was so pleased to see so many in the church, but I knew it would be that way, mam having worked as a barmaid for many years.

There were a few words and the curtains closed in front of the coffin. She was gone now, I openly wept. I went into the garden of rest where the flowers and wreaths lay. I read the cards when I could, the salty glaze obstructing my view. I found this very emotional, as I did at my dad's, but I had to read them, someone had put their heart into writing them, it was the least I could do.

They say time is a great healer, and yes it is, especially when you go to Old Trafford and thump United 3-0 in the League Cup. Then beat them again on the same ground 1-0 in the league just before Christmas, two really good days. Life was improving on the football pitch.

As Christmas 1989 passed and headed towards New Year Karen arrived home from the stables she had been working at, a job she had been doing for four or five months having learned to horse ride the previous year. She enjoyed the job and wasn't bothered that she had to work over Christmas. I was happy she had a job she really liked doing.

Karen hadn't been to a match now for three years, about the time we bought the house. It was December 27th, Karen asked if it was alright to go out on New Year's Eve.

'Yeah where we going' I asked, we often went out on New Year's Eve.

'No, I want to go alone, meet the people I work with', she said

'We always go out together', I said.

'So you don't want me to go then', Karen said.

'Well it is New Year so no', I had made my feelings felt.

'I've got something to tell you', she said.

'What?', me, Still a bit annoyed.

'I'm leaving you'.

That sense of 'did I hear you right'.

'I'm moving in with Terry'.

Terry was her new work colleague, I had met him on a few occasions, he had even been over for Sunday lunch. I felt numb, no feelings at all, nothing. We had not had one bad argument in the seven and a half years we had been together. Now she was leaving.

Karen filled a bag and left, saying 'I will come back in a few weeks' time to get some more things'. The door slammed shut, the house had never felt so empty. It was just me and Archie, my cat named after Steve Archibald.

I sat contemplating what had just happened. It dawned on me, what am I going to do, one wage, bills, mortgage, running the car. It seemed so unfair that the innocent party had the pressure of surviving. Everything was flashing through my head as reality was taking hold, but most of all I had lost my wife. It was as if she had died, especially with no inkling of what she had been up to, or I even giving it a thought. Just before she had closed the door on our lives, I asked her,

'Have you slept with him?'

'Yes'.

The answer hit hard, the twist of the already embedded knife.

Karen arrived back at the house a couple of weeks later with a van to remove some furniture, it was the realisation the marriage was over. With tears streaming down my face the furniture made its exit along with Karen. I would not see her again for seven years, then only for her mam's funeral, we didn't speak.

I hit rock bottom by February when my next-door neighbour knocked on my door carrying Archie, his body lifeless having been knocked down. It's strange how you become close to your pet, and for me Archie had given me a purpose, something to look after.

Life was certainly giving me some digs. Looking back I think I was suffering with depression, but you never gave it a thought in those days. I remember my face breaking out in a flaky eczema, and I had hardly had a spot in my teenage years.

I started to exercise, swimming my main thing, within a month or two I was swimming a mile, three times a week. Then getting worse for wear down the pub on a weekend.

Spurs certainly took a back seat, I went to only two matches after the win at Old Trafford in December. I still carried on in the Darlington programme shop, it gave me a focus and more importantly extra money. As the season ended I was beginning to get used to being on my own, coming and going as and when I pleased, I even took a couple of girls out, but nothing serious.

As the World Cup, Italia 90 finished, Spurs had two of England's best, Lineker and Paul Gascoigne, the lovable Geordie had set the world alight with his skill and his cheeky charm. Gascoigne's sending off against Germany in the Semi-Final where his emotions surfaced, made him the darling of the nation when they saw him close to tears.

Football in England was given a massive boost with Gascoigne's outpouring playing a big part. Spurs would now be box office and were the team everyone wanted to see, Gazza mania was here.

Fireworks and Lost in Blackpool

For the first time in six years I was excited at the prospect of watching Spurs. There was a buzz of expectancy for this group of players, after all we thought we had the best midfielder and striker in the country, if not in Europe. Gascoigne and Lineker were going to take us to the title thirty years from when we last won it, well that was our dream. We had ended the previous season on a roll, you could see the nucleus of a team gelling together. It was a team you wanted to watch, and with Gascoigne, it seemed that other fans wanted to see the Geordie maestro. 'He's fat, he's round, he's worth ten million pounds, Paul Gascoigne, Paul Gascoigne' we sang, and what a season he had. For that season Gascoigne was world class, running though opposition defences like they weren't there. Finally, we had hope.

Another factor, I was now coming to terms with being alone at home and had started a new job at a different printers. A mate I had gone to college with when serving my apprenticeship had set up on his own, and he asked me if I was interested in working with him. The extra forty quid a week swung it. Peter was good to work with but his drinking was always going to be an issue.

At our first game we brushed aside Man City 3-1, and the season was going well up to the end of September. As usual we began to creek and by the time of our trip to Blackpool in the FA Cup 3rd Round, the season which filled our hopes so much in August was all but a fairy tale. But remember the year was ending with a one, and our tradition of winning something in a season with a one were there for all to see. the omens were good.

In the October I had arranged and booked a trip to Amsterdam for New Year with Phil. I had no ties and nor did Phil, so we would go soon after Christmas for four nights. We'd had two really good trips there with Spurs so it seemed a good place to see what New Year's Eve would be like. My main reason to go was not to have a New Year like the year before, which was a desperate time.

New Year's Eve in Amsterdam was strange. We left the hotel at 7.30p.m. and couldn't find a pub open. We stayed in a hotel just off Dam Square so were in the heart of the city, but it was dead. We wandered around until we found a bar that was open. Going inside, the only two in, we ordered a beer.

'Where is everyone, why is it so quiet?, I asked the barman.

'It's always like this on New Year's Eve, in all of Holland until 10p.m.', he said.

'Then it livens up', I asked, hoping.

'Oh yes and very noisy', he said.

He told us every bar puts fireworks on lampposts, fences, anything they can tie them to. Not just a couple of fireworks, they would tie a roll of several hundred fireworks to them. It was a tradition in Holland to see which bar could make the most noise.

At 11p.m. everyone was in good spirits, the bars were full, with many different accents from around Europe chatting, the two of us quite merry talking to a group of actors, they were dwarfs, at least I think they were dwarfs, the bars were infused with the smell of Marijuana.

We came outside which overlooked the canal just before midnight, the bar owner lit his roll of fireworks as did every other. The noise of the city was incredible, possibly how the Blitz would of sounded, crackers going off, rockets lighting the sky, it's a memory I will keep.

The two of us headed to Dam Square which was busy, people milling around the two large Christmas trees talking to one another. I looked to the ground and picked up a used rocket firework, about a foot in length, all the outer casing was intact. I approached Phil with it and held it like a microphone.

'Hello', I said to Phil, holding the firework towards his mouth. 'Have you had a good night' I said.

'It's been great', Phil said talking into the firework, playing along.

I decide to go over to a Chinese couple with my new microphone/firework.

'Hello, I'm from the BBC', I said, holding the firework for them to talk through.

'The BBC in England', the Chinese girl shrilled.

I couldn't believe, first they thought I was a reporter, and secondly they were talking into a firework, I had to play along, I was trying not to laugh, especially when Phil came over with his firework, now they were both chatting into fireworks.

'What have you enjoyed about the night', Phil asked in a Richard Dimbleby way.

'Yes, yes we have wonderful time', They said they were so excited to be talking to the BBC!

'Could you turn this way ? ' I said. They turned.

'Give a wave to England'.

'Where is the camera ?', she asked.

'It's in the Christmas tree, hidden', I said.

They look at the tree and begin waving, I could hardly contain myself from laughing.

'Thank you', We tell them.

'Thank you, goodbye England', they shout as they leave, waving at the Christmas tree.

We tried our luck again with other people, only a few spotted it was a firework we were using, the majority were convinced they were chatting to BBC reporters. Crazy, but it was an unforgettable night. We were back to the hotel by 3a.m.

On returning from Amsterdam I would meet up again with Phil in Blackpool for the FA Cup 3rd Round. Rich, Harry and I had travelled in Col's car. Phil once again had come by train.

We parked up about half a mile from the ground and made our way to the station to meet Phil. The day was dreary and getting really windy, we met Phil and found a pub. We decided this was our one and only pub stop of the day, it was pointless wandering around in the wind. A steady flow of beer passed our lips until 2.30p.m.

Leaving the pub we literally had to fight through the wind, it seemed madness that the game would go ahead. We finally got to our open terrace, where there was little or no protection from the elements.

The game went ahead and was a complete farce. A goal kick would leave the keepers foot and go out for a throw in even though the ball was aimed down the centre of the pitch. We won a forgettable game 1-0, only because we had a little more skill against a lower league team, but we were just pleased to get through. We made our way out, and once onto the streets I soon lost touch with the others so I headed to the car. Unfortunately in my beer filled haze I didn't know where it was parked. I didn't recognise anything of my surroundings. I ran up and down streets, either fighting against the gale force wind or coming the opposite direction running faster than an Olympic sprinter. After an hour I gave up.

If only mobiles were around in 91, well they were, but you needed a suitcase to carry one in. I knew Col would wait a while, but in the bleak dark windswept evening he would have called off the search by now. I was blown down to the railway station which by then was deserted, no sign that a match had ever been on. I went to the guy at the ticket office,

'How much for a single to Darlington ?' I asked.

'Eighteen pounds' came the instant reply, like he knew every ticket price by heart.

I looked in my pocket and dragged out the little I had, eleven pounds and a few pence was the total, and no plastic cards in my possession.

'What about York ?' I asked.

'Fourteen pounds' came the reply.

'I've got eleven, get me as near to York as you can'.

'Wait there', he said, almost excited, his voice sounding joyful, pleased to have something to do.

'Right', he said. 'I can get you to York for ten pounds, twenty pence. It will be a long way round, up to Preston then across to York. I will give you two tickets, it will be the cheapest way'.

Let that be a lesson to you all if you're on a budget. I thanked the man for his research and help, a lot of others wouldn't have given a shit to my plight. I phoned Phil with the little amount of money I had left and got an evening sports paper.

'Ok if I stay at yours tonight ?' I asked Phil, who had just got back home and was surprised to hear I was in Preston.

'No problem' Phil said.

Three hours later I arrived at Phil's.

I rang Col the next day to explain what had happened. Col gave me plenty of piss taking, which went on for three years on our many Spurs trips, but this stopped when Col couldn't find my car at a game at Man City. Luckily for Col I noticed him as I was about to pass him as he was walking the dark streets of Moss Side with Steve his young son. Never laugh at other peoples' misfortune is what I say.

Wembley, Wembley

Winning the Cup in the classic 1981 replay is a night few Spurs fans will ever forget, it's my highlight and it will be to many others, but this might have been eclipsed on the 14th April 1991 when we played Arsenal in the FA Cup Semi-Final at Wembley. After our narrow win against Blackpool, then beating Oxford, Portsmouth and Notts County in which Paul Gascoigne showed his brilliance in all those games we were now due to play Arsenal in the Semi, it couldn't get any bigger, other than playing them in the Final.

The downside for me was that the Semi-Final was at Wembley. I'm a traditionalist and Wembley should only be used for the Final. I can understand the logistics of the occasion, two clubs from North London, why take it out of the capital when there is a stadium that holds 80,000, it seemed a no brainer, but we had managed for over a hundred years to play on a neutral ground that wasn't Wembley. But at the end of the day the FA probably thought a guaranteed sell out and huge corporate potential and advertising revenue, the cash cow rears its ugly head again.

We made our way to London. I had managed to get a seat alongside Richie in the upper tier.

Seating was now starting to become the norm, with Wembley being used as a blueprint for what clubs had to implement to their grounds in the near future. The Hillsborough disaster was the catalyst for the Football Association to push for club grounds to be all seater to stem the hooligan problem.

The upper tier seats were decent at Wembley as the seats themselves were put on the high steps. The lower seats were plastic bases with no backs, bolted to the shallow terrace. Was it any wonder no-one actually sat on them, but for that matter no one sat in the upper seats, well not for a game like this.

'Is Gascoigne going to have a crack, he is you know'. Barry Davies immortal words from his commentary perch to the millions watching on TV. We didn't hear those words but it's what we wanted Gazza to do, and he did, a thirty-five yarder into the top corner. Half of the ground took off in a crazy celebration. Not only were we beating the enemy, but we were also beating the eventual league champions. Arsenal were in meltdown when Lineker slipped in number two, we were in heaven, the stadium was an incessant blue and white noise. Arsenal hit back, 2-1. We heard their fans for the first

352

time, but it wouldn't be for long. Lineker poked home number three, no way back for the Arsenal. The game ended with us all singing to the red half of North London, '3-1 we've beat the scum 3-1', it rang around the ground. It seemed like everyone was singing it, young and old. The Arsenal fans were out the ground in a shot, they didn't want to hear us. The Spurs players came down to our end towards the tunnel 'Spurs are on their way to Wembley' we sang. What a day, back in the car we listened to Nottm Forest turn over West Ham 4-0.

Spurs v Forest FA Cup Final

It didn't matter how we played in the Cup Final, it would never match the Semi-Final, just because of who we had beaten. In some way it was like 'After the Lord Mayors show,' but make no mistake we wanted to win it.

After Gazza mania of the preceding summer, to finish mid-table was a disappointment, but we had seen so many false dawns, the Cup Final could be our saving grace.

I was looking for a ticket but having little luck, almost resigning myself to a day in front of the telly. Calling into my local pub, Peter the landlord asked if I was going to the Cup Final.

'I would Peter but I can't get at ticket', I said.

'Leave it with me, my brother might be able to get you one',

I called down the pub on the Thursday, two days before the Final, Peter walked in, ticket in hand, it's yours for forty quid. I knew this was well inflated from the face value, but I didn't care.

'Yes Peter, I'll take it'.

And even better it was for the Spurs end.

Peter's brother was coaching at Portsmouth, possibly obtaining it from a player hoping to make a few quid. It's ticket touting again, but I wouldn't report it, I didn't know if I might need the service again.

I made my way to my seat in the upper tier of Wembley to almost the same position in the stadium as I had stood for the game of my life ten years earlier. As I looked to the rake of empty seats yet to be filled, it seemed a lifetime ago, that unforgettable game against Man City, I didn't have the same emotion now, was it I was getting older, I had turned thirty.

Those days between 1978-1984 were possibly the happiest days of my life, well in football terms anyway. It wasn't just the football, it was everything that went with it, the music, the laughs, the scrapes, but more importantly my football mates. Now here I was about to sit my arse on a piece of plastic with total strangers either side of me, albeit Spurs fans. Football had gone plastic, the grit and essence of the game was diluting. I wanted the camaraderie back that I had in the day. Rich was in another section, John was in the Forest end.

As the plastic filled I had to make the most of it, after all, for fucks sake it's the FA Cup Final.

The game was set up by the media as Gazza taking on Cloughie, the Forest manager. Gazza had lived up to the hype of Italia 90 and taken that World Cup form through the season to single handidly take us to the Cup Final. At times he was breath-taking, his humour and being a joker endeared him to many, though hated by others, but no one could dispute his brilliance.

The media were siding with Cloughie, 'Old big head', hoping he might finally get his hands on the F.A. Cup, the only honour to elude him as player or manager. I liked

354

Cloughie, I liked his Forest teams, they played the right way, but today I wasn't wanting him to break his duck.

Gazza was flying around the pitch like he was on steroids. He then made a mad challenge on Gary Charles and ended up injuring himself so badly he is stretchered off, never to pull on a Spurs shirt again. In fact he was out of football for more than year, making his comeback for Lazio in Serie A.

Stuart Pearce thundered a thirty yarder into our top corner to make it 1-0. Lineker then missed a penalty and we're thinking here we go, it's going to be Cloughie's day. But in the 56th minute Paul Stewart, who had reinvented himself as a midfielder after a torrid time as a striker slides in an equaliser. The game went to extra time and four minutes into it Des Walker, the Forest defender headed into his own net. We hung on. We kept our record of winning something when the year ends in a one.

The Cup was lifted by Mabbsy (Gary Mabbutt), a true Spurs legend. I met up with Richie and John outside and headed up to Tottenham, it was the best place to go when we had won something. Off the tube, our first port of call was The Swan, the pub we always avoided due to it being known as a black pub, mainly Afro-Caribbean. There weren't many in and we were the only whites. The Jamaican contingent quickly clocked us and made us feel welcome. John was soon befriended by a busty fifty or so year old, and it looked like she had taken a shine to him. She didn't want John to go. He was soon dragged to the dance floor to dance to some kind of smoochy reggae music. She grinded up to John rubbing her ample charms against him. John was looking increasingly embarrassed, not a thing you often said about John. To be fair she was not unattractive, but John was pleased when the song finished, the other dreadlocked drinkers gave John a cheer.

'Drink up and let's fuck off', John pleaded.

We left The Swan.

A promise Richie and I had said a few years earlier was, that if we won the cup, we had to go in there for a drink. We hit more of the conventional pubs after that, it was a good night, but it was never going to be a night like the one against Man City ten years earlier.

Fate

I've never really believed in fate, I'm not superstitious either, but two weeks after the Cup Final my belief in fate was questioned. I was laid in the bath, early evening. It was a Friday night so I had planned to go out to the local pub, the same routine as the previous week/months. As I laid in the deep hot water of the bath I was thinking, I liked thinking in the bath, I would lie there for ages until the water became tepid and my fingers became wrinkled. Lying there I remember saying out loud, 'I'm sick of being alone'. I was still living alone and after eighteen months of it I was becoming fed up and bored of my Friday, Saturday routine, unless of course I was at a match. I'm a shy person by nature so wasn't very pushy when it came to relationships. As I laid, about to get out, the gold chain that I wore around my neck dropped off, not at the clasp, it had just snapped. I was surprised as I hadn't snagged it. The chain was my equivalent of a wedding ring off Karen. I never had liked rings so wore a gold chain instead. I lifted it out of the bath and put it on the side to get repaired at some point. I had never taken it off but I wasn't too concerned when it snapped.

Having got ready I went down the local, same old faces. Then I went onto a pub a mile away, which was a busy pub

356

for somewhere that was out of the way. In fact you needed a car to get to it, or a good walk. The pub was busier than usual, Friday was Karaoke night, not that I'm a singer. I bought a drink and as I turned around, drink in hand, I managed to spill some of it on a dark-haired girl who I had never seen before but noticed how pretty she was. I apologised for my mishap and moved over to my mates.

Later that evening I saw the girl sat with her friend.

'Who's that', I asked my mate, trying to make him hear above another Whitney Houston,

'She's called Kathryn, I went to school with her, she lives near Darlington'.

'Is she with anyone', meaning a partner.

'I don't know, but she has three kids' he said.

Three kids I was thinking, she's only in her early twenties. I'd had four pints, enough to make me less nervous. I don't know why but I was drawn to her. I made my move and sat next to her.

'Could I get you a drink?', I asked her. I know not very original.

'I'm driving but I will have an orange', She said.

After getting the drink, I sat down with her.

'Who's minding all your kids?', I asked.

'What kids', She said.

'Nigel said you had three'.

'He's having you on'.

It was a relief. We chatted for half an hour, I asked if I could see her again. She said yes, in a couple of days. I didn't know whether that was a brush off or not. She dropped me off at home.

'Hopefully I will see you again'. I said goodbye.

I took Kathryn out the following Monday to a quiet pub and had a good night. I briefly mentioned my love affair with

Tottenham with little reaction, so left it at that. I would have to ease it in slowly into her life.

The following season Kathryn asked if she could come to a match with me. 'I promise there was no badgering, her choice, I had nothing to do with it'.

Kathryn had never been to a football match. 'I'll sort it' I told her. I wanted her to experience the terrace culture as this would be the last season of having the Paxton, Park Lane and what little bit we had of The Shelf (The Ledge) as a standing terrace. The following year would see the Park Lane and Lower Shelf go to seating. I had to get her to White Hart Lane!

I arranged to take her to the game against Q.P.R. but before that we had sorted a trip to Norwich, (lads only). Our driver for the day was Andrew. He was my old boss's son where I had worked for thirteen years after leaving school. Andrew was about four years old when I started working for his dad, and within a couple of years I was getting Andrew programmes from the games I was regularly going to. It was simple progression that Andrew would end up a Spurs fan and would eventually travel with us for the next eight or nine seasons until he decided to play local Saturday/Sunday football himself.

Andrew pulled up outside my house early that Saturday morning. He hadn't long passed his driving test and had only said a couple of weeks earlier that he had got a car and was willing to drive to Norwich. Brent got us four tickets. I left the house and looked at Andrew's car. It was the first version of the Honda Civic, it was tiny. My mind skipped back to John's tiny car that we had travelled to Dundee United eleven years earlier.

We sped off!, well set off to Darlington to pick up Col and Richie. It was a beautiful August day, after picking them up we were on the motorway by 7.30a.m., and to be fair the little Honda was running like a dream, a bit slow on the hills though. Just after 11a.m. we had got to Kings Lynn, we were now thinking Norwich by midday and a few pints in some beer garden, but this was quashed when we heard a knocking noise just after we had re-fuelled.

'I don't fucking believe this', Col said, the thought of his first pint now up the spout.

'Pull over Andrew on that waste ground', I told him.

We were twenty miles from Norwich, the car limped onto the gravel.

'Have you got breakdown cover?', Richie asked, more in hope.

'No', Andrew answered.

By 1.30p.m. the car still refused to start, it seemed the only thing we were getting today was a suntan. We had almost given up on getting to the match, when our prayers were answered, a AA van pulled onto the waste ground. The driver pulled out his sandwiches, but before a bite was taken Col was tapping on his window,

'Any chance of looking at this?'.

'Are you a member?', he asked.

'No, but we're trying to get to the match at Norwich'.

He wasn't best pleased, probably thinking he should have stopped at the layby up the road, so not hassled by us.

'Go on then', he reluctantly said.

'Turn it over'.

Andrew fired it up, but nothing, it wouldn't kick over.

'Have you recently put fuel in?', he asked.

'Yeah'.

'You've got shit in it'. He messed around.

'Try that'.

The car spluttered into life.

'Keep it going'.

We piled in, thanked Mr AA, and were off. It was 2.30p.m. and the car was going well.

We arrived in Norwich at 3.00p.m., at least there was no football traffic.

'Go in the multi storey car park' we told Andrew.

We could now see Carrow Road the home of Norwich. Just as we go up the first ramp the car stopped, no questions asked we jumped out and pushed it up to level one, looked around, not a space, Level two. The beads of sweat were pouring out of us, it might have been a small car but pushing it up two ramps took some doing.

'Space over there', I shouted.

We pushed it in, locked it and were off running to the ground.

Once inside, Col was pissed off, no alcohol for sale. We were all lathered as we headed onto the terrace, missing only twenty minutes. We went on to win 1-0 which was a surprise given the day we'd had, we all thought the omens would be against us winning.

Back to the multi-storey we feared the worst, but the car started no bother, and we were off. We kept it going and passed the layby where we broke down, saw a pub and quickly knocked a few beers back. The car got us home without any more issues.

Spurs versus Q.P.R., Kathryn's first match. My main concern was to get her in so she could see. The Lower Shelf over the halfway line was where we stood.

Kathryn thought the ground was big, but of course it was by no means one of the biggest. As someone who had only seen football on TV she was impressed. At least all the fences had now gone after Hillsborough. It was a decent game and a 2-0 win. Kathryn enjoyed the atmosphere.

By the time I took her again, a mid-week game at Notts County in April, to the less glamourous surroundings of Meadow Lane, she would be watching Spurs facing the threat of relegation.

I had been to Nottingham a couple of months earlier to see us beat Forest 1-0, to put us in a strong position in the two-legged League Cup Semi-Final, but Spurs being Spurs blew it at The Lane, another Wembley visit eluding us. Retribution for Forest for the previous season's FA Cup Final.

Having also been to Villa Park to see us get a draw in the F.A. Cup 3rd Round, only to lose again at home it was now a depressing end to the season. Our one bit of good fortune was that Gary Lineker was back after missing a several weeks of the season comforting his son George, who had contracted leukaemia.

We won 2-0 at Notts County, Lineker scoring them both, beating Notts County was a major step in us avoiding relegation, especially with the new format of the Premier League about to kick off the following August, we knew we had to be in it.

Premier League, Where's the Ball, Man City

A reasonable finish to the preceding season lifted us to the heady heights of finishing in fifteenth position, but most importantly we had our name as one of the founding members of the Premier League.

What did a new name mean, well to all the foot soldiers who travelled the country supporting their clubs, it meant absolutely nothing. But to club owners it meant one thing, 'cash, cash, cash'.

Sky TV was behind the multi-million-pound deal, ploughing unbridled wealth into the fortunate twenty-two original members of its new Premier League, making those clubs richer than any club could have hoped for. That money would then pass to the players, club officials, agents and any other hangers on. In return the peasants on the terraces, or the replacement seats would be fleeced with rising admission charges for what was basically the same product as one year earlier.

Sky having put their dosh on the line were now pulling the strings, they would dictate everything, and it was us, the loyal fans who would bear the brunt. Fans having to travel colossal mileages for Sunday noon kick offs.

Football would never be the same again. The traditional Saturday 3p.m. kick off in the top division would be lost, with games sometimes spread over four days. I hated it.

Sky would say 'we have decided to show Southampton versus Newcastle, it will give Newcastle fans the chance to see their team instead of having to travel all that way'. True to a point, but you are then losing the away fans who generate the atmosphere, which in turn lifts the home support, therefore killing the spectacle that you're paying millions for. The Covid Pandemic would really show how much football needed the fans.

Don't get me wrong, Sky Sports is fantastic, it is a polished product, best camera locations, sound, commentary. But when it first came out, I for one should have boycotted it when they asked for eight quid a month subscription, because we knew that price would only go one way, up. The product was good and people paid it, and as much as I begrudged it, I was a hypocrite and also paid it because I didn't want to miss out.

It did have an effect on me watching Spurs though, and I like many others would have a lesser desire to go to a game if I knew Sky were covering it, unless it was reasonably close or an important match.

What was the first Premier League Season like in 1992. Firstly I remember it as another change of job. Peter my boss, and long-time friend, told me to start looking for another job as the work was drying up. Luckily for me I found another printing job less than a mile from where I was working. I started my new job in the September. Peter would close his printers within six months.

One of the early games I went to was Leeds United away on a Wednesday night. As we stood on the Lowfield Road away section getting hammered to the tune of 5-0, the ball was launched into our section of fans. The thousand or so of us let the ball bounce about in our section, we didn't want the Leeds player getting the ball back to take the throw in, we were already getting slaughtered so the less they had the ball the better. One Spurs fan picked the ball up and threw it in the air, the Leeds Stewards couldn't get the ball back as we punched the ball above our heads to one another. Leeds officials kicked another ball across the pitch to get the game started again. The ball we had then bounced down the stairs under the stand where the refreshments/toilets were. The stewards still thought we had it so they called in the Old Bill. Three burly officers came into our section, truncheons out.

'Where's thar fuckan ball at?', one bellowed at us.

A big guy was stood near us, his tight replica Spurs shirt hardly big enough to contain his more than adequate beer belly.

'Give it here?', the copper shouted, his glare fixed on the big guy next to us.

'What yer fucking on about?', the fat guy shouted back.

'Give it here lad', his truncheon now lifted above his head.

'It's under your shirt', the copper yelled, his annoyance there for us to see.

The big guy lifted his shirt and his flabby belly slopped over the belt of his jeans.

'It's all fucking paid for mate', the big guy said proudly.

The copper didn't see the funny side of it, as we all burst into laughter. It was the only laugh we had that night.

The season was strange. We started it badly, but as winter approached we hit form and some of our home performances were brilliant. Our two new signings Darren Anderton and Teddy Sheringham, along with the young Nick Barmby just clicked. Teddy Sheringham was a top striker, and we needed him after losing Lineker, who had left to play in Japan.

Away from home we had some crazy inept defensive frailties, letting in five at Leeds, six at Sheff Utd and six at Liverpool.

I made the trip to Goodison Park in the February, a mid-week game. One of the lads I worked with was an Everton fan, so he said he would drive down. We got tickets for the Main Stand, there were only 16,000 at the match, with around 800 Spurs fans in The Park End seats with no one allowed on the terrace below them. We won the game 2-1, with the Spurs fans rejoicing, Eric Thorsvedt our goalkeeper ran down from the opposite end to throw his gloves into the Spurs section as he always did if we won. But the fans were too high up for him to throw his gloves up to them. He suddenly jumped into the empty terrace below, then went under the stand and emerged in the seated section of Spurs fans to hand his gloves to a youngster, amid much cheering. His song was soon ringing around Goodison Park, 'I love Eric the Viking, Eric the Viking loves me'. Thorsvedt's gesture showed there was still a footballer-fan relationship, but as the Premier League years elapsed, this would grow wider and wider.

I've always had a soft spot for Man City, I don't know why. Yes I do, it's because they are like Spurs. As much as I hate to
 admit it we had lived in our neighbour's shadow. Of course, we now know that things can change and in Man City's case they are now the force of Manchester (2021), and we are now on a par or better with that lot from down the Seven Sisters Road.

Back in the early 90s City were a long way behind the Reds. Let's be honest Man Utd are one of the biggest clubs in the world and even today with City having a fantastic team they may never take United's mantle of ever being the bigger club in Manchester.

I had always enjoyed going to City, even in the mad days of Moss Side and Maine Road. There fans have always had an honesty and loyalty to their club, not unlike ours. Their support home and away had always been there in numbers.

I was in away disappointed to draw them in the 6th Round of the F.A. Cup, I hoped it might be in the Final.

The F.A. Cup was yet again keeping our season alive, no wonder we hold the old pot so dear to our hearts.

We travelled down in two cars, even though it was live on the BBC it was the sort of game not to be missed.

The City fans seemed even more up for it than us, possibly down to the fact that Man Utd were likely to go onto win the league for their first time in twenty-six years, this had United fans gloating towards the blue half of Manchester.

The pressure was on City, they hadn't won anything since the League Cup in 1976, they had try and win the cup to show they were keeping pace with the red side of Manchester.

We made our way to the Sherwood pub which was on the busy road passing the away end where we would be housed, and only a stone's throw from the Kippax, home of City's most fervent fans.

We had been going in the Sherwood for the last couple of seasons, it hadn't really got busy until around 1.30p.m., but today the place was bouncing. You could feel the excitement in the air and the tension. City knew that a win today would put them in the Semi Final for the first time since 1981, when of course they would eventually play us in the final. They had to win to stop the taunting from United fans.

The pub filled to bursting point until it spilled onto the road. The two sets of fans were getting on well. We had sold our entire allocation of 7,500 tickets so the atmosphere would be highly charged. As we left the pub at 2.30p.m. everything was good. We did have the odd anti-Jewish song thrown at us as we queued up at the turnstiles.

Once in the large North Stand behind the goal, hundreds of navy, white and yellow balloons drifted around our heads, being knocked back and forth. 'Spurs are on their way to Wembley' rang out. 'Blue moon' was sung from the City fans on the other three sides, but mainly from the huge Kippax, now one of only a few big terraces still left in the topflight in 1993.

The game kicked off, it was passionate, noise all around, it's like a game from a distant era when you had large away followings, instead of the standard two or three thousands of today.

City took the lead, the ground was in a frenzy apart from our end, but Nayim our little midfielder hits an equaliser. Sedgley then puts us ahead just before half-time, our end was bouncing, we fancied our chances now.

Second half sees Spurs kicking towards our massed ranks. Nayim hits a third but City hit back quickly, it's an epic cup tie. We were hanging on, not long left when Nayim got his hat- trick and our fourth, it's all over now.

Suddenly some City fans from the Kippax encroached onto the pitch, within seconds there was hundreds on the pitch. City fans came running to our end, a few Spurs lads jumped over and clashed, but it's only a few. Police and stewards were now all over the pitch, it was like old times, it's a shame though that a cracking cup tie should be spoilt. Police horses were now on the pitch galloping around like it's the 'Horse of Year Show', its chaos. The final whistle had already gone, our fans were taunting City fans, 'We're going to Wembley, we're going to Wembley you're not'.

It had already been decided that the Semi-Finals would be played at Wembley whichever teams were playing. The pitch was cleared of the loonies. The vast majority of City fans streamed out. To their credit some even applauded us for not going on the pitch, and for the performance, it could have been a riot.

We finally left the ground after much celebrating. After seeing what had happened on the pitch we knew this was not going to be a cakewalk outside, that underlying fear, a feeling I hadn't had for a long time. Within a couple of minutes of being on the streets we heard a roar further up the road, fights were kicking off all over, sirens blaring.

Harry, Richie, Andrew and I kept walking to the car, parked about 400 yards from the rear of the Kippax in your typical rows of terraced houses.

I had already paid a scally two quid to watch the car. I had offered a quid but he said two, 'or you don't know what might happen to your car round here'. Had I a choice? The car was safe when we returned, we jumped in, gave out a blow of the cheeks, then pulled away to join the queue of traffic.

A large group of City thugs were stood on the corner as we drove around the back of the Kippax where a coach was parked. The last of the Spurs supporters climbing aboard, then the doors closed.

I'm watching as we were stationary, not more than thirty yards from the coach. It began to pull away to join our queue of traffic, not even moving at walking pace. The group of City thugs, big lads, not kids, walked along the side of the bus, the leader had a baseball bat in hand, he slammed it against the door of the bus.

'Come on you Cockney cunts', he shouted.

Everyone on the bus was stood up peering at the menace, the door slid open, a few Spurs kicked out at the City fan with the bat.

'Get off the bus, we're only ten in number' he pleaded to the coach load.

But who would want to get off first. It's not like you were getting off en masse, one at a time and you were getting a bat across your head. No one made the move, I didn't blame them. The coach took a few more strikes before the police cavalry arrived to move them on. We got moving along the Moss Side streets, groups of City fans were all over, it wasn't the place to be loitering especially if you had Spurs connections.

A couple of years later when speaking to City fans at Maine Road, one asked if I had been to that cup match. I said 'yes, it was mad afterwards'. He said it wasn't Spurs who sent us over the edge, it was the shit United fans had been giving them. I think what he was trying to say was United were pulling away, the gulf was starting to widen, and widen it did.

When you choose your team, that's it for life, you hope things will improve and you close the gap on your neighbour, but in a way failure makes you stronger, and wins mean more to you. That loyalty from City and Spurs fans eventually brought us back to Arsenal and Man Utd, so we are now on a level. You have to keep believing that your day will come, that's what you support your team for.

Wembley, Stag Day, Oldham, Oldham, Oldham

We were Wembley bound again for the Semi-Final against our arch enemies Arsenal on a Sunday at noon, hardly the most appealing of times. The other Semi being played on the Saturday was the Steel City Derby, Sheff Utd V Sheff Wed.

Our Semi against the red half of North London was eagerly anticipated, but we knew they would want to seek revenge from two years previous.

We would finish above them in the league, us eighth, Arsenal tenth. We would then only finish above them once in the next twenty-four years.

Colin decided to drive down on the Saturday morning with Percy, Rich, Harry and I. Phil was coming down on the train. We drove down passing countless red and white, blue and white scarves fastened in by the car windows, as they dangled in the jet stream, it seemed half of Sheffield was on the road.

Brent was good enough to put us up in his large terraced Victorian house in Balham, South London, but even so we didn't all have a bed. Brent had another couple of Spurs fans staying as well as us, so the settees and floor were well used.

Once our bedding was sorted, Phil and I had grabbed a single bed each, we decided to head to the pub down the road. It was a large sprawling pub, busy with afternoon trade. Three pints later we were out to a chip shop, we didn't want to get too much to drink as we were going out later that evening. Richie had located a chip shop, his habit as strong as ever. We walked into the chip shop, Rich has already got his, Col next. The proprietor asked what I wanted.

'Saveloy and chips please'.

He loaded the chips into a cone so they exceeded the height of the said vessel, he then put a saveloy on the top. I thanked him and took the cone with the precariously balanced saveloy and left the shop. Waiting outside for the rest to be served I took a chip from the cone which totally unbalanced the saveloy, just like the game Jenga, my game was over. The saveloy headed towards the pavement but I managed to flick it up on my foot, then the other foot. I had always been decent at keepy-ups with a ball but a saveloy was a challenge, a third flick up,

'On me head Stoker' I heard Col say.

My balance having to hold the cone and the recently drunk three pints, a fourth flick wasn't going to happen. The Saveloy hit the dusty pavement looking bruised and dishevelled. I picked it up and took it into the chip shop as there wasn't a bin outside.

'It's been on the floor', I say to the man behind the counter.

'I have no more', his broken English showing his Greek or Cypriot background.

'It's ok, the chips will be fine'.

I made my way out out as a man walked in, I hear him say.

'Saveloy and chips please'.

I looked back into the shop as the owner put the bruised Saveloy on another cone of chips, I shook my head and smiled.

By 6.30p.m. we were back in the pub, which was already busy. Phil and I decided our drink of choice for the night was Beamish Stout, a lookalike for Guinness and a very heavy drink. It's a good pint, too good, it was going down so easy. By 11p.m. we decided to go back to Brent's, I was pissed, Phil was pissed. I was in bed within half an hour, and with the room spinning I was up, head over a bowl

Next morning I lifted my head off the pillow, I felt rough, it was 7a.m.

'Time to get up Phil', he was feeling rough too.

Again I think how can you feel so good on the night and so shit eight hours later. I feel better knowing Phil is rough, but not much. I skipped breakfast apart from a cup of tea which I forced down. At 9a.m. we set off to Wembley, Colin followed Brent's car. Colin said he felt okay, I was jealous. I wound down the window and stuck my head out, a trail of vomit about to be laid on Central London roads.

'God I felt ill'.

Phil was suffering as well but keeping everything down.

Once inside the stadium I went to my seat. I was in the lower seats at the tunnel end, row one, with a large mesh in front of me, the perimeter fence. Phil was about ten rows further back, ten yards to my right. To be honest the way I felt I didn't want to be there. I can't sing, in fact, I didn't want anyone to sing, my head was ready to explode.

Arsenal were the better side, our chances were few, but when they scored with only a couple of minutes left it was a sickener, even in my condition. But that's football and Arsenal got their revenge for two years earlier. I could hear the chant from the opposite end, 'One nil, we've beat the scum one nil'. We left the ground and got back to the car. We got out of London, but to top it all we break down and end up on the back of a recovery wagon. Let the season end now.

The Mags were back, Newcastle had gained promotion to the Premier League. Let's be honest, they were playing how every supporter wanted his/her team to play like, swashbuckling, attacking, they were exciting to watch. Kevin Keegan was managing them exactly how he liked to play. Their first game back in the elite level was against us at St James' Park. I couldn't believe my bad luck, as I had purchased a ticket to see U2 at Roundhay Park, Leeds. My dilemma was which one should I go to. My trip to Newcastle would have to wait for another season, U2 won the day. If I hadn't been such a big fan of the band it would have been no contest. With one eye on the score while going for several beers in Leeds with the York lads. At 4.50p.m. the result came through. Teddy Sheringham won it for us. The concert would be that much better now

Kathryn and I had set a date to get married, October 16th, which yet again would fall on the day of a match that I always would go to, Man Utd at Old Trafford. I could hardly change the Wedding date. It was decided that the trip to Sheff Utd in September would be my football stag day as Sheffield was always a good place for a drink. Six of us made the trip on the train, Phil, Richie, Pete, Harry, Andrew and me. The drinks were soon flowing as we went from bar to bar, making our way towards the ground.

At 2p.m. we were like a bunch of giggling juveniles.

'In here Phil', I shouted.

We were outside the pub directly behind the away end, which was strictly home fans only, no Spurs fans in this one.

'Sorry lads', the burly bouncer on the door said. We had no colours on our attire. Phil and Pete were doing the talking or slurring.

'We not Spurs fans, we from York and Harrogate' they said in their Yorkshire accent. Although not as broad as South Yorkshire, it seemed to throw the bouncer off his guard.

'Yeah go on then', he said.

We entered the pub, into the heaving throng of Yorkshire men, we were it seemed the only Spurs fans present, but it mattered little for our craving for the next pint.

'Five pints and three cigars', Phil ordered.

Richie had dropped out the round early doors when looking for a chip shop. You always knew when Phil was pissed as the cigars would be purchased. One to Pete, one to me, Phil already asking a Blades fan for a light, none of us smoked. Richie didn't want one and Harry thought it might stunt his growth.

A group of United fans left for the match so we jumped into their seats. We were so drunk we couldn't stop laughing, anything we talked about was funny.

The plume of cigar smoke had got a lad interested on the other side of the room, he kept giving us the eye until he came over.

'Have you got any of that gear left, it looks fucking mint the way you lot are laughing'.

'What?' I said.

'Thar weed yer smoking, it looks fuckin good gear'.

373

He looked pissed off when I told him it was a slim panetella cigar.

We left the pub ten minutes before kick-off and tried to put our sensible heads on for a minute. If the police or stewards saw what we were really like we would have ended up in the back of the Yorkshire constabulary riot van. Once inside our leash was off. Spurs had been given the whole end, but with it only half full we had loads of room. Sheringham scored, we all jumped up and ended up in a pile on the terrace, the legs had gone.

The game ended 2-2. We headed to the station for a few beers and brought them outside to sit on the benches on the platform. We saw Harry getting slated by a couple of Sheff Utd fans and it was getting heated. I walked over to see what was going on,

'What's your problem?', I asked one of them.

'You lot, Spurs fans from the North'.

'So what I said'.

He backed off noticing I had a pint glass in my hand. I guess he thought I might take a swing at him with the glass, it was the last thing I would ever do, but with my drunken state he maybe thought it. They walked off down the platform but got on the same train as us to York. After half an hour of the journey one of the Sheff Utd fans walked down the train and apologised to Harry for having a go at him on the platform in Sheffield, fair play to him, we accepted and shook hands. We changed again at York and connected with the high-speed train bound for Scotland. I got seated and was soon dozing off with the motion of the train but woke with a start, I felt sick. I left my seat and headed through the sliding door, only to see the toilet was engaged.

'Oh no not engaged'.

I wouldn't make the next carriage, the sick was already starting to come into my mouth, nothing for it, the window was pulled down, I put my head out into the hundred mile an hour jet stream and emptied the contents of my stomach. What I didn't realise was the projectile vomit had left my mouth and had come straight back through the window without even touching me. I looked around and the toilet door was covered in sick. A farm muck spreader could not have covered the door any better. I made a hasty retreat to my seat, thinking thank god the person hadn't come out at the same time, instead they may have possibly heard a slight brushing sound on the door as the vomit splattered it. What would they have thought when they came out of the toilet to see the sticky mess that wasn't there two minutes earlier. A stag day to remember.

This whole season was a nightmare. Once Teddy Sheringham got injured it was a relegation battle, which was a shame for Ossie Ardiles who had taken over the manager's hot seat. We had such high hopes for Ossie, the fans loved him, but he was out of his depth. The signing of Kevin Scott from Newcastle showed how desperate we were, as he ran around like a cart horse, it was no wonder Keegan moved him on. So bad was our form at The Lane we only managed four league wins on our own patch.

My wedding in October was a wonderful day, Kathryn was already expecting as we tied the knot. Phil was my best man, with all my Spurs mates making it, apart from John.

Phil had some good ammunition for his speech, standing up to a chorus of 'Yido, yido, yido'. What the other guests made of that I wasn't sure. A good day was had by all and I even managed to nip to my room to watch Spurs lose to Man Utd on 'Match of the Day'.

By the time we were due to play the away game at Oldham in March we were just above the relegation zone. Andrew drove down with Rich and me, we had arranged to pick Phil up at Wetherby. Just before getting to Wetherby we heard that the game had been called off.

The game at Oldham was re-arranged, a midweek fixture a couple of weeks later. With our tickets still valid I drove this time, picking up Andrew and Richie. Phil was again being picked up at Wetherby.

Making good time we got to Wetherby before the arranged time of 4p.m. There was no sign of Phil, we waited until 4.30p.m. Phil still hadn't turned up so we decided to go without him.

Parking up in Oldham by 6.30p.m. we went into the pub we were in the previous season, which was friendly and very cheap, three pints came to a little over £2.50. One more pint and we set off to the ground.

'It's quiet', I said.

Even the pub wasn't that busy. Oldham only averaged 12,000 but Spurs fans always got to the grounds early and I didn't see many around.

'This can't be off again?', I said to the others.

After all it wasn't a bad night weather wise. We got to the road that led to the stadium, we could see the away section but not a sole about. A voice from across the road shouted, 'waterlogged again'.

No wonder Phil wasn't at Wetherby. Back to the car we headed off home, dropping into the outskirts of Leeds to get fish and chips, at least Richie was pleased. Sitting in the car I said it's a long way for two pints and fish and chips, but at least we were home for 10.00p.m.

The game with Oldham was scheduled again for May 5th a Thursday night live on Sky. There was no chance we were going to miss this game. We were now on the cusp of relegation, as were Oldham, the winner had every chance of staying up. The four of us travelled again, relieved that Phil was now in the car as we headed back to the same pub, which was packed with Spurs fans. Getting to the ground the atmosphere was upbeat, we needed to win and the team needed us. Our 3,000 in the crowd of 14,000 were relentless in the noise they made, it never stopped. Steve Perryman who was now Ossie's assistant was even applauding our efforts during the game.

The pitch was heavy with thick mud in the eighteen-yard box. When we scored I remember this big lad behind me jump on the back of the seat, then walked down the tops of the seats. We were only about six rows from the front, he then climbed onto the pitch to embrace our goal scorer, but as he ran towards him his feet went and he did one of those slapstick falls where your legs go high into the air. He landed in the thick mud, where he wallowed like a happy pig, until led away by Stewards. We won 2-0. Oldham are relegated which was a shame as it was always a good away day, but we stayed up.

Our final home game was against Q.P.R. which we lost, but the Oldham game saved us. A special night where you knew the prize was massive. It may not have been a trophy season, but nights like that are equal or even better. Coming out of Boundary Park we were on a high, the support that night was unbelievable. It was a good way to end the first twenty seasons of watching Spurs.

Printed in Great Britain
by Amazon